Krakow

Wesoła, Kleparz and Biskupie
Pages 130–141

QUARTER

WESOŁA, KLEPARZ
AND BISKUPIE

Okół and Stradom Quarters
Pages 76–89

OKÓŁ
AND STRADOM
QUARTERS

| 0 metres | 400 |
| 0 yards | 400 |

KAZIMIERZ
QUARTER

Kazimierz Quarter
Pages 120–129

DK EYEWITNESS TRAVEL

Krakow

Main Contributor **Teresa Czerniewicz-Umer**

Penguin
Random
House

Produced by Wydawnictwo
Wiedza i Życie, Warsaw

Managing Editor Ewa Szwagrzyk
Series Editor Joanna Egert
DTP Designer Paweł Pasternak
Consultant Jan Ostrowski
Production Anna Kożurno-Królikowska

Contributors
Teresa Czerniewicz-Umer,
Andrzej Betlej, Piotr Krasny,
Robert Makłowicz, Craig Turp

Photographers
Andrzej Chęć, Wojciech
Czerniewicz, Piotr Jamski,
Dorota and Mariusz Jarymowicz

Illustrators
Andrzej Wielgosz, Piotr Zybrzycki,
Paweł Mistewicz

Printed and bound in China

First published in the UK in 2000 by
Dorling Kindersley Limited
80 Strand, London WC2R 0RL, UK

17 18 19 20 10 9 8 7 6 5 4 3 2 1

Reprinted with revisions
2003, 2007, 2010, 2013, 2015, 2018

Copyright 2000, 2018 © Dorling
Kindersley Limited, London
A Penguin Random House Company

Mosaic detail in the Church of the
Sacred Heart of Jesus

Introducing Krakow

Pretty gardens at Wawel Royal Castle

◀ **Title page** Wawel Royal Castle, skirted by the Planty   **Front cover main image** Peering at the Church of St Mary from the Cloth Hall
Back cover main image Boats docked alongside Wawel Royal Castle

Contents

Detail, Benedictine Abbey in Tyniec

Café seating at the Cloth Hall, with views
of the Market Square

HOW TO USE THIS GUIDE

This Eyewitness Travel Guide is intended to help you make the most of your stay in Krakow. It provides detailed practical information and expert recommendations. *Introducing Krakow* tells you about the geographical location of the city, establishes Krakow in its historical context and describes events that take place throughout the year. *Krakow at a Glance* is an overview of the city's attractions. *Krakow Area by Area* guides you through the city's sightseeing areas and describes

the main sights with maps, photographs and illustrations. It recommends short excursions out of Krakow and offers three walks around the city. Information about hotels, restaurants, shops and markets as well as cafés, bars, entertainment and sport can be found in *Travellers' Needs*. The *Survival Guide* has advice on everything, including using your mobile phone, getting around on public transport and obtaining medical assistance.

Krakow Area by Area

Krakow has been divided into six colour-coded sightseeing areas. Each area begins with a short portrait, which sums up the area's character and history, and a list of key sights. Sights are numbered and located on an *Area Map*. The *Street-by-Street* map that follows focuses on the most interesting part of the area. Finding your way around is made simple by the numbering system.

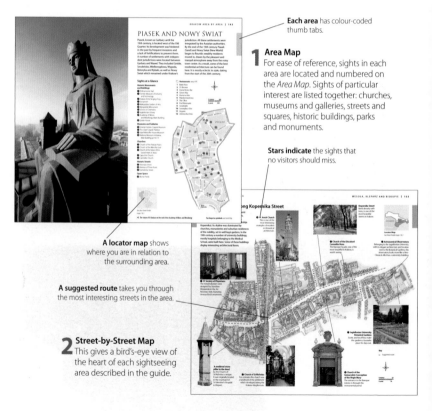

Each area has colour-coded thumb tabs.

1 Area Map
For ease of reference, sights in each area are located and numbered on the *Area Map*. Sights of particular interest are listed together: churches, museums and galleries, streets and squares, historic buildings, parks and monuments.

Stars indicate the sights that no visitors should miss.

A locator map shows where you are in relation to the surrounding area.

A suggested route takes you through the most interesting streets in the area.

2 Street-by-Street Map
This gives a bird's-eye view of the heart of each sightseeing area described in the guide.

Krakow Area Map

This colour-coded map *(see pp18–19)* indicates the six main sightseeing areas described in this guide. Each of these is more fully covered in the *Area by Area* section *(see pp58–153)*. In *Krakow at a Glance* this same colour coding allows you to locate the most interesting places. You will also be able to orientate yourself during the three suggested walks *(see p168)*.

Numbered circles locate the listed sights on the *Area Map* and within the descriptive section.

Practical information provides everything you need to know to visit each sight. Map references pinpoint the sight's location on the *Street Finder* map *(see pp230–39)*.

3 Detailed Information

Each of the most interesting sights is described in depth. You will find them listed in order following the numbering on the *Area Map*. Practical information, including map references, opening hours and telephone numbers, is also provided.

The visitors' checklist provides useful information you may need to plan your visit.

The boxes contain detailed information on a particular subject related to the sight.

Numbered circles point out key features of the sight.

4 Krakow's Main Sights

Historic buildings are dissected to reveal their interiors. Museums and galleries have colour-coded floor plans enabling you to find important exhibits.

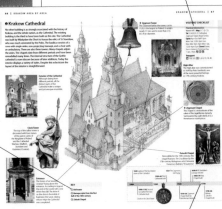

A timeline indicates important dates in the history of the building.

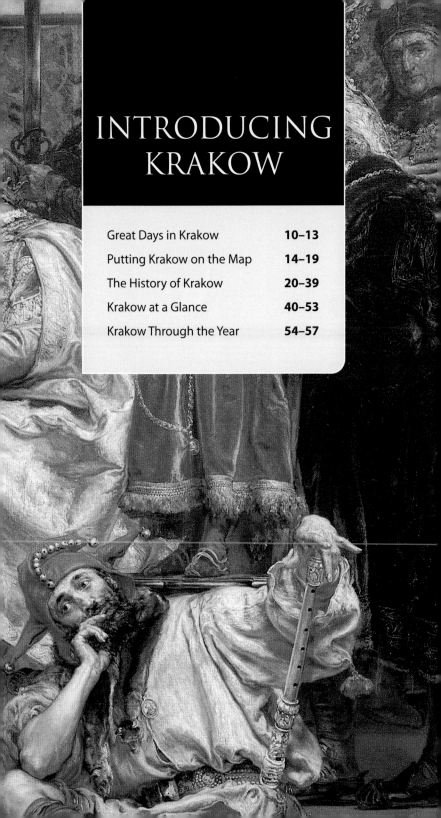

INTRODUCING KRAKOW

GREAT DAYS IN KRAKOW

There are three themes that define the most visited city in Poland – its royal past, Judaism and culture. Some of Krakow's most important sights are along the Royal Route to the Wawel Castle, while the Kazimierz district, home to the city's Jews since the 14th century, is seeing a welcome revival after the tragedy of the Holocaust. As Poland's cultural capital, many museums here house artistic treasures. Krakow is also a surprisingly green city, full of parks and meadows particularly suited to children. The four days on pages 10–11 are designed to uncover the city from these three different viewpoints; the price guides include travel, food and admission fees. The itineraries on pages 12–13 show visitors how to make the most of their time based on length of stay.

Walking the Royal Route

Two Adults allow at least 340zł

- **Explore Krakow's Old Quarter**
- **Great views from the Town Hall Tower**
- **Authentic Polish cuisine**
- **Impressive churches and a cathedral**

Morning

Starting early to avoid the crowds, especially in summer, there is no better way to enter Krakow's Old Quarter than through the 700-year-old **St Florian's Gate** (see p113), one of the few remnants of the city's original defences. Stroll along **Floriańska Street** (see p116), once Krakow's main commercial thoroughfare and still very much a thriving shopping street; it's lined with cafés and fashion boutiques that sell international brands. Krakow's **Market Square** (see pp100–103) is both the geographical and

St Florian's Gate, part of the defensive walls that surrounded the city

spiritual heart of the city, and is surrounded on all sides by historic treasures; **St Mary's** (see pp94–7) and **St Aldabert's** (see p99) churches are worth a look. Listen out for the short bugle call played from the north, south, east and west sides of the left tower of the Church of St Mary every hour. Climb the 70-m- (230-ft-) high **Town Hall Tower** (see p99) for superb panoramic views and wander around the market inside the 14th-century **Cloth Hall** (see pp104–5). For lunch, enjoy some classic Polish dishes at Krakow's oldest restaurant, **Wierzynek** (see p194).

Afternoon

One of Krakow's oldest streets, **Grodzka** (see p80) is a cobbled route of different, but harmonious, architectural styles. Admire the remodelled **Royal Arsenal** (see p81) and the modest but charming **Church of St Giles** opposite (see p81). A little further down, don't miss the **Church of St Martin** (see p81), set slightly back from the street, or the impressively preserved Romanesque **Church of St Andrew** (see p80). Take a look inside the **Church of Saints Peter and Paul** (see pp82–3), an early Baroque masterpiece modelled on the Jesuit Church of Il Gesù in Rome. At the end of the Royal Route is **Wawel Hill** (see pp62–3), and late in the afternoon, after the majority of visitors have gone, you can stroll the hill at leisure. Be sure to visit the wonderful **Wawel Cathedral** (see pp66–71), and to wander around the Renaissance-style inner courtyard of the **Wawel Royal Castle** (see pp72–3).

The 16th-century interior of the Old Synagogue, Kazimierz

Jewish Krakow

Two Adults allow at least 180zł

- **The history of Krakow's Jewish population**
- **Great kosher food**
- **World War II Jewish ghetto**
- **The famous Schindler Factory**

Morning

Start your day at the **Old Synagogue** (see p124), damaged during World War II, but now restored to its original 16th-century design. The exhibition inside serves as a good introduction to the history of Jews in Krakow. Nearby are two cemeteries: the **New Jewish Cemetery** (see p125), created in the 19th century as a resting place for the city's wealthiest Jews, and **Remu'h Cemetery** (see pp124–5) in the courtyard of the Remu'h synagogue. For a kosher lunch head to **Klezmer Hois** (see p194).

Afternoon

Stroll over the **Father Bernatek** footbridge *(see p159)* to the Podgórze district. The Nazis moved the Jews here from Kazimierz in 1941, squeezing them into a ghetto in the area around Bohaterów Getta and Rynek Podgórski. The **Pharmacy Under the Eagle** *(see p158)* at Bohaterów Getta 18 contains memories of ghetto life. At Lipowa 4 is the former **Schindler's Factory** *(see p158)*, featured in the film *Schindler's List*. An exhibition details stories from Krakow's Polish and Jewish inhabitants during World War II. The adjacent MOCAK art gallery *(see p159)* is an unmissable introduction to contemporary Polish culture.

Flowers in bloom on the Planty greenbelt

City of Culture

Two Adults allow at least 230zł

- Admire treasures and jewels at the Royal Castle
- Visit the former home of Pope John Paul II
- Explore the Collegium Maius
- Beautiful Secessionist architecture

Morning

Head straight for the **Wawel Royal Castle** *(see pp72–3)* to see the Royal Apartments and check out the collections of royal insignia and suits of armour in the Crown Treasury and Armoury. Next, stroll down to the charming **Kanonicza Street** *(see p81)*, lined with houses displaying

The courtyard of the Jagiellonian University, in the Collegium Maius

a variety of architectural styles, and the **Palace of Bishop Erazm Ciołek** *(see p84)*, which houses a spectacular collection of ecclesiastical art dating from the 14th to the 18th century. On the same street is the **Archdiocesan Museum** *(see p84)*, a building popular with pilgrims interested in the life of Pope John Paul II, who lived here in the 1950s. For lunch, head to **Kurka Wodna** *(see p192)* for outstanding modern Polish food.

Afternoon

A walk through the southern part of the **Planty** *(see pp170–71)*, past the bronze statue of Copernicus, to the Jagiellonian University and Museum in the **Collegium Maius** *(see pp108–9)*, is the perfect post-lunch stroll. Enjoy the glorious courtyard and take the 30-minute guided tour of the building, then take a quick peek inside the **Church of St Anne** *(see pp110–11)*. If you have an appetite for more art, head to the **Bunker of Art** *(see p107)*, home to cutting-edge exhibitions. Next, pay a visit to the **Słowacki Theatre** *(see p117)*. It is officially closed unless there is a performance on, but the doorman may just let you in to admire the lovely Secessionist interior. Round off this cultural day with dinner at **Jazz Club U Muniaka** *(see p208)*, Krakow's best jazz café.

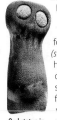
Owl statue in the Planty

A Family Day

Family of Four allow 545zł

- The magical and mysterious Dragon's Lair
- Picnic lunch in the park
- Shopping in the Cloth Hall
- Cycle round the city

Morning

Few children will fail to be intrigued by the **Dragon's Lair** *(see p65)* on Wawel Hill, a warren of tunnels, nooks and crannies. They can then shop for chocolate at **Wawel** *(see p201)* before you head next door to the deli to buy bread, sausage and cheese for a picnic lunch. Then visit the **Cloth Hall** *(pp104–5)*, which sells excellent wooden toys.

Afternoon

Tram 20 will take you out to the family-friendly Jordan Park, where you can linger over lunch while the kids take a paddle-boat on the lake. If you still have some energy, take a bike tour around the sights of the city with Krakow Bike Tour (www.krakowbiketour.com). The tour starts from ul. Grodzka 2 at 3pm. After such an active afternoon, you might want an early dinner; try **U Babci Maliny** *(see p193)*, a cosy basement restaurant serving traditional Polish fare.

2 Days in Krakow

- Stroll around the buzzing Market Square
- Admire the tombs of Poland's kings in Wawel Cathedral
- Explore the mixed Jewish-Christian heritage of the Kazimierz Quarter

Krakow's Market Square, with St Adalbert's Church to the left

Day 1

Morning Start with a circuit of the **Market Square** (pp92–3) before exploring the covered stalls of the Renaissance **Cloth Hall** (pp104–5). Join the crowds milling around at the foot of the **Mickiewicz Statue** (p93), then head for the sumptuously decorated **Church of St Mary** (pp94–7). Try to arrive by 11:50am to observe the ritual unveiling of Veit Stoss's **High Altar** (pp96–7).

Afternoon Walk south through the Okół district along **Grodzka Street** (p80) to **Wawel Hill** (pp60–75), site of **Wawel Cathedral** (pp66–71) and **Wawel Royal Castle** (pp72–3). Admire the stunning views from the ramparts before taking the spiral steps down to the **Dragon's Lair** cave (p65). Finish the day with a stroll on the Vistula riverbank just below.

Day 2

Morning Explore the multicultural past of the **Kazimierz Quarter** (pp120–29) with a stroll around its atmospheric streets and piazzas, notably the former market square of **Szeroka Street** (pp122–3). Visit the **Old Synagogue** (p124) and the **Remu'h Synagogue** (p124) for an evocative taste of Jewish Krakow, then stop at one of the area's many restaurants for lunch.

Afternoon Cross the footbridge at the end of Mostowa Street to reach **Schindler's Factory** (p158), now a moving museum recalling the fate of many Krakovians during World War II. Head back northwards via the western half of Kazimierz,

with its churches of **Corpus Christi** (p125) and **St Catherine** (p128). In the evening, stay in Kazimierz to enjoy the numerous cafés and bars of this bohemian quarter.

3 Days in Krakow

- Step back into Krakow's Middle Ages with a visit to the Rynek Underground
- Tour the former royal apartments of Wawel Royal Castle
- Spend a day at the Auschwitz-Birkenau memorial museum

Day 1

Morning Soak in the sights of the **Market Square** (pp92–3), including the subterranean history museum **Rynek Underground** (p99). Enjoy the rich interior of the **Church of St Mary** (pp94–7) before

The statue of Apollo topping the façade of the Palace of Art

strolling up **Floriańska Street** (pp116–17) towards the **Barbican** (p116), pausing to admire the 19th-century paintings and furnishings at the **Matejko House** (p116). From here, walk west the **Planty** (pp170–71) towards Szczepański Square.

Afternoon Delve into Krakow's artistic heritage with a visit to the ornate **Palace of Art** (p107) and the nearby **Bunker of Art** (p107). Walk south through the atmospheric University quarter to the **Collegium Maius** (pp108–9) and the Baroque splendour of the **Church of St Anne** (pp110–11). Finish at the **Franciscan Church** (pp88–9), famous for its beautiful Art Nouveau frescoes by Stanisław Wyspiański.

Day 2

Morning Devote a few hours to **Wawel Hill** (pp60–75). Explore the royal tombs in **Wawel Cathedral** (pp66–71) before choosing to see at least one of the many museum collections located in **Wawel Royal Castle** (pp72–3).

Afternoon Take a stroll around the former Jewish quarter of **Kazimierz** (pp120–29), calling in at renovated synagogues such as the **Tempel** (p124), the **Isaak's** (p124) and the **Remu'h** (p124). Walk through the **Remu'h Cemetery** (pp124–5) and the **New Jewish Cemetery** (p125), filled with reminders of Kazimierz's rich Jewish past. If time allows, cross the river and visit **Schindler's Factory** (p158).

Day 3
Morning Take the bus to Oświęcim for a guided tour of the former **Auschwitz** concentration camp (pp164–5).

Afternoon Visit the nearby killing fields of **Birkenau** (pp166–7) before returning to Krakow by bus.

5 Days in Krakow

- Immerse yourself in Krakow's monument-packed Old Town
- Descend into the amazing underground world of the Wieliczka Salt Mines
- Enjoy woodland walks in Las Wolski forest

Day 1
Morning Explore the **Market Square** (pp92–3), touring the Gallery of Polish Art on the top floor of the **Cloth Hall** (pp104–5) before climbing the **Town Hall Tower** (p99) for views of the Old Town skyline. Admire the altars of the **Church of St Mary** (pp94–7), then take a peek at **St Barbara's Church** (p98) just behind it. Stand beneath the towers of the Church of St Mary on the hour to hear a trumpeter playing the *hejnał* bugle-call (p94).

Afternoon Walk south along **Grodzka Street** (p80), pausing to examine the churches of **St Andrew** (pp80–81) and **Saints Peter and Paul** (pp82–3).

Wawel Royal Castle at Wawel Hill seen from across the Vistula River

Detour into pretty **Kanonicza Street** (p81), where you can visit the medieval art collections of the **Archdiocesan Museum** (p84) and the **Palace of Bishop Erazm Ciołek** (p84). Afterwards, spend a leisurely hour or two walking the complete circuit of the **Planty** (p170–71).

Day 2
Morning Devote the morning to as many museum collections within **Wawel Royal Castle** (pp72–3) as you have time for. If time is at a premium, prioritize the State Rooms and the Private Royal Apartments. Try to arrive early, since there may be queues for tickets.

Afternoon Head for **Kazimierz** (pp120–29) and visit the area around **Szeroka Street** (pp122–3), site of the original Jewish quarter. Afterwards, visit the western part of the Kazimierz district, with the **Church of**

St Catherine and the **Paulite Church "On the Rock"** (p128).

Day 3
Morning and afternoon
Reserve the whole day for a bus trip to the **Auschwitz-Birkenau** memorial museum (pp164–7), taking time to walk through the extensive Birkenau site.

Day 4
Morning Catch a swift suburban train to **Wieliczka** to take a guided tour of the spectacular man-made caverns of the **Salt Mines** (p160).

Afternoon Return to Krakow by train and take the tram to **Nowa Huta** (p156). You can then stroll from the centre of this 1950s-era suburb to the medieval **Mogiła Monastery** (p156) nearby. Again taking the tram, call at the **Polish Aviation Museum** (p156) on your way back to the city centre.

Day 5
Morning Explore the extensive art and history collections of the **National Museum in Krakow** (pp150–51). Be sure to leave enough time for the modern paintings on the top floor.

Afternoon Walk, cycle or catch a bus to the Zwierzyniec district in order to scale the **Kościuszko Mound** (p173). Follow this up with a stroll or mountain-bike ride around the **Las Wolski** forest (pp174–5), pausing to visit either **Krakow Zoo** (p175) or the **Camaldolese Monastery** (p174).

Kościuszko Mound and the fortification surrounding it

Putting Krakow on the Map

The old part of Krakow (Kraków), with the Royal Castle on Wawel Hill, is regarded as a fascinating historic town rich in heritage. The historic quarters constitute only a small part of present-day Krakow, the largest urban development in the Lesser Poland (Małopolska) region. The geographical position makes Krakow an ideal base for excursions to the Polish mountains, Auschwitz or the picturesque Krakow-Częstochowa Valley. The town is also well positioned for international connections to Prague, Brno, Bratislava, Vienna and L'viv.

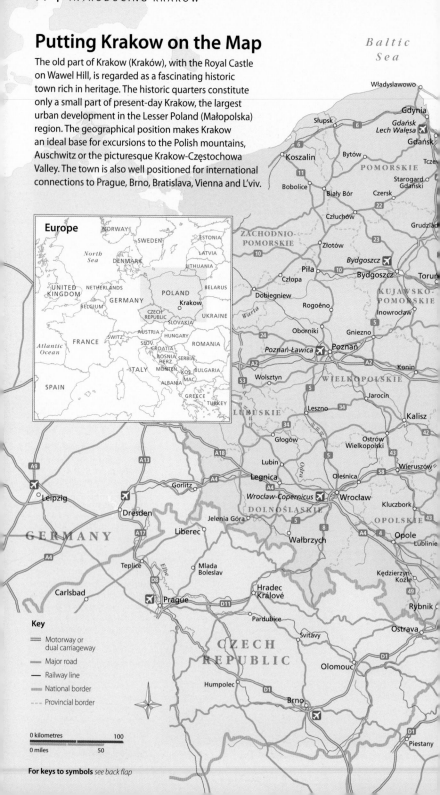

Key

══ Motorway or dual carriageway

── Major road

── Railway line

▬▬ National border

- - - Provincial border

0 kilometres   100

0 miles   50

For keys to symbols *see back flap*

Krakow and Environs

See next page

See map above

Krakow and its Environs

Until the early 20th century the conurbation of Krakow occupied a relatively small area on the banks of the Vistula (Wisła) River and was made up of several small towns (Kleparz, Kazimierz, Garbary and Podgórze). Greater Krakow was established in 1910 after the incorporation of the extensive lands of Rakowice, Prądnik, Czarna Wieś, Krowodrza, Bielany, Dębnik, Płaszów and Prokocim. A new industrial district of Nowa Huta was constructed outside Krakow after World War II. Long walks in Krakow are always interesting as all the historic quarters have their own unique character.

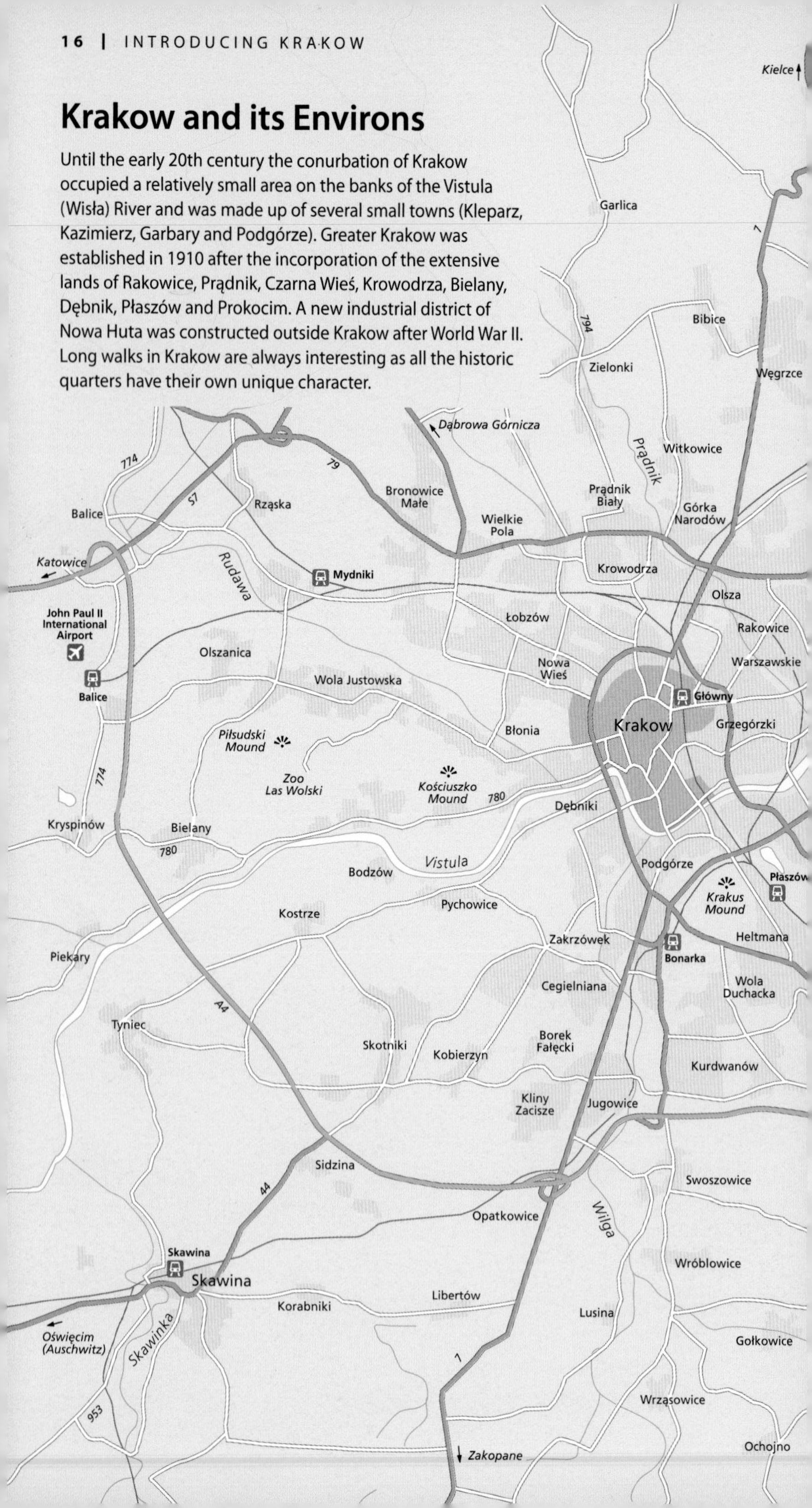

Kielce

Garlica

Bibice

Zielonki

Węgrzce

↑ Dąbrowa Górnicza

774

79

Š7

Rząska

Bronowice Małe

Witkowice

Prądnik

Prądnik Biały

Balice

Wielkie Pola

Górka Narodów

Katowice ←

Rudawa

Mydniki

Krowodrza

Olsza

John Paul II International Airport

Łobzów

Rakowice

Olszanica

Wola Justowska

Nowa Wieś

Warszawskie

Balice

Głowny

774

Piłsudski Mound

Błonia

Krakow

Grzegórzki

Zoo Las Wolski

Kościuszko Mound

780

Kryspinów

Bielany

Dębniki

780

Vistula

Podgórze

Płaszów

Bodzów

Krakus Mound

Piekary

Kostrze

Pychowice

Zakrzówek

Heltmana

A4

Cegielniana

Bonarka

Wola Duchacka

Tyniec

Skotniki

Kobierzyn

Borek Fałęcki

Kurdwanów

Kliny Zacisze

Jugowice

Sidzina

Swoszowice

44

Opatkowice

Wilga

Skawina

Wróblowice

Skawina

Korabniki

Libertów

Lusina

Gołkowice

Oświęcim (Auschwitz)

Skawinka

7

Wrząsowice

953

↓ Zakopane

Ochojno

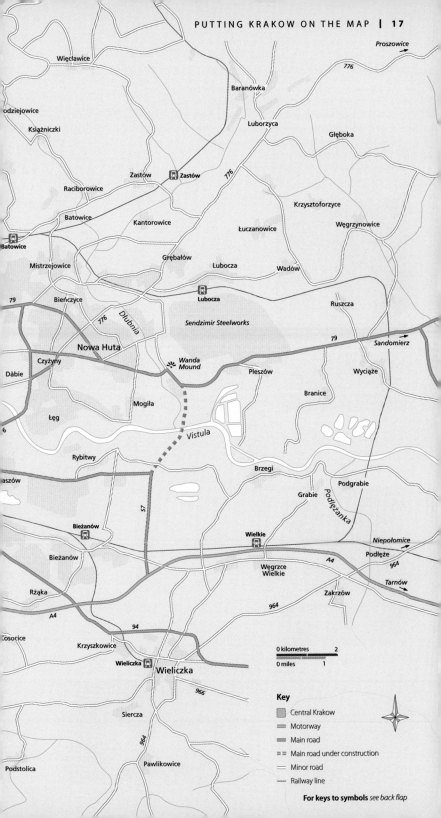

Central Krakow

Central Krakow is divided into six main sightseeing areas, each of which has its own chapter. Krakow's impressively well-preserved churches, cathedrals and palaces can be found in the Old Quarter and atop Wawel Hill. The south of the city is ideal for exploring Jewish history, while the streets surrounding the Old Quarter are replete with eclectic architecture and modern developments.

Church of St Mary
With its asymmetrical silhouette, this church is Krakow's best-known landmark *(see pp94–7).*

Zygmunt Chapel
This 16th-century chapel is regarded as the greatest example of Renaissance architecture north of the Alps *(see pp67–8).*

Old Synagogue
This Renaissance synagogue in the Kazimierz quarter is the most outstanding building of the Jewish district *(see p124).*

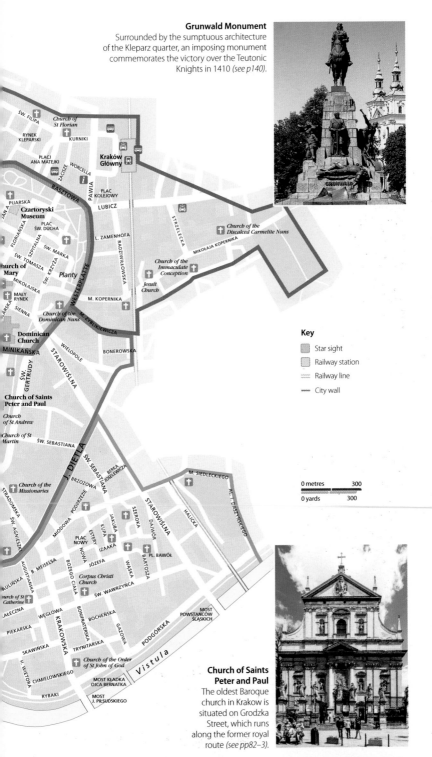

Grunwald Monument
Surrounded by the sumptuous architecture of the Kleparz quarter, an imposing monument commemorates the victory over the Teutonic Knights in 1410 *(see p140)*.

ŚW. FILIPA
Church of St Florian
RYNEK KLEPARSKI
KURNIKI
PLACJ ANA MATEJKI
ZACISZE WORCELLA
Kraków Główny
PAWIA
PLAC KOLEJOWY
BASZTOWA
LUBICZ
PIJARSKA
Czartoryski Museum
PLAC ŚW. DUCHA
L. ZAMENHOFA
FLORIAŃSKA
ŚW. SZPITALNA
ŚW. MARKA
RADZIWIŁŁOWSKA
STRZELECKA
MIKOŁAJA KOPERNIKA
Church of the Discalced Carmelite Nuns
ŚW. TOMASZA
ŚW. KRZYŻA
Planty
Church of the Immaculate Conception
Church of Mary
MIKOŁAJSKA
WESTERPLATTE
M. KOPERNIKA
Jesuit Church
MAŁY RYNEK
SIENNA
M. ZYBLIKIEWICZA
Church of the Dominican Nuns
Dominican Church
MINIKAŃSKA
STAROWIŚLNA
WIELOPOLE
BONEROWSKA
ŚW. GERTRUDY
Church of Saints Peter and Paul
Church of St Andrew
Church of St Martin
ŚW. SEBASTIANA
J. DIETLA
ŚW. SEBASTIANA
BERKA JOSELEWICZA
M. SIEDLECKIEGO
BRZOZOWA
Church of the Missionaries
STRADOMSKA
PODBRZEZIE
STAROWIŚLNA
HALICKA
MIODOWA
SZEROKA
JAKUBA
KUPA
DAJWÓR
ŚW. AGNIESZKI
PLAC NOWY
ESTERY
IZAAKA
NOWA
JÓZEFA
WĄSKA
PL. BAWÓŁ
BARTOSZA
AUGUSTIAŃSKA
B. MEISELSA
BOŻEGO CIAŁA
Corpus Christi Church
ŚW. WAWRZYŃCA
Church of St Catherine
LELECZNA
WĘGLOWA
KRAKOWSKA
BONIFRATERSKA
BOCHEŃSKA
GAZOWA
PODGÓRSKA
MOST POWSTAŃCÓW ŚLĄSKICH
PIEKARSKA
SKAWIŃSKA
TRYNITARSKA
Church of the Order of St John of God
H. WIETORA
CHMIELOWSKIEGO
Vistula
RYBAKI
MOST KŁADKA OJCA BERNATKA
MOST J. PIŁSUDSKIEGO
AL. T. GASZYŃSKIEGO

Key
- Star sight
- Railway station
- Railway line
- City wall

0 metres — 300
0 yards — 300

Church of Saints Peter and Paul
The oldest Baroque church in Krakow is situated on Grodzka Street, which runs along the former royal route *(see pp82–3)*.

For keys to symbols *see back flap*

THE HISTORY OF KRAKOW

One of the oldest cities in Poland, Krakow is also among the country's largest. For many centuries, it was the capital city and Polish rulers resided at Wawel Castle. The royal court moved to Warsaw in 1609, after parliamentary sessions and the election of kings began to take place there. Krakow retained an important place in Polish cultural life until the Partitions of Poland in the late 18th century. Deprived of its former status, Krakow suffered a significant decline in its fortunes.

It is more than 400 years since Krakow ceased to be the seat of national government, and yet the city maintains its leading role in preserving Polish national identity. Wawel Royal Palace, the seat of Polish kings, and the cathedral that bore witness to their coronations and houses their tombs, as well as the Paulite Church "On the Rock" in whose crypt prominent Poles are buried, belong to the most treasured national heritage. The 600-year-old Jagiellonian University, formerly known as the Academy of Krakow, is the oldest and one of the most important universities in the country and a pillar of Polish culture. Bearing in mind the small population of Krakow (approximately 760,000), visitors may be surprised by the great number of theatres, cabarets, concert halls and art galleries, which are always popular with regular audiences.

Polish historic cities suffered badly during World War II but Krakow's architecture escaped relatively unscathed, largely because the German Governor General had headquarters here. Despite surviving the war, for many years Krakow's treasures were left in a state of neglect, hidden beneath peeling plaster, cracking paint and layers of dirt caused by pollution. Fortunately, most buildings have now been renovated and returned to their former splendour, attracting plenty of visitors to the city.

Krakow's medieval Market Square remains at the heart of the city. It is the venue for some of the city's most important events and the traditional meeting place for locals and visitors alike, all of whom enjoy Krakow's unique atmosphere and culture.

A 19th-century lithograph of Krakow with the Kościuszko Mound (in the foreground), Museum of Krakow

◀ *Kościuszko's Defeat against the Russian-Prussian Force at Maciejowice in October 1794* by R. Weibezahl

Krakow's Origins

Krakow is one of the oldest cities in Poland. Archaeological findings provide evidence of a Palaeolithic settlement, as well as those from the Neolithic period, and the Bronze and Iron Ages. The Celtic people and invaders from the east, namely the Scythians and Huns, also left important artifacts. In the early centuries AD Krakow and Lesser Poland bordered and traded with the Roman Empire. Written accounts date only from the 9th century and pertain to the Vistulan settlers who, by the end of the same century, came under the rule of the Great Moravian Empire. Polish rulers from the House of Piast gained control over the region towards the end of the rule of Mieszko I (around 992).

Extent of the City
AD 1000   Today

An imaginary view of Wawel Castle

The cave in Wawel Hill

King Krak
The legendary founder of Krakow is believed to have lived in the early 8th century.

The Dragon of Wawel
This woodcut comes from Sebastian Münster's Cosmographia universalis *of 1544 and shows the legendary dragon and his slayer, the cobbler Skuba, below Wawel Castle.*

Earthenware with String Ornaments
These earthenware containers were among the 1st-century artifacts excavated at Nowa Huta while constructing the new town.

c. 200,000 BC Earliest evidence of settlements in the Krakow area

c. 1300 BC Lusatian culture flourishes in Lesser Poland

Palaeolithic stone tool

200,000 BC	20000	0	AD 200

c. 50,000 BC Evidence of a settlement on Wawel Hill

1st–4th century AD Krakow settlers trade with the Roman Empire

Saints Cyril and Methodius

Methodius and his brother Cyril are two of the three Patrons of Europe. Together they converted the pagans of Moravia to Christianity, which spread gradually among neighbouring Slav lands, including Poland.

Wawel means a hill surrounded by marshes

Where to See Prehistoric Krakow

Very little has survived from prehistoric times in Krakow. There are, however, two mounds worth a visit: Krakus Mound dominating the southern quarters, and Wanda Mound near Mogiła village. The Archaeological Museum *(see p85)* houses many interesting artifacts from southern Poland, and Krakow and the region surrounding it in particular. The figure of the four-faced pagan idol Światowid is of special interest.

Krakus Mound contains, according to legend, a tomb of Krak, the ancient ruler of Krakow. In reality it was more likely to have been used as a religious site of the Celts.

Światowid

This statue represents a four-faced idol holding a cornucopia. Evidence of ancient pagan cults has been found at the Wawel and other sites.

Iron Treasures

Iron objects in the form of elongated axes found at Wawel Hill were used as a form of payment in the 11th century.

600–1000 Vistulans establish their state, possibly with Krakow as the capital

965 Ibrahim Ibn Yaqub, an Arab traveller, comments on Krakow as a Czech city

| 400 | 600 | 800 | 1000 |

Early medieval earthenware vase

before 885 The Vistulans' state loses its independence. Krakow becomes part of the Great Moravian Empire

before 992 Mieszko I adds the former state of the Vistulans to his other territories

Krakow in the Early Middle Ages

Following the establishment of a bishopric in 1000 and the construction of the cathedral, Krakow became one of the most important centres of the Polish state. After the destruction of other centres in Lesser Poland (Małopolska) by the Czechs in the first half of the 11th century, Kazimierz the Restorer and his successors made Krakow their main seat. Following the death of Bolesław the Wrymouth Poland was divided into duchies, and the Dukes of Krakow gained suzerain position. From 1138 to 1320 the dukes aimed to unite the remaining provinces. Krakow was sacked by the Tatars in 1241, but was quick to recover.

Extent of the City
1253   Today

Bishop Stanisław in prayer

Szczerbiec
According to legend this is the sword of Bolesław the Brave with which he struck the Golden Gate of Kiev on entering the city in 1018. The sword was actually made in the 13th century. Today it is housed in the Crown Treasury as one of the most treasured regalia.

Denarius of Bolesław the Brave
Following the establishment of Krakow's bishopric in 1000, Bolesław made this city one of his seats.

c. 1038 Kazimierz the Restorer makes Krakow the capital of Poland

1000 Bishopric of Krakow established

1020 Construction of first cathedral in Krakow begins

1079–98 Construction of St Andrew's Church

c. 1044 Benedictine Abbey at Tyniec is established

1079 Martyrdom of St Stanisław

Coat of arms of the Chapter of Krakow

1090–1142 Construction of second cathedral at Wawel

| 1000 | 1025 | 1050 | 1075 | 1100 | 112 |

The Supposed Mitre of St Stanisław
This ornate 13th-century mitre decorated with pearls, sapphires and rubies testifies to the riches of metropolitan Krakow, one of the most important bishoprics in medieval Poland.

Where to See Romanesque Krakow

Krakow is rich in Romanesque architecture. Some buildings have survived in their original form, though they have often been enlarged and refurbished. The Church of St Andrew *(see pp80–81)* dates from this period, as does St Adalbert's *(see p99)* and the remains of the earliest buildings at Wawel, including the Rotunda of the Virgin Mary *(see p65)* and the little Church of the Holy Redeemer *(see p172).*

King Bolesław the Bold

The Church of St Adalbert was, according to legend, consecrated by Adalbert before his missionary journey to Prussia in 997.

Kazimierz the Restorer after Jan Matejko
It can be said that Krakow owes its capital status to this ruler, who settled here around 1038 and established a central administration.

The Crypt of St Leonard is a remnant of Krakow's second cathedral. It was built by Władysław Herman between 1090 and 1142.

The Death of Bishop Stanisław

The conflict between Bishop Stanisław of Szczepanów (later canonized) and Bolesław the Bold ended with the murder of the bishop in 1079 and the exile of the king. Both events contributed to the weakening of Poland. The cult of St Stanisław began in the 15th century. This scene decorates a 16th-century chasuble (priest's vestment) commissioned by Piotr Kmita.

1138 Bolesław the Wrymouth grants Krakow the status of a capital of the suzerain province

1173 Bolesław the Curly is the first Piast to be buried at Wawel

Cloister at the Dominican Church

1241 Tatars led by Batu Khan destroy Krakow

| 1150 | 1175 | 1200 | 1225 | 1250 |

1141–1320 Polish dukes fight for Krakow

Benedictine Abbey at Tyniec

1250 Consecration of the Dominican Church

Gothic Krakow

The charter granted to Krakow in 1257 facilitated urban development and allowed for a new and more structured plan. A Gothic defence wall surrounded the city, and Krakow began to flourish anew following the coronation of Władysław the Short in 1320. The new satellite towns of Kazimierz and Kleparz both received municipal charters. The architectural panorama of Krakow was substantially transformed by the building of many new churches and the cathedral (the third on Wawel Hill) in the 14th and 15th centuries. The foundation of the Krakow Academy, and its subsequent renewal, contributed greatly to the development of culture and intellectual activities.

Extent of the City
1370   Today

The coat of arms of the Piasts

The Diptych Reliquary
A double leaf Gothic reliquary containing the relics of saints is decorated with the image of the Virgin Mary and that of Christ.

Saints Stanisław and Wacław shown standing on the battlement walls are patron saints of Wawel Cathedral and the Kingdom of Poland.

A View of Late Gothic Krakow, 1493
This townscape from the 15th-century *World Chronicle* by Hartmann Schedel is the earliest known view of Krakow.

1285 Construction of Krakow's defence walls begins

Coat of arms of Kazimierz

1364 Krakow Academy founded by Kazimierz the Great

1312 Revolt of German burghers, led by Albert

1340 Construction of Corpus Christi Church begins

1250	1275	1300	1325	1350

1257 Duke Bolesław the Chaste grants Krakow her charter on 5 June

Crown of Kazimierz the Great (replica)

1335 Kazimierz the Great grants Kazimierz its charter

1366 Kleparz (Florencja) receives its charter

Krakow's Charter
The municipal status granted to Krakow was modelled on the Magdeburg law and contributed to uniform urban development.

The coats of arms shown on both sides of the gate are those of Bolesław the Chaste who granted Krakow her charter.

Krużlowa Madonna
This beautiful Madonna with Child is an interesting example of the influence of International Gothic on wood sculpture of Lesser Poland in the 15th century.

Seal of the Royal City of Krakow
The 14th-century Great Seal of Krakow (shown here with the image reversed) features the emblem of Poland, thus stressing the role of Krakow as its capital.

Where to See Gothic Krakow

Some of the biggest attractions in Krakow are the Gothic buildings, such as the Barbican *(see p116)*, St Florian's Gate *(see p113)* and the Collegium Maius *(see pp108–9)*, and large churches such as St Mary's *(see pp94–5)*, the Dominican Church *(see pp118–19)*, St Catherine's *(see p128)* and Corpus Christi *(see p125)*. Some smaller churches, such as the Holy Cross *(see p117)*, are equally interesting. The works by Veit Stoss are gems of Gothic art.

The cathedral *(see pp66–71)* is the burial place of kings and the seat of the local archbishop.

The Church of the Holy Cross has a single nave whose interior is covered with palm vaulting.

1386 Grand Duke Jogaila of Lithuania becomes King Władysław II Jagiełło of Poland

Mace of the rector of Krakow Academy

1473 First Polish printing house of Łukasz Straube issues a calendar

| | 1400 | 1425 | 1450 | 1475 | 1500 |

ore 1400 Collegium Maius is stablished

1400 Władysław Jagiełło re-establishes the Krakow Academy

1477–89 Veit Stoss works on the high altar at St Mary's

Coat of arms of the Jagiellonians

1492 Kazimierz Jagiellończyk dies

Renaissance Krakow

Krakow, the capital city, developed rapidly in the 16th century and began to change in appearance. The Cloth Hall, the city landmark, was remodelled in the Renaissance style, and the rich merchants of Krakow also began to modernize their houses. The art and culture of the Italian Renaissance was assimilated by the royal courts of King Aleksander and King Zygmunt the Old and his second wife Bona Sforza. Bartolomeo Berrecci, Giovanni Maria Padovano and other outstanding Italian masters established their workshops in Krakow during this time.

Extent of the City
1572　　Today

Shield with the Polish eagle

Royal orb　　Royal sceptre

"The Sword Makers" from the Baltazar Behem Codex
This Codex of 1505 contains laws and privileges of the town guilds and is illustrated with 27 illuminations showing craftsmen at work.

A Tapestry with Satyrs
This is one of 160 tapestries commissioned in the 16th century by Zygmunt August for the Wawel Collection.

1502–5 Erection of King Jan Olbracht's monument, the first work of Renaissance art in Poland

1505 Baltazar Behem Codex made

Head in the Hall of Deputies

1525 Homage paid by the Prussians to the Polish King in the Market Square on 10 April

1543 The treatise *De revolutionibus* by Copernicus is published

1500	1510	1520	1530	1540

1504 Rebuilding of the Wawel Castle starts

1513 First Polish book in print from the Ungler House

1521 Zygmunt's Bell is hung

1519 Bartolomeo Berrecci begins work on Zygmunt's Chapel in the cathedral

NICOLAI CO
PERNICI TORINENSIS
DE REVOLVTIONIBVS ORBI-
um cœlestium, Libri VI.

Detail of the title page from Copernicus's treatise

A Renaissance Portal
The first post office in 16th-century Poland, serving the Krakow-Venice route, was situated in the house of Prospero Provana. Today the building houses the Hotel Pod Różą.

Cock of the Marksmen's Brotherhood
This gilt masterpiece, made in 1565, belonged to the members of the Brotherhood whose aim was to support soldiers responsible for the defence of the town.

Oval recess with Renaissance decoration

Monument of Zygmunt August
King Zygmunt August was a patron of the arts. It was through his commissions that the Royal Castle at Wawel was enriched with an outstanding collection of tapestries. The king's monument was made by Santi Gucci between 1574 and 1575, in Hungarian red marble.

Where to See Renaissance Krakow

Renaissance architecture was introduced by Italian masters during the rebuilding of Wawel Royal Castle in the early 16th century. The Zygmunt Chapel *(see pp66–71)*, the Montelupis Monument at St Mary's Church *(see pp94–5)* and a number of houses at Kanonicza Street *(see p81)* are among the finest examples of Renaissance art and architecture in the city.

The arcaded courtyard at Wawel Royal Castle is one of the most beautiful in Europe *(see pp72–3)*.

The Renaissance Cloth Hall *(see pp104–5)*, topped with a characteristic parapet, displayed the prosperity of Jagiellonian Krakow.

Tomb of Stefan Batory

After 1550 Santi Gucci comes to Poland

1595 Santi Gucci works on the tomb of King Stefan Batory

1550	1560	1570	1580	1590

1569 Polish-Lithuanian commonwealth established

1586 First secular secondary school is opened

1595 Archconfraternity of The Passion established

1556–1559 Giovanni Maria Padovano rebuilds the Cloth Hall

1574 Coronation of the first elected king, Henri de Valois

1596 Royal court moves from Krakow to Warsaw

Baroque Krakow

The 17th and 18th centuries saw the decline of Krakow. After the king had moved his residence to Warsaw, he was followed by the noblemen who held high office. Foreign incursions and occupations, wars and the First Partition of Poland in 1772 all added to the city's woes. Despite a number of attempts at reform towards the end of the rule of Stanisław August Poniatowski, Krakow became a provincial, underdeveloped frontier town, though the atmosphere was enlivened by royal coronations and funerals. The failure of the Kościuszko Insurrection of 1794 and the subsequent Third Partition of Poland in 1795 brought an end to Krakow's prominence.

Extent of the City
☐ 1700   ☐ Today

The Evangelists with their symbols: eagle, angel, lion and ox.

Hood of the 1669 Coronation Cape
The eagle (the emblem of the Commonwealth) on the *cappa magna* of Bishop Tomicki, made for the coronation of Michał Wiśniowiecki, was embroidered with pearls and sapphires.

Figures of the Holy Doctors of the Church

Epitaph of King Władysław IV
The monumental and sombre interior of the Vaza Chapel in the cathedral is decorated with black marble and features splendid memorial plaques of the Vaza dynasty.

King David
This late Baroque dancing figure in the Corpus Christi Church was made by Anton Gegenbaur in the second half of the 18th century.

1626–9 Canopy of St Stanisław is erected in the cathedral

1619 Church of Saints Peter and Paul is completed

1661 First Polish newspaper "Merkuriusz Polski" published by Jan Alexander Gorczyn's Press

Title page of "Merkuriusz Polski"

MERKVRIVSZ POLSKI.

| 1600 | 1620 | 1640 | 1660 | 1680 |

1609 Zygmunt III Vaza finally abandons his Krakow residence in favour of Warsaw on 25 May

Zygmunt III Vaza

1655–7 Swedish, then Transylvanian, armies occupy Krakow

1676 University Press is established after Krakow Academy buys Piotrowczyks' Press

1664–76 Vaza Chapel in the cathedral is completed

Memorial Plaque of Bishop Denhoff
Memorial plaques of bishops in the cloister adjoining the Franciscan Church date from different periods. This plaque was made in the early 18th century, probably to a design by Baldassare Fontana.

Where to See Baroque Krakow

The Church of Saints Peter and Paul *(see pp82–3)*, Krakow's earliest Baroque church, as well as later churches, including St Anne's *(see pp110–11)* and the Church of the Order of St John of God *(see p128)*, represent the best of Baroque architecture from Tylman von Gameren and Kacper Bażanka, among others.

A silver sarcophagus with the Bishop's mitre and crozier is a reliquary of St Stanisław.

Kołłątaj's Panoramic Map of Krakow
Hugo Kołłątaj led the reform of the university. In 1785 he also created this precise map of Krakow, which shows all the land owned by the city.

The Church of Saints Peter and Paul is one of the finest early Baroque churches in Central Europe.

Canopy of St Stanisław
This canopy in Wawel Cathedral was inspired by a number of unexecuted designs for the great baldachin in St Peter's in the Vatican.

The façade of the Church of the Missionaries *(see p89)* was inspired by Roman Baroque architecture, in particular by the work of Bernini and Borromini.

Medal of Virtuti Militari

1788 Astronomical Observatory established

1794 Tadeusz Kościuszko takes his oath in the Market Square on 24 March

1734 Coronation of August III Wettin, the last to take place in Krakow, on 17 January

1768–72 Confederates of Bar fight for Krakow

| 00 | 1720 | 1740 | 1760 | 1780 | 1800 |

1705 St Anne's Church is consecrated

1777–8 Hugo Kołłątaj reforms the Krakow Academy

1791 Kazimierz and Kleparz incorporated into Krakow

1702–05 Krakow is invaded several times by the Swedes

1795 Wawel Royal Castle made into barracks for the Austrian army

Hugo Kołłątaj

Krakow in Galicia

In 1772 Austria occupied the southern part of Poland, called Galicia. After a period of Austrian occupation, Krakow was briefly incorporated into the Duchy of Warsaw. The Russian occupation followed. In 1815 the Republic of Krakow, which included the area round the city, was established, but by 1846 Krakow was under Austrian rule again. After a period of suppression, Galicia received extensive autonomy from the 1860s onwards. During the 19th century Krakow was the only Polish territory to enjoy relative freedom. It embarked upon a mission of safeguarding traditions and celebrating past historic successes, thus becoming the spiritual capital of Poland.

Extent of the City

▨ 1818   ☐ Today

Sarcophagus of Prince Józef Poniatowski
Of all the famous Poles who died abroad, Józef Poniatowski was the first to have his body brought back to receive a solemn funeral, which turned into a patriotic demonstration.

A beggar woman receiving alms

Emperor Franz Joseph

The Opening of the Sarcophagus of Kazimierz the Great by Jan Matejko
An accidental discovery of the remains of the king prompted his second funeral in 1869, which became an event on a national scale, reminiscent of the glorious past.

The Entry of Emperor Franz Joseph in 1880

Franz Joseph was a popular ruler with the people of Krakow. He was believed to be behind the development of the city and its autonomy. A series of watercolours by Juliusz Kossak (1824–99), such as this one, depicts his stay in Krakow.

Ruins of the fire-damaged Dominican Church

1813–15 Krakow occupied by the Austrians

1846 Krakow Uprisin Krakow become part of Austr

| 1800 | 1810 | 1820 | 1830 | 1840 |

1809 Krakow incorporated into the Duchy of Warsaw

1810–14 City walls demolished

1820–23 Kościuszko Mound constructed

1815 "Free, independent and strictly neutral city of Krakow" and her region established as the Republic of Krakow

Coat of arms of Galicia

House of Jan Matejko
Jan Matejko, whose particular genre of history painting imprinted in the nation's mind an image of its past, lived in this house *(see p116)*.

Inhabitants of Krakow greeting the Emperor

Where to See 19th-Century Krakow

The architecture of Krakow in the 19th century was eclectic. The Renaissance Revival style predominated (for example the Academy of Fine Arts, *see p138*), and was often influenced by the monumental architecture of Vienna, the place where many of Krakow's architects trained. The university buildings are a good example of Gothic Revival in which the historic style is blended with vernacular features.

The Church of the Felician Nuns is one of the few buildings in the Romanesque Revival style *(see p146)*.

Design for the Mickiewicz Monument
This model by Antoni Kurzawa was never fully executed. It is held at the National Museum in Krakow.

The Collegium Novum is a prestigious Gothic Revival building designed by Feliks Księżarski *(see p106)*.

The Krakow Uprising
The uprising of 1846 was intended to spark a revolt in all parts of partitioned Poland, but was suppressed by the Austrians.

1866 Local government established in Krakow with Józef Dietl as Mayor

1854 Society of Friends of Fine Arts established

1872 Academy of Skills established

1876 Czartoryski Collection opens to the public

1883–7 Collegium Novum built

1850	1860	1870	1880	1890

1850 Great fire of Krakow

Apparatus for condensing oxygen

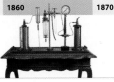

1883 Two Krakow scientists, Z. Wróblewski and K. Olszewski, condense oxygen

1893 Słowacki Theatre opens

Modernist Krakow

At the end of the 19th century Greater Krakow was established and became a place of mass excursions from other parts of occupied Poland. People came to see the newly re-established university and the repossessed Wawel, which was then undergoing restoration. It was the period of "art for art's sake", and Krakow became a mecca for Polish artists. Modern life concentrated around artistic cafés, such as the Paon and the Jama Michalika, which were also venues for cabarets. The latter café housed the Zielony Balonik Cabaret. The ambience in Krakow was one of melancholy and decadence but life, permeated by patriotic Neo-Romantic symbolism, was lived here to the full. The outbreak of World War I put an end to this unique bohemian era.

Extent of the City
▦ 1900　▢ Today

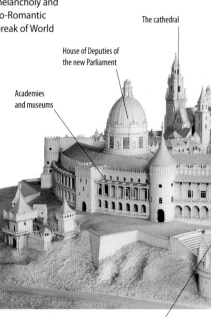

The cathedral

House of Deputies of the new Parliament

Academies and museums

An amphitheatre modelled on the Barbican in Krakow

Helenka
Stanisław Wysplański often painted portraits of his friends and family; this is a 1900 painting of his daughter.

"Życie"
This is the masthead of the magazine of the Polish Modernist movement. The contributors were the leading authors of the time.

1897 "Życie" weekly is established

1898 Stanisław Przybyszewski arrives in Krakow

1901 Palace of Art, the seat of the Society of Friends of the Fine Arts, is built

1903–5 Old Theatre (Teatr Stary) rebuilt in the Art Nouveau style

| 1895 | 1897 | 1899 | 1901 | 1903 | 19 |

1895 Adam Mickiewicz's statue is unveiled

1898–1900 Stanisław Wyspiański decorates the Franciscan Church with murals and stained glass

1901 Premiere of *The Wedding* by Stanisław Wyspiański

Wyspiański's Art Nouveau murals in the Franciscan Church

Poster by Stanisław Wyspiański
This poster announces a lecture by S. Przybyszewski followed by a play by M. Maeterlinck.

Marionettes from the Zielony Balonik Cabaret
This cabaret and New Year's satirical show, staged by Karol Frycz, ridiculed the narrow-mindedness and hypocrisy of the middle classes.

Reconstructed churches of St George and St Michael

Stadium modelled on Roman architecture

Polish Acropolis by Stanisław Wyspiański

The idea behind this design for the rebuilding of the entire Wawel Hill was to transform the Royal Castle into a political, social, academic and cultural centre of the liberated Poland. Its architecture was intended to reflect a synthesis of Polish history.

Where to See Modernist Krakow

Modernist Krakow was, above all, a city of literature and painting. Architecture from this period is scarce. There are, however, some magnificent buildings, such as the spider House "Pod pająkiem" (*see p153*) and the Palace of Art (*see p107*). Art Nouveau interiors of exceptional beauty can be found at the Franciscan Church with its stained glass and murals, designed by Wyspiański (*see pp86–7*), the Society of Physicians building (*see p134*) and the prestigious former Museum of Industry and Technology (*see p146*).

During the rebuilding of the Old Theatre (Teatr Stary) in the Art Nouveau style its façade was decorated with a stucco floral frieze (*see p107*).

The façade of the Church of the Discalced Carmelite Nuns, with its elaborate decoration, is in sharp contrast to its austere interior.

1906 Krakow sports clubs, Wisła and Cracovia, established

1907 Stanisław Wyspiański dies

1910 Riflemen's Union formed by Józef Piłsudski

1912 First cinema opens in Krakow

A late 19th-century armchair

| 1907 | 1909 | 1911 | 1913 | 1915 |

1906 Building of the Chamber of Commerce and Industry completed

1910 Grunwald Monument unveiled

The sphere at the top of the Chamber of Commerce and Industry Building

1914 First Cadre Brigade of the Polish Legions marches out of Krakow on 6 August

Krakow in the Years 1918–1945

When World War I ended in 1918, Poland regained its independence after 123 years of foreign occupation. In the period between the two World Wars Krakow provided political leaders, bureaucrats and army officers to the new Polish Republic. Above all the city was a cultural and academic centre. Art Nouveau traditions were still present in the arts but soon gave way to a new generation of artists, such as the Formists, Capists (the Polish variant of Post-Impressionists), the avant-garde Krakow Group and the Cricot Theatre. During World War II the German Governor General had his headquarters in Krakow, and this was reason enough for the city to be spared destruction.

Extent of the City

☐ 1938   ☐ Today

Kościuszko Mound

Marshal Józef Piłsudski

Tribune

Józef Piłsudski
The Commander by Konrad Krzyżanowski portrays well the personality and character of this uncompromising Polish soldier and politician.

Portrait of Nena Stachurska
This portrait is by S. I. Witkiewicz, who was one of the most unconventional artists of the 20th century. He painted under the influence of various drugs.

Figures decorating the Academy of Mines and Metallurgy Building
The first school of its type in liberated Poland was established to educate specialists for the industry in Silesia.

1918 Austrian Army disarmed in Krakow. Polish Liquidation Commission created on 31 October

1925 Tomb of the Unknown Soldier blessed

1923 Workers' unrest in Krakow

Jagiellonian Library

1918	1921	1924	1927	1930

1919 Academy of Mines and Metallurgy established

Banner which was raised in liberated Krakow

1927 Juliusz Słowacki's remains brought to Krakow and buried at Wawel

1921 Church of the Sacred Heart of Jesus at Wesoła consecrated

1930–9 Jagiellonian Library completed

Funeral of Marshal Piłsudski
The funeral of the Commander, who was buried at Wawel in 1935, was the biggest state event in interwar Poland.

Demolition of Mickiewicz's Statue
During the German occupation all monuments of importance were demolished, including those of Mickiewicz, Kościuszko and Grunwald.

A military band gallops at the head of the troops.

The Cavalry Parade

The parade of the cavalry of the Second Republic took place at Błonie on 6 October 1933 to celebrate the 250th anniversary of the Battle of Vienna, where the Polish cavalry saved the Austrian capital from the Ottomans. Wojciech Kossak painted this grand event.

Auschwitz (Oświęcim)

The name Oświęcim may have little meaning for most foreigners but the German name, Auschwitz, is a synonym for the crimes of Nazism. During World War II the Nazis established Auschwitz *(see pp164–5)* and the nearby Birkenau (Brzezinka) *(see pp166–7)* concentration camps. Just over 1.1 million people (90 per cent of them Jewish) were murdered in these camps. The Auschwitz camp was set up in 1940 to house Polish political prisoners and slave labourers. It was enlarged to include Soviet POWs, and in 1942 became an extermination camp for Jews and Gypsies, who were brought here from all over Europe. A cynical inscription over the gate leading into the Auschwitz camp reads *"Arbeit macht frei"* ("Work makes you free").

It was in the Auschwitz Death Block that Maksymilian Kolbe, a Franciscan priest, gave up his life for another inmate. Kolbe (who was later canonized) was sentenced to death by starvation.

In the old barracks of Auschwitz there are exhibitions telling the history of the camp. Temporary displays are also organized. Birkenau, 3 km (1.8 miles) away, is largely as the Germans left it. Only some of the original 300 barracks remain, along with the loading platform where new prisoners were unloaded from railway wagons and segregated.

1933 Cricot, the Artists' Theatre, is established

1935 Piłsudski is given a state funeral at Wawel

1938 Dietl's statue erected

1939 Outbreak of World War II on 1 September

1943 Jewish ghetto liquidated

1945 Soviet troops enter Krakow on 18 January

1933 | **1936** | **1939** | **1942** | **1945**

Statue of Józef Dietl

1937 Teaching commences at the Academy of Mines and Metallurgy

1941 Jewish ghetto established

1939 Krakow occupied by the Nazis on 6 September

Krakow after 1945

After World War II ended Krakow did not willingly accept the new Soviet-imposed regime. In 1946 the celebrations of the 3 May Constitution turned into clashes with tragic consequences. Many Krakovians claim that the industrial suburb of Nowa Huta, with its immense steelworks *(see p156)*, was built to "punish" the city for rejecting the 1946 Communist referendum. In fact, the site was chosen because of good rail links, proximity to the river, and Krakow's engineering and scientific heritage. It is also false to claim that pollution from Nowa Huta was meant to damage Krakow's ancient monuments. Krakow's problem with air quality is largely the result of domestic heating furnaces and vehicle fumes.

Tadeusz Sendzimir Steelworks
Formerly known as the Lenin Steelworks, the mills were expected to become a bastion of the Communist proletariat. Paradoxically, they became one of the main centres of opposition.

Banner of the Vatican

Papal high altar

Holy Mass during the Pope's Visit

The political transformation of Poland which took place after 1989 was welcomed in Krakow. The Mass celebrated in 1991 by Pope John Paul II in Market Square attracted unprecedented numbers of worshippers.

Mistrzejowice Church
Built between 1976 and 1983, the church was decorated with sculptures by Gustaw Zemła.

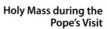

1946 Bloody suppression of 3 May celebrations

Builders' Brigade by H. Krajewska

1956 Piwnica pod Baranami Cabaret established

1967 Construction of the Ark of God Church in Nowa Huta begins

1978 Krakow included in the UNESCO World Heritage List

1980 Solidarity established

1945 | 1950 | 1955 | 1960 | 1965 | 1970 | 1975 | 1980

1949 Construction of Nowa Huta begins

1950 Nowa Huta becomes a borough of Krakow

1956 Cricot 2 Theatre established

1957 Celebrations of the city of Krakow's 700th anniversary

1964 600th anniversary of the Academy of Krakow

John Paul II

1978 Karol Wojtyła, the Metropolitan of Krakow, elected as Pope John Paul II

Demonstrations in Nowa Huta
During the period of martial law, street demonstrations in the workers' suburb of Nowa Huta often ended in riots.

Extent of the City
⬛ 1945   ☐ Today

Nobel Prize for Wisława Szymborska
The Krakow poet was awarded the 1996 Nobel Prize for Literature.

St Mary's Church

Polish banner

Where to See Modern Krakow

Very few postwar buildings in Krakow deserve notice. However, some examples of ecclesiastical architecture, namely the Abbey of the Fathers of the Resurrection designed by Dariusz Kozłowski, and two churches in Nowa Huta – the Ark of God and Mistrzejowice Church, are exceptional. An extensive programme of building renovation in old Krakow has been undertaken. Outstanding contemporary buildings include the Małopolska Garden of Arts and the Cricoteka building in Podgórze.

Sculpture Decorating the Tomb of Tadeusz Kantor
The theatre of Tadeusz Kantor (1915–90) had a Polish, as well as a European, dimension. This sculpture on his tomb was originally designed for his play *Wielopole, Wielopole.*

The Ark of God Church in Nowa Huta *(see p156) is an example of modern ecclesiastical architecture, rich in impressive forms and symbolic content.*

1981 Martial law declared in Poland on 13 December (lifted on 22 July 1983)	**1991** International Cultural Centre established **1992** European Month of Culture celebrations take place in Krakow in June	**1996** Wisława Szymborska is awarded the Nobel Prize for Literature		**2005** Pope John Paul II dies in Rome	**2010** A plane crash kills President Lech Kaczyński and his wife; Bronisław Komorowski elected president of Poland		
1985	**1990**	**1995**	**2000**	**2005**	**2010**	**2015**	**2020**
1981 Citizens Committee for the Rescue of Krakow established	**1993** Czesław Miłosz, the winner of the Nobel Prize for Literature, becomes an honorary citizen of Krakow		**2004** Poland joins the European Union (EU)		**2014** Canonization of Pope John Paul II	**2016** Krakow hosts Catholic World Youth Day	

A book by Czesław Miłosz

KRAKOW AT A GLANCE

Included on the very first UNESCO World Heritage List, Krakow has long been a destination for visitors from all over the world. Ranging from the remarkably well-preserved medieval centre to the museums and synagogues exploring the history of Krakow's Jewish community, there is much to see here, and more than a hundred of the city's sights are described in the Area by Area section of this book. To help make the most of your stay, the following 12 pages are a guide to the very best museums and galleries, as well as notable churches, that Krakow has to offer, with cross-references to full entries included for each sight. Furthermore, listed below are ten of the most popular tourist attractions to start you off.

Krakow's Top Ten Tourist Attractions

Wawel Royal Castle
See pp72–5.

Wawel Cathedral
See pp66–71.

Kościuszko Mound
See p173.

Church of St Anne
See pp110–11.

Church of St Mary
See pp94–7.

Market Square
See pp100–103.

Planty
See pp170–71.

Collegium Maius
See pp108–9.

Remu'h Cemetery
See pp124–5.

Cloth Hall
See pp104–5.

◄ The splendid Art Nouveau ceiling designed by Stanisław Wyspiański in the Franciscan Church

Krakow's Best: Museums and Galleries

Krakow has dozens of museums, which are very varied in character. The Royal Castle at Wawel offers visitors the chance to see collections housed in the royal chambers which date from the time when the Polish kings resided here. The National Museum has rich collections of Polish art housed in a number of branches in the city centre. Schindler's Factory is one of the most visited museums in Poland.

National Museum in Krakow, Main Building
One of the best collections of 20th-century Polish art is housed here. The collection of Modernist art is particularly rich, and includes excellent sculptures by Konstanty Laszczka.

PLASEK AND NOWY ŚWIAT

KARMELICKA

KRUPNICZA

SMOLEŃSK

ZWIERZYNIECKA

F. STRASZEWSKIEGO

Vistula

WAW HIL

Museum of Krakow
This museum in Krzysztofory Palace is devoted to the history of the city. Krakow is famous for her portable Christmas cribs, and the collection housed here is of great beauty.

Japanese Centre of Art and Technology
This modern building houses a collection of works from the Far East, much of which was donated by Feliks Manggha Jasieński. The *netsuke* (a kind of button) shown takes the form of a tiger.

| 0 metres | 500 |
| 0 yards | 500 |

Archaeological Museum
Many archaeological finds from the Lesser Poland area, as well as Egyptian mummies, are displayed here.

House of Matejko
In the family house of Jan Matejko, some of his works, including this study for Joan of Arc, as well as his extraordinary collection of "antiquities", are brought together.

Gallery of 19th-Century Polish Art in the Cloth Hall
In 1879 Henryk Siemiradzki presented the National Museum with its first gift, his painting *The Torches of Nero*.

Old Synagogue
A collection of Judaica, one of the best in Central Europe, is housed in this Renaissance synagogue.

Schindler's Factory
The former factory of Oskar Schindler houses a fascinating yet sobering exhibition exploring the Nazi occupation of Krakow.

Royal Castle in Wawel
This royal residence houses an outstanding art collection which includes paintings, sculptures, gold work, arms and Oriental art. The tapestries are of particular interest.

Exploring Krakow's Museums and Galleries

Krakow's museum collections tell the history of the city and Polish culture in great detail. There are also a few specialized foreign collections. A visit to all the many museums would require several weeks but it is possible to concentrate on just the most important collections and still get to know the city well. For contemporary art, head to the Museum of Contemporary Art in Krakow (MOCAK) and the Bunker of Art.

St Stanisław's Reliquary, found in the Cathedral Museum

The History of Poland and Krakow

The former residence of Polish rulers, **Wawel Royal Castle** is the best known of Krakow's museums. Visitors can explore the Armoury and Crown Treasury, and view outstanding tapestries and paintings. Worth a visit is the archaeological display "Lost Wawel", which shows the Rotunda of the Virgin Mary (Krakow's first church). A computer-generated model of Wawel gives

visitors an overview of the early 10th-century construction.

The history of the former capital of Poland is told at the **Museum of Krakow** in Krzysztofory Palace. The collections here include the insignia of municipal governments and those of guilds, seals featuring Krakow's coat of arms and many townscapes showing Krakow in the past.

The Jagiellonian University Museum is housed in the **Collegium Maius**, the oldest of the university's buildings. The museum brings together scientific equipment, of which some items are unique, as well as memorabilia left by former professors. Many rooms have retained their original furnishings.

Kazimierz was a thriving Jewish district until it was dismantled during World War II. The **Old Synagogue**, with its rich collection of Judaica, including liturgical objects, is dedicated to Jewish heritage. On the

opposite side of the Vistula, in Podgórze, is **Schindler's Factory**, which explores the fate of Krakow's citizens under Nazi occupation.

The election of the Archbishop of Krakow, Karol Wojtyła, to the pontificate was an important event in the history of the city. A room recreated in the **Archdiocesan Museum** commemorates the years spent by Karol Wojtyła in Krakow.

The courtyard of the Collegium Maius, home to the Jagiellonian University Museum

Polish Art

In 1879 Henryk Siemiradzki presented Krakow with his painting *The Torches of Nero*. He thus initiated the establishment of the **National Museum in Krakow**. Poland was then still an occupied country and the intention was to raise patriotic awareness and the morale of the Poles. Only Polish art and works relating to the history of Poland were included. As a result, the museum has only a limited selection of Western art. Its collection of historical Polish art, on the other hand, is unparalleled. The museum has a dozen branches throughout the city. Nineteenth-century Polish art, housed at the **Cloth Hall**

Deputies' Hall in the Royal Castle at Wawel

The main building of the National Museum in Krakow

Gallery, is also of great interest. Twentieth-century painting and sculpture can be admired in the main building. The museum has a programme of temporary monographic exhibitions concerned with the life and work of great Krakow artists such as Jan Matejko, Stanisław Wyspiański and Józef Mehoffer.

The museum in the wonderfully restored former **Palace of Bishop Erazm Ciołek** houses religious art through the ages. A section devoted to Orthodox religious art displays a beautiful collection of icons from Poland's eastern borderlands.

Contemporary Polish and non-Polish art can be seen at the popular **Museum of Contemporary Art in Krakow (MOCAK)**, as well as at the **Bunker of Art**, which is considered Krakow's most important gallery. Housed in a small, elegant white building, the **Józef Czapski Pavilion** is dedicated to the versatile 20th-century artist. The pavilion's colourful display includes his personal diaries and photos, as well as archival film and interview footage documenting the social and political climate of Europe during Czapski's lifetime. The **Cricoteka** displays the works of 20th-century painter and designer Tadeusz Kantor. The museum is housed in a striking modern building on the river bank.

The **Archdiocesan Museum** has a magnificent collection of Polish sacred art. The museum also organizes exhibitions of works on loan from leading church treasuries throughout Poland as well as other countries.

Foreign Art

Western art, including *Landscape with the Good Samaritan* by Rembrandt, Romanesque gold work from the Maas region and Meissen porcelain, can be found at the **Czartoryski Museum**. The museum is closed for renovation until at least 2020; during this time, its most celebrated master-piece, *The Lady with an Ermine* by Leonardo da Vinci, is on display at the National Museum in Krakow.

The **Szołajski House** hosts changing exhibitions of inter-national art, many of them featuring famous names and grand historical themes. The European branch of the Cloth Hall Gallery houses the museum's collection of western art, which displays important works by Brueghel the Younger and Lorenzo Lotto.

The Mangha **Japanese Centre of Art and Technology** covers Japanese art. A bequest of objects from the Far East presented by Feliks Manggha Jasieński constitutes the core of the collection, which also includes works by contemporary artists.

Local Culture and Natural History

The **Archaeological Museum** displays important objects found in the 19th century in Galicia (*see p32*), which was then under Austrian occupation. One of them is the statue of Światowid fished out of the Zbrucz River. Other objects found during the construction of Nowa Huta and renovation works at Kanonicza Street were also added. There is also a notable collection of Egyptian mummies.

The **Ethnographic Museum** houses a large collection of folk art from the Lesser Poland region. Temporary exhibitions, which take place at the Krakowska Street branch, are always of interest.

An extremely well pre-served rhinoceros (*coelodonta antiquitatis*) from the Ice Age is a highlight of the **Natural History Museum**.

Tin-glazed majolica plate (c. 1545) from the collection of the Czartoryski Museum

Krakow's Best: Churches

The skyline of Krakow is dominated by the spires of its churches, each representative of centuries of changing architectural and artistic styles. Though many churches were dismantled or destroyed in the 19th century, plenty remain for visitors to explore, including some 40 in the historic centre alone.

PLASEK AND
NOWY ŚWIAT

LOBZOWSKA

KARMELICKA

KRUPNICZA

SMOLEŃSK

WAWEL
HILL

Vistula

Church of St Anne
This church was created by two outstanding artists at the end of the 17th century – the architect Tylman van Gameren and the sculptor Baldassare Fontana.

Franciscan Church
Magnificent murals and stained glass by Stanisław Wyspiański decorate the Gothic interior of this church.

Wawel Cathedral
This cathedral is a place where the history of the Polish state meets that of the Church and where national memorabilia are treasured.

| 0 metres | 500 |
| 0 yards | 500 |

Piarist Church
The Rococo façade of this church is flat, though it is richly decorated.

Church of St Mary
The most important church in the centre of historic Krakow, St Mary's is famous for its retable, made between 1477 and 1489, and its interior decoration, which dates from later years.

LUBICZ

OLD QUARTER

WESOŁA, KLEPARZ AND BISKUPIE

MIKOŁAJA KOPERNIKA

OKÓŁ AND STRADOM QUARTERS

STAROWIŚLNA

JÓZEFA DIETLA

KRAKOWSKA

KAZIMIERZ QUARTER

ŚW. WAWRZYŃCA

Vistula

Dominican Church
This memorial plaque of Callimachus (Italian humanist, secretary to the Royal court), made after 1496 to the design of Veit Stoss, is to be found here. The remaining furnishings are mostly Neo-Gothic.

St Catherine's Church
While visiting this church one should not miss the south porch decorated with stonework and tracery.

Church of Saints Peter and Paul
This is the finest early Baroque church in Poland from the leading architects of the late 16th century. It is decorated with exquisite carved statues and stuccowork.

Exploring Krakow's Churches

Krakow's churches represent many different styles, from the Romanesque and Gothic through Baroque and later eclecticism to the modern. Fortunately the majority of churches were saved from wartime destruction and have not been damaged. Today their splendid interiors impress visitors to the city. Visitors should note that Krakow's churches are not only tourist attractions but also places of pilgrimage and worship. The relics of a number of saints and blessed, as well as many pious figures who enjoy a local cult, are laid to rest in churches throughout the city.

St Andrew's Church

Pre-Romanesque and Romanesque

The earliest stone churches in Krakow date from the second half of the 10th century. They were built on the site of today's **St Adalbert's Church** and at Wawel, where the remnants of a number of rotundas have been found. Today the

reconstructed Rotunda of the Virgin Mary *(see p65)*, originally from the late 10th century, can be visited. Built around 1079, **St Andrew's** is exceptional among the Romanesque churches. The **Church of the Holy Redeemer** dates from around the same period. The Crypt of St Leonard beneath Wawel Cathedral is a remnant of the second cathedral built between 1090 and 1142. The remnants of the Church of St Gereon and the Chapel of St Mary of Egypt are also at Wawel.

Gothic

Slender silhouettes of Gothic churches enhance the city. Some buildings were, however, demolished in the 19th century during the programme of "tidying up" the old architecture. The **Franciscan Church** is the oldest to have survived. Its irregular plan of a Greek cross with an asymmetric nave is unusual. The **Church of the Holy Cross**, begun

Gothic vault in the nave of the Corpus Christi Church

around 1300, is worth visiting for its palm vaulting supported by a single pillar. **Wawel Cathedral** is certainly a major attraction. This three-aisled basilica with a transept and ambulatory, surrounded by chapels, was constructed between 1320 and 1364. The Monastery, **Church of St Catherine** and the **Corpus Christi** were both founded by Kazimierz the Great, while the **Dominican Church** was rebuilt during his reign. All three churches share the same structural and stylistic characteristics and were probably constructed by the same stonemasons, who moved from one site to another. **St Mary's**, the city's main civic church, is also Gothic. It was under construction from the end of the 13th century until the late 15th century.

Towers, Domes and Spires in Krakow

The outlines of many church domes and spires dominate the skyline of old Krakow. They also bear witness to the historic and artistic changes that the city has undergone. The Gothic spires of St Mary's and Corpus Christi are among the tallest and most picturesque. Baroque styles are more common and include the Church of Saints Peter and Paul, St Anne's and the Cathedral Clock Tower.

Towers of the Church of St Andrew

Slender Gothic spire of St Mary's Church

Baroque dome of St Anne's Church

Renaissance and Mannerist

There is no complete church in Krakow in either the pure Renaissance or Mannerist styles, but the Zygmunt Chapel, built from 1519 to 1533, is regarded as the greatest example of Italian Renaissance north of the Alps. The chapel, with its spatial design and decoration, provided a model which was followed faithfully throughout Poland for many years.

Renaissance monuments by Jan Michałowicz of Urzędów and Giovanni Maria Mosca ("Il Padovano") can be seen in a number of churches. The career of the Italian Mannerist Santi Gucci, an equally fine artist, spans the last decades of the 16th century.

Baroque

Although in the 17th century Polish kings no longer resided in Krakow, many new ecclesiastical foundations were undertaken. The Jesuit **Church of Saints Peter and Paul** was the most magnificent. The church was completed by the royal architect Giovanni Battista Trevano in

Baroque façade detail of the Church of the Missionaries

1609–19. The imposing Zbaraski Chapel in the **Dominican Church**, built between 1629 and 1631, is another fine example of early Baroque. The Canopy of St Stanisław and the Vaza Chapel, both in **Wawel Cathedral**, exemplify the best of the High Baroque style. In the first half of the 17th century the interiors of many Gothic churches, such as St Mark's (see p112) were remodelled in the Baroque style. The century that followed brought about further architectural masterpieces, including **St Anne's Church**. A mention must also be made of the **Church of the Missionaries** whose exterior and interior were both modelled on Roman architecture, the **Piarist Church** with its airy façade, and the **Church of the Order of St John of God** whose façade displays dynamic articulation.

Neo-Classical and Eclectic

The late 18th-century choir and the high altar in the Church of the Norbertine Nuns are the only examples of ecclesiastical Neo-Classicism in Krakow. No building activity was undertaken until Galicia became autonomous, and new churches were only constructed in the second half of the 19th and first half of the 20th centuries. The **Church of the Felician Nuns** was built between 1882 and 1884 to designs by Feliks Księżarski, and the **St Joseph's Church** (1905–09) was designed by Jan Sas Zubrzycki. The **Church of the Sacred Heart of Jesus** designed by Franciszek Mączyński and decorated with sculptures by

Decoration of the porch of the Church of the Sacred Heart of Jesus

Xawery Dunikowski and Karol Hukan, is an excellent example of 20th-century architecture.

Modern

A variety of designs were applied to modern churches of the second half of the 20th century. Amongst the most interesting are the **Ark of God** in Nowa Huta (architect Wojciech Pietrzyk, 1967–77), the Church of St Maksymilian Kolbe in Mistrzejowice (architect Józef Dutkiewicz, 1976–83) and the Church of St Jan Kanty at Bronowice Nowe.

Finding Krakow's Churches

Late Baroque clock tower of Wawel Cathedral

Neo-Gothic spire of St Joseph's Church in Podgórze

Modern spire of the Ark of God Church in Nowa Huta

Exploring Krakow's Cemeteries

All over Europe the cult of commemorating the dead resulted in the establishment of many large cemeteries, with beautiful sculptures often decorating the tombs. Krakow is no different in this respect. Numerous cemeteries and mausolea in church crypts have been established here over the years. They were already regarded as tourist attractions in the 19th century and continue to be visited by those touring the city today.

The Jerzmanowski Mausoleum, Rakowicki Cemetery

Christian Cemeteries

At the end of the 18th century a Krakovian noted that: "Every time one looks through the window one cannot but see graves and crosses in the centre of the city." At that time cemeteries used to be located near churches. The one at St Mary's was the largest. It was relocated at the end of the 18th century and the original burial site transformed into Mariacki Square. Many tombstones and epitaphs, often medieval, which commemorate those who died centuries ago, have survived on the exterior walls of the churches of St Mary and St Barbara. A number of mausolea, built as chapels by the patrician families of Krakow, also survive on the former site of St Mary's Cemetery.

The **Rakowicki Cemetery** was established outside the city in 1803 and is the oldest cemetery in use. It occupies a vast plot and its layout is transparent. Many old trees give the place a park-like appearance. Some tombstones, especially those made around 1900 by the best Polish sculptors of the time, are true works of art.

In 1920 a **Military Cemetery** was set up by the Rakowicki Cemetery (they have since merged). Polish soldiers who fell in the years 1914–20 and in September 1939, as well as British and Commonwealth airmen who lost their lives in World War II, all rest here.

The **Salwator Cemetery** is a far more modest place with no great monuments, but rather smaller tombstones decorated with small-scale but nevertheless interesting bas-reliefs. It is, however, a lovely place, picturesquely situated on a high hill and rich in varied fauna. One of the best times of year to visit Krakow's cemeteries is a few days either side of All Saints' Day, when they glow under candlelight at night.

Jewish Cemeteries

For many centuries Jews constituted a substantial part of the population of Kazimierz, the so-called Jewish city. They were interred at the **Remu'h Cemetery**, established in 1533. This small plot, squeezed between buildings, has many layers of tombs

The graves of British airmen, Military Cemetery

Monuments and Tombs

The monuments in Krakow's cemeteries show different ways in which people wished to commemorate the deceased. The medieval monuments show a stiff figure lying on a death bed placed under a canopy. The canopy symbolizes Heaven awaiting the soul. Elements glorifying the deceased were introduced into Baroque monuments. Female figures with attributes personified the virtues. Neo-Classical monuments were influenced by ancient sculpture. Fine sculptures and symbolic content are characteristic of the monuments in the Art Nouveau style.

Sarcophagus of Kościuszko in Wawel Cathedral's crypt (1818)

Sarcophagus of Jan III Sobieski in Wawel Cathedral (1760)

Monument of Kazimierz the Great (died 1370) in Wawel Cathedral

which have been placed here over hundreds of years. The tombstones are engraved with Hebrew inscriptions and symbolic images that identify the religion and social rank of the deceased. The dense accumulation of tombstones within a tiny and bare space contributes to the unique character of this Jewish cemetery.

Established in the 19th century, the **New Jewish Cemetery** was given, like other cemeteries, a park-like appearance. Tombstones are scattered over a wide area and surrounded by luxuriant vegetation. It is one of the few Jewish cemeteries in Poland still in use.

Tombstones lined up in the small Remu'h Cemetery

Crypts with Tombs of Great Poles

During the Partitions period (1795–1918) a number of celebrated Poles received state funerals. These events were intended to raise the patriotic feelings of the Polish people.

The Angel of Vengeance on the Monument to Victims of the 1848 Bombardment of Krakow (1913)

The Vaza Crypt in Wawel Cathedral

Church crypts were open to the public and transformed into pantheons of Poland's greatest citizens. **Wawel Cathedral's Crypt** contains the most solemn royal tombs of all. The crypt is divided into galleries in which Polish rulers, leading poets and national heroes rest. Tadeusz Kościuszko and Prince Józef Poniatowski were interred here during the occupation of Poland; President Lech Kaczyński and his wife, who were killed in a plane crash in 2010, are also buried here.

The **Crypt in the Paulite Church "On the Rock"** is a resting place for those who made great contributions to the arts and sciences. The eminent historian Jan Długosz was buried here in the 15th century.

Monastic Cemeteries

The crypts found beneath monastic churches are unique to Krakow. Their character reflects the unusual burial practices of particular religious orders.

The corpses in the **Crypt in the Church of the Reformed Franciscans** have been mummified naturally owing to the crypt's construction and ventilation. One can see here the corpses of poor friars lying on sand with their heads resting on a stone, as well as lay people in rich clothes resting in elaborate coffins. Over 700 laymen and around 250 Franciscan friars were buried here. The **Camaldolese**

Catacombs beneath the church in Bielany are different. Here, the corpses are laid at first in niches cut out in a wall and then bricked up. Some years later the bones are removed and placed in an ossuary with the exception of the skull, which is taken by one of the monks for the purposes of contemplation. The Camaldolese crypt strikingly shows that in the face of death all are equal.

Mummified monks in the crypt of the Church of the Reformed Franciscans

Krakow's Famous Residents

Many leading personalities of Polish academic, cultural and public life were born in Krakow. Eminent scholars were educated at or drawn to the Jagiellonian University, which was sometimes called "a gem of all knowledge". Famous artists and writers chose to live here, attracted by the unique atmosphere of the city, which was enlivened by old traditions. The cult of such great figures as writer and artist Stanisław Wyspiański, theatre director Tadeusz Kantor and painter Jan Matejko is still alive.

Helena Modrzejewska (1840–1909)
This famous actress began her career at the Old Theatre (Teatr Stary) She is buried in Krakow.

Stanisław Wyspiański (1869–1907)
Best known for his play *The Wedding,* Wyspiański was a dramatist, painter and designer. His great artistic visions are embedded in the Polish perception of national identity. He was born at Krupnicza 26.

PLASEK AND NOWY ŚWIAT

Wisława Szymborska (1923–2012)
This prominent poet was awarded the 1996 Nobel Prize for Literature. Szymborska's links with Krakow span more than 50 years. She lived at Krupnicza 22 in her youth.

Stanisław Lem (1921–2006)
One of the most widely read science-fiction authors in the world, Lem was also an essayist and critic. He studied medicine in Krakow.

Andrzej Wajda (1926–2016)
A leading film and theatre director, Wajda was educated in Krakow. He was the main instigator of the Japanese Centre of Art and Technology, one of the city's best museums. Wajda won an Oscar for Lifetime Achievement in 2000.

John Paul II (1920–2005)
Before his elevation to the papacy, Karol Wojtyła was Suffragan Bishop, then Archbishop of Krakow from 1963 to 1978. He lived in the Archbishop's Palace on Franciszkańska 3.

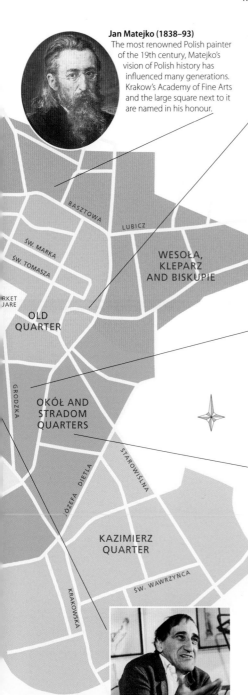

Jan Matejko (1838–93)
The most renowned Polish painter of the 19th century, Matejko's vision of Polish history has influenced many generations. Krakow's Academy of Fine Arts and the large square next to it are named in his honour.

Krzysztof Penderecki (born 1933)
World-renowned composer and conductor, Penderecki was educated in Krakow. He was a Professor and Rector of the Music Academy.

Sławomir Mrożek (1930–2013)
An outstanding playwright and satirist, Mrożek began his career in Krakow as a journalist. After many years abroad, he returned and settled here in 1996. He is buried in the Church of Saints Peter and Paul.

Czesław Miłosz (1911–2004)
A poet, leading thinker, Nobel Prize winner and honorary doctor of the Jagiellonian University, Miłosz was made an honorary citizen of Krakow in 1993. In his final years he lived at W. Bogusławskiego 6.

Tadeusz Kantor (1915–90)
A leading European artist and theatre director, Kantor established the world-famous Cricot 2 Theatre. For many years he worked at Kanonicza 5.

WESOŁA, KLEPARZ AND BISKUPIE

OLD QUARTER

OKÓŁ AND STRADOM QUARTERS

KAZIMIERZ QUARTER

BASZTOWA

LUBICZ

ŚW. MARKA

ŚW. TOMASZA

RKET JARE

GRODZKA

JÓZEFA DIETLA

STAROWIŚLNA

KRAKOWSKA

ŚW. WAWRZYŃCA

0 metres 500
0 yards 500

KRAKOW THROUGH THE YEAR

Steeped in history, Krakow is a city where old traditions are maintained. Embraced by the Planty, which replaced the medieval walls, the Old Quarter remains at the heart of the city. At hourly intervals, a bugle call from the tower of St Mary's Church echoes across Market Square, the location of many festivals and celebrations throughout the year. In addition to these perennial events, Krakow's large student population helps to ensure a constant buzz of exciting cultural activity. There is something for everyone here. Press listings and other local media, as well as tourist agencies, are good sources of information.

A bouquet of traditional Polish Easter palms for sale on Palm Sunday

Spring

At the foothills of the Tatra Mountains, vast fields of crocuses announce the arrival of spring. In Krakow, the new season is heralded by people spilling onto the city's pavements, all enjoying the warmer weather, splendid sights and al fresco dining.

Easter
Palm Sunday (Sun before Easter). The blessing of palms in churches. A competition for the largest and best decorated palm takes place in Lipnica Murowana village, 41 km (25 miles) east of Krakow.
Misteria Paschalia (Easter week). This popular music festival celebrates sacral classical music.
Holy Saturday is a day when baskets with food are taken to the church for a blessing, and symbolic tombs of Christ are venerated.

Easter Sunday is the most important Catholic feast.
Easter Monday. The Emmaus Fair takes place in Zwierzyniec and people are splashed with water (Śmigus-dyngus) throughout the city.

April
Paka Cabaret Festival. A varied programme where amateur and professional satirical performers, Polish and foreign, all take part.

May
3 May Constitution Day celebrates the first Polish Constitution of 1791 with a Mass said in Wawel Cathedral followed by the laying of wreaths at the Tomb of the Unknown Soldier. Afterwards, there are fairs and picnics.
Procession from Wawel to the Paulite Church "On the Rock" (first Sun after 8 May, Feast of St Stanisław). The Primate and bishops lead the procession and carry the relics of the patron saints of Poland, joined by the faithful in regional costumes.
Photomonth (mid-May). Contemporary photography is celebrated with exhibitions in various locations around town.
Juvenalia. Krakow is ruled by students for a couple of days.
Krakow Film Music Festival (late May). Movie soundtracks performed by full orchestras, featuring many international guest musicians.
Krakow Film Festival (May-Jun). The oldest film festival in the country.

Archconfraternity of the Passion

Since 1595 the Good Friday processions of the Archconfraternity of The Passion have taken place in the Franciscan Church. The Brothers wear black habits with hoods covering the face. The ritual has remained unchanged for centuries. The Archconfraternity had the right to pardon those condemned to death.

Brothers in Procession

Average Daily Hours of Sunshine

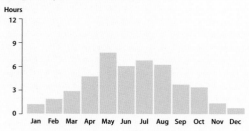

Hours

Sunshine Chart
Visitors should expect sunshine from May through to August. While May is the sunniest month of the year, December is the gloomiest.

Summer

Summer heat may be difficult to bear in Krakow. This is because of the city's location in a valley and its humid microclimate. Many bars, cafés and restaurants in the Old Quarter and Kazimierz are open and busy till the early hours of the morning. Crowds of visitors are attracted not only by the heritage but also the nightlife and cultural events.

June
Corpus Christi (Boże Ciało) *(Thu in May or June).* A great procession proceeds from Wawel to the Market Square. On Thursday, a week after Corpus Christi, *Lajkonik* canters around the town *(see p98)*.
Dragon Parade, Market Square. A colourful parade of dragons is held on the square, followed by a "battle of the dragons" son et lumiere show by the river.
Enthronement of the "king" Marksman, Market Square. The Marksmen's Brotherhood has existed since the Middle Ages. It

is made up of burghers who are members of craftsmen guilds. Their leader is the winner of the annual shooting competition. The outgoing leader passes the silver cock to the new "king" during a colourful ceremony.
Midsummer's Eve (Wianki) Sat preceding the eve of St John's Feast *(24 Jun)*. Candle wreaths are set adrift on the Vistula by Wawel and there are fireworks displays.
International Music Festival of Military Bands *(even-numbered years)*. The festival features gala shows of drill, parades in period uniforms and many concerts.

July
Ulica International Street Theatre Festival. Pantomime, puppet shows and acrobatics take place throughout the Old Quarter.
Summer Opera Festival. The festival showcases the best of Krakow Opera House's repertoire, with some outdoor performances in the Wawel Royal Castle courtyard.

Poster announcing events during the Jewish Culture Festival

Krakow Jazz Festival (Stary Jazz w Krakowie) *(Jul–Aug)*. A real treat for fans of traditional jazz.
Jewish Culture Festival *(early Jul)*, Kazimierz. Outstanding Jewish festival featuring Klezmer concerts, film, theatre and panel discussions.

August
The Assumption of the Virgin Mary (Święto Wniebowzięcia Matki Boskiej) *(15 Aug)*. A Solemn Mass is said in the cathedral. This is also the national holiday of the Polish Soldier, marking the 1920 victory over the Bolshevik Army.
Krakow Live Festival. This rock-pop festival is held in a field near the Polish Aviation Museum and attracts top international names.
International Folk Art Fair (Targi Sztuki Ludowej), *(12 days in Aug)*, Market Square. Folk artists and craftsmen from Poland and other countries demonstrate their handicrafts and folklore. One day is dedicated to concerts of folk music by the Polish Highlanders.

Colourful costumes at the Dragon Parade

Average Monthly Rainfall

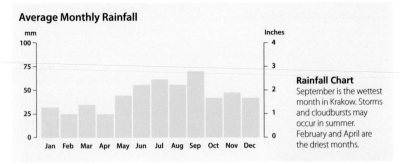

Rainfall Chart
September is the wettest month in Krakow. Storms and cloudbursts may occur in summer. February and April are the driest months.

Autumn

On dry and sunny autumn days Krakow is beautifully shrouded in colours; the Planty chestnut trees turn golden and market stalls display baskets full of wild mushrooms from the woodlands of the mountain foothills.

Students return to Krakow by the end of September to take part in the inaugural celebrations of the new academic year. The hymn *Gaudeamus Igitur* can be heard sung at many colleges, and in particular at the Jagiellonian University, Poland's oldest university, established in 1364.

Flowers and candles on top of tombs ahead of All Saints' Day

September
Sacrum Profanum Festival
(early to mid-Sep). This annual festival is devoted to 20th-century music of all sorts, whether classical, pop or avant-garde. It has previously included appearances by the likes of Kraftwerk, Aphex Twin and Sigur Rós. Important buildings in the city are adapted and tailored to suit the festival's needs.

October
Unsound *(early Oct)*. Held in a variety of atmospheric spaces around the city, this vibrant festival features electronic, experimental, independent and club music from around the world.

A marching band celebrating national Independence Day

November
All Saints' Day (Dzień Wszystkich Świętych) *(1 Nov)*. Many Krakovians visit cemeteries to lay flowers and light candles on the graves. The views of the old Rakowicki Cemetery or of the beautifully located cemetery on the Hill of the Holy Redeemer (św. Salwator) are unforgettable. It is an old custom of Krakow to be able to buy, on this day only, so-called Turkish honey (caramelized sugar with walnuts or pistachios) at the entrance to cemeteries. Children, especially, look forward to this event.
All Souls Jazz Festival (Krakowskie Zaduszki Jazzowe). Oldest jazz festival in post-Communist Europe, with concerts in the Philharmonic hall and jazz clubs.
Independence Day (Święto Niepodległości) *(11 Nov)*. After a Mass at the Wawel Cathedral, wreaths are laid at the Tomb of the Unknown Soldier by the Grunwald Monument in Matejko Square.
"Etude" International Film Festival (Międzynarodowy Festiwal Filmowy Etiuda) *(late Nov)*. This festival sees the screening of short

Average Monthly Temperature

Temperature Chart
Average maximum and minimum temperatures are show here. July and August are the hottest months with the temperature often exceeding 20°C, sometimes even reaching 30°C. Temperatures can plummet in winter but on average linger around freezing.

films by students from art schools and film schools from all over the world.

Winter

Krakow under a blanket of snow is a wonderful sight, but winter also brings misty and bitingly cold days.

Every year on the first Thursday of December a competition for the best Christmas crib (*szopka*) takes place by the Mickiewicz Monument in Market Square. The winning cribs are later displayed at the Museum of Krakow in Krzysztofory Palace. The tradition of making Christmas cribs, unique to Krakow, can be traced back to medieval Christmas plays.

Nativity scenes at churches are also worth visiting. The one outside the Franciscan Church, with real people and animals, is best known. It can be seen only on Christmas Eve and Christmas Day.

Stalls selling handmade Christmas decorations and traditional delicacies fill the Market Square during the Christmas Fair.

Carol singers in traditional costume in Floriańska Street at Christmas time

Spectacular display of fireworks on New Year's Eve

December
Christmas Eve (Wigilia) *(24 Dec)*. The evening begins with a meat-free meal. Midnight Masses are said and the Zygmunt Bell rings at Wawel.
Christmas (Święto Bożego Narodzenia) *(25 and 26 Dec)*. Christmas Day and the day after are public holidays. Masses are celebrated in all churches.
New Year's Eve (Sylwester) *(31 Dec)*. A crowd, several thousand strong, gathers in Market Square to see in the New Year. The Wielopolski Palace, the seat of local government, is the venue for one of the grandest balls in Poland. Distinguished guests arrive from all over the world, and the proceeds go to charity.

January
New Year's Day (Nowy Rok) *(1 Jan)*. Public holiday. A month of balls and parties begins on this day.

Christmas decoration

February
"Fat Thursday" (Tłusty czwartek) *(last Thu before Lent)*. Everybody eats doughnuts. The *Gazeta w Krakowie*, the local supplement to the *Gazeta Wyborcza*, rates the bakeries to help people choose the best doughnuts in Krakow.
Shrovetide (Ostatki), *(last Sat and Tue of the Carnival season, before Ash Wednesday)*. This is a time of parties before Lent.

Public Holidays

New Year's Day (1 Jan)
Epiphany (6 Jan)
Easter Monday (Mar/Apr)
Labour Day (1 May)
Constitution Day (3 May)
Whit Sunday (7 weeks after Easter)
Corpus Christi (Thu, usually around 8 weeks after Easter)
Assumption (15 Aug)
All Saints' Day (1 Nov)
Independence Day (11 Nov)
Christmas (25 & 26 Dec)

The Father Bernatek bridge over the Vistula River ▶

KRAKOW
AREA BY AREA

WAWEL HILL

One of Krakow's – and Poland's – most important sites, Wawel Hill has a chequered history that dates back to ancient times. Once inhabited by the Vistulan people, it was first designated the seat of political power by Kazimierz the Restorer, and later became the official royal residence for Poland's kings and queens in the 14th century. As rulers moved into Wawel, they each made their own additions and changes to the castle and cathedral, and both are a veritable mixture of architectural styles, from the Romanesque to the Baroque. The Renaissance-style castle courtyard is a highlight as is the electic interior of the cathedral. The capital was moved from Krakow to Warsaw at the end of the 16th century and, although royal coronations and funeral ceremonies continued to take place at Wawel, the site steadily entered a period of decline. From 1795, it became home not to rulers but to the military: the Austrian army were garrisoned here until the early 20th century and during World War II it became the headquarters of the Nazi Governor General. Fortunately, substantial restoration work from the mid-20th century has seen Wawel regain its former magnificence, and it remains a major stop for visitors to the city.

Sights at a Glance

Churches

❸ *Wawel Cathedral pp66–71*

Historic Sights, Buildings and Monuments

❶ Fortifications and Towers
❷ Statue of Tadeusz Kościuszko
❼ Archaeological Site
❽ Dragon's Lair

Museums

❹ Cathedral Museum
❺ *Wawel Royal Castle pp72–3*
❻ "Lost Wawel" Exhibition

0 metres 100
0 yards 100

PODZAMCZE

ŚW. IDZIEGO

WAWEL

Vistula

BERNARDYŃSKA

See also Street Finder maps 3, 5 & 6

◀ The grounds of Wawel Cathedral, on Wawel Hill

For keys to symbols *see back flap*

Street-by-Street: Wawel Hill

The Wawel is exceptional because of its first-class collections and its unique atmosphere. To savour it unhindered by large crowds you should plan an early-morning visit when the cathedral and castle courtyard are nearly deserted. Visitors from every corner of the world gather here before noon, thereby enlivening the place. A trip to the cathedral, where a variety of styles intermingle, as well as to the Royal Castle, is a must.

❷ Statue of Tadeusz Kościuszko
The statue of Kościuszko stands at the entrance to Wawel Castle. Kościuszko was the general who led the Insurrection of 1794 against the Russian army. His ashes rest in the cathedral crypt.

The Coat of Arms Gate

❹ Cathedral Museum
The museum houses a collection of sacred art, as well as a selection of insignia and memorabilia of the Polish kings, including the coronation robe of Stanisław August Poniatowski.

❽ Dragon's Lair
This cave, consisting of a number of interconnecting chambers, and a sculpture of a fire-belching dragon is a much loved attraction. It is particularly popular with children.

Key

 Suggested route

❶ Fortifications and Towers
The compact but varied defence system on Wawel Hill was constructed from the 15th to the 19th centuries.

⑤ ★ Wawel Royal Castle
A visit to the castle takes in its interior with its display of 16th-century tapestries, regalia, gold treasures and lavish Oriental objects.

Locator Map
See Street Finder maps 3, 5 & 6

PIASEK AND NOWY ŚWIAT

OKÓŁ AND STRADOM QUARTERS

WAWEL HILL

The "Hen's Claw" Wing (Kurza Stopka) is the most prominent remnant of the medieval castle. It was erected during the reign of Jadwiga and Władysław II Jagiełło.

③ ★ Wawel Cathedral
The 19th-century sarcophagus of St Jadwiga, the Queen of Poland, is among many monuments associated with the history of the Church and Nation.

⑥ "Lost Wawel" Exhibition
Arranged in the former royal kitchen in the cellars, this special exhibition includes among its most interesting exhibits a reconstruction of the Rotunda of the Virgin Mary.

0 metres 50
0 yards 50

⑦ Archaeological Site
The foundations of medieval buildings are exposed on this site.

❶ Fortifications and Towers

Wawel Hill. **Map** 3 C1 (5 C5). 🚌 504.
🚃 6, 8, 10, 13, 18.

The fortifications surrounding Wawel Hill date from different periods. Three massive towers – the Thief's Tower (Złodziejska), Sandomierz and Senator's Towers (the latter also called Lubranka) are dominant features of the architectural silhouette of the Wawel. They date from the second half of the 15th and early 16th centuries, when the royal residence was rebuilt by the Jagiellonians. New, mainly earth fortifications designed by Jan Pleitner were erected under Władysław IV between 1644 and 1646 on the castle's northern terrace. The southeast bastion and redan (fortification of two parapets) were constructed in the early 18th century for King August II. Later in the century star-shaped fortifications designed by Bakałowicz and Mehler were built on the side of the Vistula River. The Austrians expanded the system between 1849 and 1852. Two round towers, forming part of the Austrian additions, have survived. The Wawel Castle was thus transformed into a citadel surrounded by a complex defence system.

The Sandomierz Tower, one of the three Wawel defence towers

The Coat of Arms Gate and part of the fortifications surrounding Wawel Hill

❷ Statue of Tadeusz Kościuszko

Wawel Hill. **Map** 3 C1 (5 C5). 🚌 504.
🚃 6, 8, 10, 13, 18.

The statue of Tadeusz Kościuszko, general and main leader of the 1794 Uprising in Poland *(see p31)* and a participant in the American Revolution, was erected in 1921. It was designed by Leonard Marconi and completed by Antoni Popiel. The statue was destroyed by the Germans in 1940. The present reconstruction was donated in 1960. When approaching the Władysław bastion, where the statue stands, you can see a number of plaques mounted in the brick wall. These commemorate the donors who contributed to the restoration works carried out within the castle during the inter-war years. Also of interest is the Coat of Arms Gate by Adolf Szyszko-Bohusz.

Stirrup that belonged to the Grand Vizier Kara Mustafa, Cathedral Museum

❸ Wawel Cathedral

See pp66–71.

❹ Cathedral Museum

Wawel 3. **Map** 3 C1 (5 C5). **Tel** 12 429 33 21. 🚌 504. 🚃 6, 8, 10, 13, 18. **Open** 9am–5pm Mon–Sat (Nov–Mar: to 4pm). 📷

The Cathedral Museum was established in September 1978 by the then Archbishop Karol Wojtyła, the Metropolitan of Krakow. The display consists of objects from the cathedral's Crown Treasury. Among the exhibits are a sword, which was purposely broken in two places at the funeral of the last Jagiellonian king, Zygmunt August; the coronation robe of Stanisław August Poniatowski; the replica of the royal insignia found inside the royal coffins buried beneath the cathedral, and the stirrup of the Grand Vizier Kara Mustafa which was presented to the cathedral by King Jan III Sobieski following his victory at the Battle of Vienna (1683). The outstanding collection of reliquaries, church vessels and vestments includes objects found in the tomb of Bishop Maur, as well as memorabilia of John Paul II.

❺ Wawel Royal Castle

See pp72–3.

❻ "Lost Wawel" Exhibition

Wawel Hill 5. **Map** 3 C1 (5 D5). **Tel** 12 422 51 55. 🚌 504. 🚃 6, 8, 10, 13, 18. **Open** Apr–Oct: 9:30am–1pm Mon, 9:30am–5pm Tue–Fri, 10am–5pm Sat & Sun; Nov–Mar: 9:30am–4pm Tue–Fri, 10am–4pm Sat & Sun. **Closed** public hols.
🆆 wawel.krakow.pl

This special exhibition, arranged in the basement of the former royal kitchen (now occupied by the administration office), will appeal to those interested in the medieval history of Wawel. There were possibly ten churches on Wawel Hill in the past. The Rotunda of the Virgin Mary (Sts Felix and Adauctus), unearthed in 1917 during excavations carried out by Adolf Szyszko-Bohusz, is of great interest. The excavations also brought to light the remnants of a man's body as well as some articles of jewellery nearby. It is believed that the circular rotunda formed part of the first palatium (the seat of the first ruler of Wawel), and was built sometime in the late 10th or early 11th century. Its plan resembles a quatrefoil, with strong evidence of Czech influences in the design of the structure. The rotunda was almost completely destroyed in the 19th century.

The exhibition also includes a virtual computer model of the Wawel architecture, which enables visitors to travel into the past to the early 10th century. The computer reconstruction of selected medieval buildings, based on archaeological, architectural, photographic and conservational evidence, shows the state of current research into the early history of Wawel. The models of the so-called Rotunda B, the Rotunda of the Virgin Mary and other buildings, including the palatium, the Church of St Gereon and the cathedral, give a clear picture of the overall layout.

The 6-m- (20-ft-) high dragon statue, one of the most popular attractions in Wawel Hill

❼ Archaeological Site

Wawel Hill. **Map** 3 C1 (5 C5). 🚌 504. 🚋 6, 8, 10, 13, 18.

The archaeological site is an open area where foundations of medieval buildings can be seen. The buildings were numerous and once formed a small town. A vicarage in the Renaissance style was among them. All the buildings were demolished by the Austrians in 1803–04 and replaced by a drill ground. The lower parts of the walls of St Nicholas, the small Romanesque church rebuilt in the Gothic style during the reign of Kazimierz the Great, are of particular note. This church was an interesting example of a single nave church, supported on one central column. The plan of the small church of St George is also easy to discern.

❽ Dragon's Lair

Wawel Hill. **Map** 3 C1 (5 C5). **Tel** 12 422 51 55. 🚌 504. 🚋 6, 8, 10, 13, 18. **Open** Apr, Sep & Oct: 10am–5pm; May & Jun: 10am–6pm; Jul & Aug: 10am–7pm.

Within Wawel Hill there are a number of rock caves. The earliest records of these caves date from the 16th century and are thought to be associated with criminality. A pub and a brothel were here in the 18th century. In the 19th century the Austrians sealed the entrance when constructing the fortification walls.

The "lair" is open only during the summer months. Some 135 spiral steps lead down into the den, and there are 145 m (476 ft) of tunnels in total, of which only a part can be visited. The bronze statue of the dragon, designed by Bronisław Chromy, which stands at the exit, was made in 1972.

According to legend, the inhabitants of ancient Krakow were terrorized by a dragon until one day a brave shoemaker, named Skuba, cheated the monster with a sheep stuffed with sulphur. The dragon swallowed the bait. When the sulphur heated its gut, the dragon drank so much water from the Vistula that its body burst. To reward the shoemaker King Krak gave him the hand of his daughter in marriage.

The metal monster belches fire and is seen as a major attraction by younger visitors.

The archaeological site, in front of Wawel Cathedral

❸ Wawel Cathedral

No other building is as strongly associated with the history of Krakow, and the whole nation, as the cathedral. The third building to occupy this site, the existing cathedral was built by Władysław the Short to house the relics of St Stanisław, who was much venerated by the Poles. The internal structure of the Gothic cathedral is now obscure because of later additions. Today, the interior displays a variety of styles but despite this eclecticism the layout is straightfoward. The basilica consists of a nave with single aisles, non-projecting transept and a choir with an ambulatory. Many chapels, dating from different periods and some having been remodelled many times, adjoin the aisles. Make sure to climb the Zygmunt Tower to see the bell and take in views of the city.

Exterior of the Cathedral
Although dating from different periods, all the distinct parts of the cathedral make a unique and picturesque ensemble.

Clock Tower
The top of the tallest tower is decorated with four statues of the patron saints of the Kingdom of Poland and the cathedral: Wacław, Adalbert, Stanisław and Kazimierz (Casimir).

Entrance
The bones of an "ancient creature" hang above the entrance. According to legend the end of the world will come when they fall. The letter K on the door is the initial of Kazimierz the Great, during whose reign the cathedral was completed.

KEY

① **Bell tower**

② **Baroque spire from the first half of the 18th century**

③ **Załuski Chapel**

★ **Zygmunt Tower**
The Zygmunt bell in the tower, cast in 1520, is the largest in Poland. It weighs nearly 11 tons and is more than 2 m (6.5 ft) in diameter.

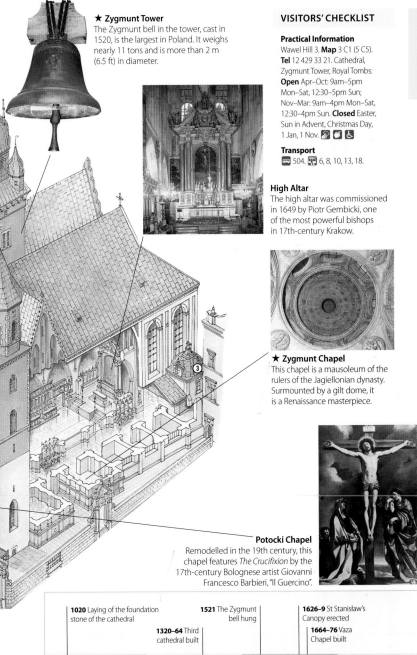

VISITORS' CHECKLIST

Practical Information
Wawel Hill 3. **Map** 3 C1 (5 C5).
Tel 12 429 33 21. Cathedral, Zygmunt Tower, Royal Tombs:
Open Apr–Oct: 9am–5pm Mon–Sat, 12:30–5pm Sun; Nov–Mar: 9am–4pm Mon–Sat, 12:30–4pm Sun. **Closed** Easter, Sun in Advent, Christmas Day, 1 Jan, 1 Nov.

Transport
504. 6, 8, 10, 13, 18.

High Altar
The high altar was commissioned in 1649 by Piotr Gembicki, one of the most powerful bishops in 17th-century Krakow.

★ **Zygmunt Chapel**
This chapel is a mausoleum of the rulers of the Jagiellonian dynasty. Surmounted by a gilt dome, it is a Renaissance masterpiece.

Potocki Chapel
Remodelled in the 19th century, this chapel features *The Crucifixion* by the 17th-century Bolognese artist Giovanni Francesco Barbieri, "Il Guercino".

1020 Laying of the foundation stone of the cathedral

1320–64 Third cathedral built

1521 The Zygmunt bell hung

1626–9 St Stanisław's Canopy erected

1664–76 Vaza Chapel built

| 1000 | 1250 | 1500 | 1750 |

1090–1142 Second (so-called Herman) cathedral built

Clock on the Clock Tower

1519–33 Zygmunt Chapel built by Bartolomeo Berrecci

1758–66 Bishop Załuski's Chapel built

Interior of the Cathedral

Wawel Cathedral is exceptional not only for the works of art which are housed here, but also because it has borne witness to many historical events such as coronations, royal weddings and funerals, as well as thanksgiving ceremonies. One of the most important churches in Poland, the cathedral is still a spiritual centre today. It enjoys not only high sacred status, but it also acquired symbolic importance during the occupation of Poland when it became a treasury of objects commemorating national glory. The great Polish playwright Stanisław Wyspiański chose the cathedral as a dramatic setting for his play *Deliverance*.

② Poets' Crypt
Adam Mickiewicz and Juliusz Słowacki, two of the foremost Polish poets, are buried here. The remains of Mickiewicz were laid here in 1890 and those of Słowacki in 1929.

⑦ Zygmunt Chapel
The splendid double Monument of King Zygmunt the Old (top; by Santi Gucci, 1574–75) and his son, King Zygmunt August (below; by Bartolomeo Berrecci, 1530s) is the outstanding artistic feature of the cathedral.

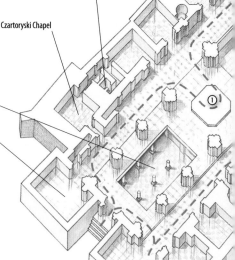

Entrance to the crypt

Czartoryski Chapel

The Cathedral Crypt
houses the tombs of kings and distinguished Poles.

Chapel of the Holy Trinity

⑧ Sarcophagus of King Kazimierz Jagiellończyk
One of the most affecting works of Veit Stoss, this was made in 1492, the year of the king's death.

① Canopy of St Stanisław
This altar, the largest in the cathedral, is dedicated to Poland. It was probably designed by Giovanni Battista Trevano. The silver reliquary in the form of a coffin, containing the relics of St Stanisław, was made by Peter von der Rennen from 1669 to 1671.

Treasury

Sacristy

Chapel of the Virgin
(Batory Chapel)

③

④

④ Tomb of King Stefan Batory
The work of an outstanding sculptor, Santi Gucci, this tomb was created in 1595. It is a fine example of Mannerist decoration.

⑤

⑤ Tomb of King Jan III Sobieski
Overloaded with Baroque decoration, the tomb of King Jan III (died 1696) and his wife was made in 1760 to the designs of Francesco Placidi.

⑥

⑥ Tomb of King Jan Olbracht
Created from 1502 to 1505, the decoration of the recess around the tomb is the earliest example of Renaissance art in Poland. The design is modelled on a Roman triumphal arch. The sarcophagus retains late Gothic forms.

⑦

③ Crucifix of Queen Jadwiga
According to legend the Queen prayed in front of this expressive crucifix (c.1380), which has become a place of mass pilgrimage. The relics of the Queen, who became a saint, rest in the altar.

Key

 Suggested route

Exploring Wawel Cathedral

Wawel Cathedral requires more than one visit to do justice to the magnificent building. Its interior with its variety of styles, from medieval to modern, is simply overwhelming. It is worth returning here for a careful visit to all the chapels in the aisles, and to the monuments and tombs of the kings and prominent people in the crypt. The artistic backdrop adds to the spirituality of the cathedral, which is above all else used for worship. To avoid the crowds, the best time to visit is in the early morning or just before closing time.

Chapels

The chapel of the Holy Cross, erected on the initiative of King Kazimierz Jagiełłończyk and his wife Elisabeth von Habsburg, has retained much of its medieval character. The cycle of old Russian wall paintings is one of the largest ensembles to have survived. It is of the Pskov School. Two triptychs of the Holy Trinity and the Virgin Mary of Sorrows both date from the second half of the 15th century. The most interesting furnishing is the tomb of Kazimierz made by Veit Stoss with Huber of Passau. The king is shown in majestic resplendence, yet it is also a dignifed image of death. The stained-glass windows were designed by Józef Mehoffer in the Art Nouveau style.

The Zygmunt Chapel (1519–33), designed by Bartolomeo Berrecci, is of exceptional beauty and is considered one of the purest examples of the Italian Renaissance outside Italy. The chapel was modelled on the best Italian architectural and decorative works and contains sculptures, stuccos and paintings designed by some of the most renowned artists of the age. The silver altar was made between 1531 and 1538 in Nuremberg by Melchior Baier to the designs of Peter Flötner. The royal tombs are equally interesting. The interior is peaceful and majestic and conveys the spirit of 16th-century humanism. Bishop Tomicki's Chapel is also Renaissance in style. Remodelled by Bartolomeo Berrecci from 1526 to 1535, the chapel played an important role as a model for mausolea for the nobility and gentry. The Chapel of the Virgin Mary (King Stefan Batory's Chapel) houses a 17th-century Baroque tabernacle with the Holy Eucharist. The sandstone tomb of Batory and the royal stalls were designed by Santi Gucci.

The Vaza Chapel, probably also designed by the same architect, exemplifies a 17th-century interior: monu-mental, heavy forms executed in black marble with large epitaphs. It acts as a reminder of the fragility and transcience of earthly life.

Among the chapels constructed in the 18th century, two are of particular interest. The Lipski Chapel (1743–7), designed by Francesco Placidi, catches the light and plays with shadows. The decoration of Bishop Załuski's Chapel (1758–66) employs the allegory of the passage through the gate (note the enlarged entrance).

The *Crucifixion* by Guercino and the statue of the Risen Christ by Bertel Thorvaldsen are to be seen in the sepul-chral Chapel of Bishop Filip Padniewski. This Renaissance chapel was remodelled in the 19th century for the Potocki family. The statue of Włodzimierz Potocki in the Holy Trinity Chapel is also by Thorvaldsen.

The altar in the Zygmunt Chapel

Intricately carved stalls in the choir of the Cathedral

Furnishings

As well as the canopy of St Stanisław, particularly noteworthy are the epitaphs of the bishops of Krakow placed on the pillars, and decorated with busts of the deceased. Marcin Szyszkowski, Piotr Gembicki, Jan Małachowski and Kazimierz Łubieński all rest here, providing eternal company for the relics of St Stanisław. The Baroque stalls in the choir were made around 1620; additions were made in the 19th century. The bas-relief epitaph of Cardinal Fryderyk Jagiellończyk shows superb craftsmanship. It was made after 1503 in the Vischer workshop in Nuremberg. The throne of Bishop Piotr Gembicki has splendid Baroque decoration. The organ loft, made around 1758 to the design of Francesco Placidi, is also of much interest.

Sarcophagi and Tombs

The cathedral is a resting place for Polish rulers, and all its medieval tombs follow a particular model. They show a figure lying in state on a massive sarcophagus, decorated with allegorical figures of the king's subjects lamenting the death of their sovereign. A dog, symbolizing fidelity, is usually placed at the king's feet, and the head of the ruler rests on a lion, the symbol of power. A stone canopy is suspended over the tomb. The tomb of Władysław the Short,

dating from the mid-14th century is the earliest sarcophagus of this type. Kazimierz Jagiellończyk was the last to have such a monument erected.

Two tombs of a much later date were inspired by this early type of sepulchre. The beautiful and majestic tomb of Queen Jadwiga is one of them. It was executed with great delicacy in white Carrara marble by Antoni

The tomb of Władysław Jagiełło

Madeyski in 1902. The tomb is one of the most visited places of pilgrimage in the cathedral. The other sarcophagus, also by Madeyski, was erected in 1906. It is a cenotaph (tomb without a corpse) commemorating King Władysław III Warneńczyk, who was killed in 1444 at the Battle of Varna against the Ottomans.

His body was never found, giving rise to stories about his miraculous salvation.

Royal Tombs

The Royal Tombs were placed in the crypt following the construction of the Zygmunt Chapel, which is a mausoleum. Zygmunt the Old and his sons are buried in the crypt under the chapel. Earlier rulers were buried in the cathedral, except Bolesław the Brave, Bolesław the Bold, Przemysław II, Louis of Anjou, Władysław III Warneńczyk and Aleksander Jagiellończyk. A crypt was also constructed for the Vaza dynasty. Later rulers were buried beneath the Chapel of the Holy Cross and in St Leonard's crypt. In 1783 the last Polish king, Stanisław August Poniatowski,

commissioned a grandiose sarcophagus for Jan III Sobieski. The elected kings Henri de Valois, August II of Saxony and Stanisław August Poniatowski do not rest in the Wawel. Two national heroes, Kościuszko and Prince Józef Poniatowski, were laid here during the Partitions of Poland. State funerals of Piłsudski and General Sikorski took place in the cathedral in the 20th century.

The sarcophagi of the Vaza kings

❺ Wawel Royal Castle

Little is known about the earliest Wawel residence. The Romanesque palatium was probably built by Kazimierz the Restorer; later Władysław the Short started to construct a new building but it was only completed by Kazimierz the Great. The present Renaissance castle was constructed in the first half of the 16th century. At the start of the 17th century the apartments in the north wing were remodelled in the early Baroque style. After the royal court moved from Krakow to Warsaw, the castle fell into ruin and further devastation was caused by the occupying foreign powers. Early in the 20th century the castle was given back to Krakow, and restoration was begun.

Castle Guide

The Crown Treasury and Armoury are situated on the ground floor together with a number of state rooms. The remaining state rooms and other apartments are on the first and second floors. After leaving the Senators' Hall a visit to the "Orient in the Wawel Collections" exhibition on the first and second floors in the west wing is recommended.

Crown Treasury and Armoury
This 11th-century chalice belonged to the Abbots of Tyniec and is now in the Treasury. Adjacent to the Treasury is the Armoury with its rich collection.

Senators' Hall

Senators' Staircase

First floor

The Castle Courtyard
A mix of architectural styles can be found at the castle. One of the highlights is the beautiful Renaissance-style courtyard, built in the 16th century.

Key

- ☐ Royal Apartments
- ☐ Treasury
- ☐ Armoury
- ☐ "Orient in the Wawel Collections" Exhibition
- ☐ Non-exhibition area

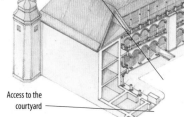

Access to the courtyard

Entrance to the Crown Treasury and Armoury

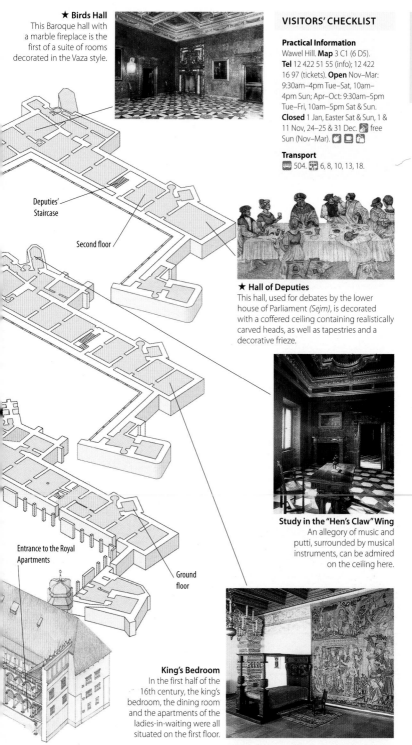

★ Birds Hall
This Baroque hall with a marble fireplace is the first of a suite of rooms decorated in the Vaza style.

VISITORS' CHECKLIST

Practical Information
Wawel Hill. **Map** 3 C1 (6 D5).
Tel 12 422 51 55 (info); 12 422
16 97 (tickets). **Open** Nov–Mar:
9:30am–4pm Tue–Sat, 10am–
4pm Sun; Apr–Oct: 9:30am–5pm
Tue–Fri, 10am–5pm Sat & Sun.
Closed 1 Jan, Easter Sat & Sun, 1 &
11 Nov, 24–25 & 31 Dec. free
Sun (Nov–Mar).

Transport
504. 6, 8, 10, 13, 18.

Deputies' Staircase

Second floor

★ Hall of Deputies
This hall, used for debates by the lower house of Parliament *(Sejm)*, is decorated with a coffered ceiling containing realistically carved heads, as well as tapestries and a decorative frieze.

Study in the "Hen's Claw" Wing
An allegory of music and putti, surrounded by musical instruments, can be admired on the ceiling here.

Entrance to the Royal Apartments

Ground floor

King's Bedroom
In the first half of the 16th century, the king's bedroom, the dining room and the apartments of the ladies-in-waiting were all situated on the first floor.

Cobbled Grodzka street, one of the oldest streets in Krakow ▶

OKÓŁ AND STRADOM QUARTERS

Okół was probably the earliest settlement at the foot of Wawel. Timber-built houses and a palisade enclosure were already here in the 10th century. The settlement expanded along the so-called Salt Route which led from Hungary to Greater Poland. It became an elite quarter because of its proximity to the Royal Castle and the cathedral;

high-ranking clergy resided here and many churches were built.

The development of Stradom, situated between Okół and Kazimierz, was hindered by its location on peat marshes and the vicinity of the Wawel fortress. The mid-17th century, however, saw the construction of splendid churches and palaces, and by the end of the 1800s the area was developing rapidly.

Sights at a Glance

Churches and Monasteries
- ③ Church of Saints Peter and Paul *pp82–3*
- ④ Church of St Andrew
- ⑤ Church of St Martin
- ⑦ Church of St Giles
- ⑯ Franciscan Church *pp88–9*
- ⑱ Church of the Bernardine Nuns
- ⑲ Bernardine Church
- ㉑ Church of the Missionaries

Museums and Galleries
- ⑩ Archdiocesan Museum
- ⑪ Palace of Bishop Erazm Ciołek
- ⑬ Cricoteka
- ⑭ Archaeological Museum
- ㉒ Natural History Museum

Historic Parks
- ㉓ Dietl Plantations

Historic Monuments and Buildings
- ② Collegium Iuridicum
- ⑥ Royal Arsenal
- ⑨ Deanery
- ⑫ Statue of Piotr Skarga
- ⑮ Wielopolski Palace
- ⑰ Statue of Józef Dietl
- ⑳ Częstochowa Seminary

Historic Streets
- ① Grodzka Street
- ⑧ Kanonicza Street

Restaurants *see p192*
1. Balaton
2. Il Calzone
3. Copernicus
4. Kurka Wodna
5. Miód Malina
6. Pod Aniołami
7. Pod Baranem
8. Pod Nosem
9. Smak Ukrainski
10. Trattoria La Campana

See also Street Finder maps 1, 3 & 6

◀ Statues of the Apostles at the entrance to the Church of Saints Peter and Paul

For keys to symbols *see back flap*

Street-By-Street: Okół

South of the medieval centre of Krakow is the
historic Okól district, a picturesque area with
curving streets lined with some outstanding
buildings. Fortunately the great fire
of Krakow in 1850 did not damage
the buildings in Okół, and much
of the original architecture can
still be seen here.

❷ **Collegium Iuridicum**
This sculpture, *Luca di Nara*,
in the courtyard is by
Polish-born Igor Mitoraj.
It was presented to the
Jagiellonian University
by the artist, who
now lives in Italy.

❹ **Archaeological Museum**
The collection here includes prehistoric
Polish artifacts as well as exhibits from
ancient Egypt.

❸ **Cricoteka**
The Cricot 2 Theatre
was originally
located in this
Gothic house.

⓫ **Palace of Bishop
Erazm Ciołek**
This beautiful building is
now home to the National
Museum's collection of Polish
art from the Middle Ages to the
beginning of the 19th century.

⓾ **Archdiocesan Museum**
The collection consists of objects from
churches in the Krakow Archdiocese
that are no longer used in the liturgy.

SENACKA

KANONICZA

❾ **Deanery**
The arcaded courtyard
of this small house,
formerly a canonry,
gives the impression
of a magnificent
Renaissance residence.

❽ **Kanonicza Street**
One of Krakow's prettiest
Gothic-Renaissance streets,
lined with the handsome
town houses that once
belonged to the city's clergy.

❸ ★ Church of Saints Peter and Paul
This early Baroque Jesuit church is a masterpiece of 17th-century Polish architecture. The façade, with its rich sculptural decoration, is remarkable.

Locator Map
See Street Finder maps 1, 3 & 6

❶ Grodzka Street
The town houses situated along one of the oldest streets in Krakow were once palaces.

❹ ★ Church of St Andrew
This is the best preserved example of Romanesque architecture in Krakow.

❺ Church of St Martin
This small early Baroque church was transformed into the Augsburg Protestant Church in the early 19th century.

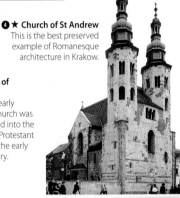

Key

— Suggested route

❼ Church of St Giles
This is a rather modest Gothic church dating from the first half of the 14th century.

❻ Royal Arsenal
This entrance to the Arsenal is one of the most beautiful 17th-century doorways in Krakow.

0 metres   50
0 yards   50

Historic Grodzka Street, lined with picturesque buildings

❶ Grodzka Street
Ulica Grodzka

Map 1 C5 (6 D4). 🚊 1, 6, 8, 10, 13, 18, 20.

Grodzka is one of the oldest streets in Krakow. In the past it formed part of the important Salt Route from Hungary to Greater Poland. As part of the Royal Route it bore witness to coronation and funeral processions of Polish kings.

Grodzka Street was once lined with many palaces and a few churches. These palaces were rebuilt and converted into town houses. Grodzka is a lovely street full of character, owing to its irregular plan, varying width and diverse architecture.

❷ Collegium Iuridicum
ul. Grodzka 53. **Map** 1 C5 (6 D4). **Tel** 12 633 63 77. 🚊 1, 6, 8, 10, 13, 18, 20. **Open** 10am–1pm Tue & Thu, 11am–2pm Sun.

The Collegium Iuridicum of the Academy of Krakow was founded early in the 15th century through the bequest of Queen Jadwiga. The excavation work carried out at the site has confirmed that the building had replaced a large trade hall, probably built in the 14th century on the orders of Władysław the Short. The remnants of the hall have survived in the basement.

The college was renovated and remodelled several times, with works funded by many people, including Jan Rzezsowski, who served as Bishop of Krakow from 1471 to 1488. The elaborate doorway decorated with the

Two-tier arcaded courtyard of the Collegium Iuridicum

university's emblem was made around 1680. The college was entirely rebuilt after a fire in 1719 and the two-tier arcaded courtyard added. Since 1992, the Institute of the History of Art of the Jagiellonian University has been housed here.

In the summer months concerts and theatrical performances take place in the courtyard, which features a sculpture by Igor Mitoraj.

❸ Church of Saints Peter and Paul
Kościół św. św. Piotra i Pawła

See pp82–3.

❹ Church of St Andrew
Kościół św. Andrzeja

ul. Grodzka 56. **Map** 1 C5 (6 D4). 🚊 1, 6, 8, 10, 13, 18, 20. **Open** 7:30am–5pm daily and during services.

The Church of St Andrew in Okół is regarded as one of the finest examples of Romanesque architecture in Poland. It was built between 1079 and 1098 as a foundation of Sieciech, the powerful Palatine to Duke Władysław Herman. It was rebuilt around 1200, and the towers and aisles were extended and a transept added. According to the chronicler Jan Długosz this was the only church in Krakow to resist the Tatar invasion of 1241. Around 1702 it was remodelled in the Baroque style to the designs of Baldassare Fontana, who also covered the internal walls and vaulting with stuccowork. Mural paintings by Karl Dankwart complete the decoration. Among furnishings worth noting are the pulpit, in the form of a boat, and the high altar with an imposing ebony tabernacle decorated with silver ornaments.

The treasury in the convent adjoining the church houses some priceless objects, such as a portable mosaic depicting the Virgin Mary from the end of the 12th century, 14th-century

Church of St Andrew with its two spires

marionettes used in Christmas nativity plays, and early medieval reliquaries.

❺ Church of St Martin
Kościół św. Marcina

ul. Grodzka 58a. **Map** 6 D4. **Tel** 12 446 64 30. 🚊 6, 8, 10, 13, 18. **Open** 10am–1pm Mon–Sat and during services.

The first church on this site was probably built in the 12th century. In 1612 the Discalced Carmelite Nuns were brought here. The old church was demolished and in 1637–40 the nuns commisioned a new, rather small church in the early Baroque style. After the convent was closed down, the church was taken over by the Protestant community. The interior was converted according to the needs of the Lutheran liturgy. The high altar features a 14th-century crucifix and *Christ Calming the Storm*, painted by Henryk Siemiradzki in 1882.

❻ Royal Arsenal
Arsenał Królewski

ul. Grodzka 64. **Map** 6 D5. 🚊 6, 8, 10, 13, 18. **Closed** to the public.

In the first half of the 16th century Zygmunt the Old built an arsenal and a cannon foundry next to the city wall. They formed part of Krakow's fortifications. The present building was remodelled in 1927 by the architect Stanisław Filipkiewicz, who juxtaposed the Baroque structure of the arsenal with an austere extension thus achieving an interesting effect.

❼ Church of St Giles
Kościół św. Idziego

ul. Św. Idziego 1. **Map** 6 D5. 🚊 6, 8, 10, 13, 18. **Open** 10am–1pm Tue–Fri.

According to historic evidence made popular by a song by Ewa Demarczyk (of the Piwnica pod Baranami Cabaret), this church was "built in 1082 by Władysław Herman and his wife Judith, after they bore a child through the intervention of St Giles". The present church was built in the early 14th century. In 1595 the Dominicans took over and soon remodelled it.

Among the furnishings, the stone stalls are particularly interesting. They were made in 1629 by reusing fragments of the Renaissance tomb of St Jacek (otherwise known as St Hyacinth) from the Dominican Church.

❽ Kanonicza Street
Ulica Kanonicza

Map 1 C5 (6 D4). 🚊 1, 6, 8, 10, 13, 18, 20.

Kanonicza Street formed the last stretch of the Royal Route leading towards Wawel. From the 14th century onwards it was lined with the houses of Krakow's canons, who were given the use of these houses for life when they took up office in the Chapter of Krakow. Each successive inhabitant tended to modernize their house. As a result, Gothic houses acquired arcaded Renaissance courtyards, Baroque doorways or Neo-Classical façades. The canons could afford to spend lavishly owing to their elite status within the church.

The great diversity of architectural styles which can be found within the gently curving little Kanonicza Street gives it a picturesque character.

Decorative bas-relief plaque of 1480 on the Długosz House, Kanonicza Street

❸ Church of Saints Peter and Paul

This church, modelled on the Jesuit Church of Il Gesù in Rome, is considered to be one of the most magnificent early Baroque churches in Central Europe. The history of its construction and the name of the architects involved are the subjects of an ongoing debate among architectural historians. The foundation stone was laid in 1596. The leading Jesuit architect, Giovanni de Rosis, contributed the design, and works were carried out by Giuseppe Brizio and Giovanni Maria Bernardoni. In 1605 the church neared its completion but, due to some structural problems, a number of walls had to be dismantled and rebuilt to an altered design. The court architect Giovanni Battista Trevano was put in charge of the second stage.

Cartouche with an Eagle
This exquisitely carved coat of arms belonged to the main founder of the church, King Zygmunt III Vaza.

Organ Gallery
The late Baroque organ gallery with a curved balustrade, designed by Kacper Bażanka, is in contrast with the austere and monumental architecture of the church. It is located inside, just above the main entrance.

Statues of the Apostles
This railing was designed by Kacper Bażanka and is decorated with copies of statues originally carved by David Heel between 1715 and 1722.

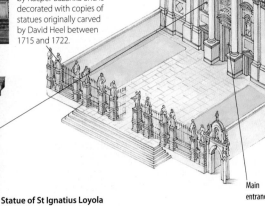

Main entrance

Statue of St Ignatius Loyola
The founder of the Society of Jesus is depicted in this late Baroque sculpture by David Heel. The adjoining statues are of Stanisław Kostka, Francis Xavier and Aloysius Gonzaga.

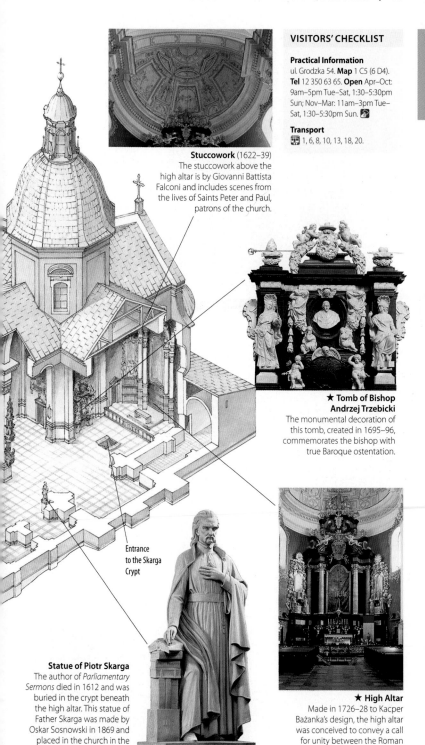

Stuccowork (1622–39)
The stuccowork above the
high altar is by Giovanni Battista
Falconi and includes scenes from
the lives of Saints Peter and Paul,
patrons of the church.

★ **Tomb of Bishop
Andrzej Trzebicki**
The monumental decoration of
this tomb, created in 1695–96,
commemorates the bishop with
true Baroque ostentation.

Entrance
to the Skarga
Crypt

Statue of Piotr Skarga
The author of *Parliamentary
Sermons* died in 1612 and was
buried in the crypt beneath
the high altar. This statue of
Father Skarga was made by
Oskar Sosnowski in 1869 and
placed in the church in the
early 20th century.

★ **High Altar**
Made in 1726–28 to Kacper
Bażanka's design, the high altar
was conceived to convey a call
for unity between the Roman
Catholic and Orthodox Churches.

Massive portal of the medieval Deanery

❾ Deanery
Dom Dziekański

ul. Kanonicza 21. **Map** 1 C5 (6 D4).
🚋 1, 6, 8, 10, 13, 18, 20.

This house is considered to be the most beautiful of all the canons' houses in Krakow. The medieval house was completely rebuilt in the 1580s, probably by the architect and sculptor Santi Gucci. The arcaded courtyard with its magnificent decoration, carved in stone, the impressive portal and the *sgraffiti* on the façade all date from this period. The statue of St Stanisław in the courtyard was added in the 18th century. In the 1960s this was home to the future Pope and then Suffragan Bishop of Krakow, Karol Wojtyła.

❿ Archdiocesan Museum
Muzeum Archidiecezjalne

ul. Kanonicza 19. **Map** 1 C5 (6 D4).
Tel 12 421 89 63. 🚋 1, 6, 8, 10, 13, 18, 20. **Open** 10am–4pm Tue–Fri, 10am–3pm Sat & Sun. 🚫 📷

This house is traditionally associated with the residence of St Stanisław while he was a canon in Krakow, hence the name, St Stanisław's House.

It was actually built in the 14th century but entirely remodelled in the late 18th century. The Archdiocesan Museum is now housed here. It runs a programme of temporary exhibitions of sacred art based on loans from church treasuries in the Krakow Archdiocese. Interesting goldwork displays have taken place here.

Part of the Archdiocesan Museum is given over to the room of Karol Wojtyła, who became Pope John Paul II. The room has been faithfully reconstructed here as it stood originally in the adjoining Deanery, where he lived.

⓫ Palace of Bishop Erazm Ciołek
Pałac biskupa Erazma Ciołka

ul. Kanonicza 17. **Map** 1 C5 (6 D4). **Tel** 12 433 59 20. 🚋 1, 6, 8, 10, 13, 18, 20. **Open** 10am–4pm Tue–Sun. 🎟 free on Sun (permanent collection).

This museum was once home to the great diplomat and patron of the arts Bishop Erazm Ciołek (1474–1522). A magnificently distinguished residence, it has been extensively renovated and now houses the National Museum's large and notable collection of Polish Art. The house was built in a mix of Gothic and Renaissance styles, while the collection within ranges from the 12th to the 18th centuries. The latter includes stunning exhibits such as late-Gothic altarpieces, Gothic statuary and a room dedicated to the highly ceremonial funerary culture of 17th-century Poland. Fixed to the ceilings of the galleries are beautifully restored examples of ceiling painting taken from ancient wooden churches.

A separate section on the opposite side of the courtyard houses one of the oldest and most valuable collections of Orthodox religious icons in Central Europe. The icons featured here are mostly from the eastern parts of Poland where significant Orthodox- and Uniate-Christian populations still live.

Karol Wojtyła's room in the Archdiocesan Museum

⓬ Statue of Piotr Skarga
Posąg Piotra Skargi

Plac Marii Magdaleny. **Map** 1 C5 (6 D4). 🚎 1, 6, 8, 10, 13, 18, 20.

Dominating the small piazza that connects Kanonicza with Grodzka is a modern statue of the leading Polish Jesuit Piotr Skarga (1536–1612). Skarga was a powerful orator and preacher, something captured admirably in this animated sculpture by Czesław Dźwigaj.

⓭ Cricoteka

ul. Kanonicza 5. **Map** 1 C5 (6 D4). 🚎 1, 6, 8, 10, 13, 18, 20.

The former canon's house at 5 Kanonicza Street has retained much of its Gothic form. In 1980 it became the home of the renowned avant-garde theatre Cricot 2. This theatre was founded in 1955 on the initiative of Tadeusz Kantor, the outstanding painter and stage designer. It became famous for performances which were permeated by a symbolic representation of man's existence. The most unusual sets added a surreal flavour to the performances. The collection of stage designs and props, costumes, photographs of the performances, as well as drawings and paintings by Kantor that used to be displayed here can now be seen at the modern Cricoteka museum in Podgórze *(see p159)*.

⓮ Archaeological Museum
Muzeum Archeologiczne

ul. Poselska 3. **Map** 1 C5 (6 D4). **Tel** 12 422 71 00. 🚌 504. 🚎 1, 6, 8, 10, 13, 18, 20. **Open** 9am–3pm Mon, Wed & Fri; 9am–6pm Tue & Thu; 11am–4pm Sun (Jul & Aug: 11am– 6pm Mon-Fri, 10am–3pm Sun). 🎟 free on Sun.

Begun in 1850 and known then as the Museum of Antiquities, the Archaeological Museum is housed in the former Friary of the Discalced Carmelites, founded in 1606. Its collection includes artifacts that tell the earliest history of the Lesser Poland region. The statue of the idol Światowid, salvaged from the Zbrucz River, jewellery found in the tomb of a Scythian princess in Ryżanówka, gold objects from the tomb of a Hun from Jakuszowice and iron objects used as a form of payment *(see p23)* are the highlights of the collection. There are also Egyptian mummies.

The basement of the museum (accessed via a doorway in the garden) was once the site of St Michael's Prison, one of Krakow's most notorious jails. The cells here were used by the Austrian, Nazi and post-war Communist authorities to incarcerate Polish political prisoners. In 1945, a group of imprisoned soldiers was rescued following heroic action by the Home Army (AK). The cells here were also used to hold Nazi war criminals, including Rudolf Höss, commandant of Auschwitz, and Amon Göth, head of the Płaszów concentration camp *(see p159)*.

Elaborate porch at the entrance to the Wielopolski Palace

⓯ Wielopolski Palace
Pałac Wielopolskich

Plac Wszystkich Świętych. **Map** 1 C5 (6 D3). **Tel** 12 616 12 07. 🚎 1, 6, 8, 10, 13, 18, 20. **Open** by prior telephone arrangement only.

This palace was transformed into a seat of municipal administration in the second half of the 19th century. Following remodelling work in 1907–12 by architect Jan Rzymkowski, the building acquired a simplified modern form. A porch supported by pseudo-Romanesque columns was added to the wall facing Poselska Street. An Art Nouveau frieze with coats of arms of various cities can also be seen here.

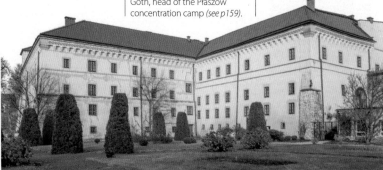

Archaeological Museum and garden

⑯ Franciscan Church

The Franciscans arrived in Krakow in 1237 and the construction of this church was undertaken in 1255 as a foundation of Duke Bolesław the Chaste and his wife the Blessed Salomea. After the Swedish invasion, which caused much damage, the church was rebuilt in the Baroque style. The great fire of Krakow in 1850 damaged the church again and it was rebuilt partly in the Neo-Romanesque and partly in the Neo-Gothic style. The work of Stanisław Wyspiański on the interior decoration is of prime importance. Around 1900 the artist executed the Art Nouveau murals and designed a series of unusual stained-glass windows in expressive colours.

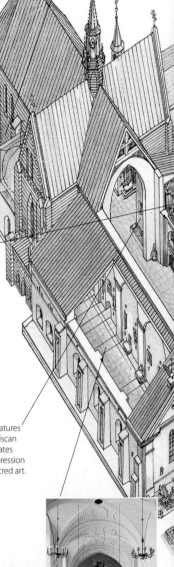

A 13th-century wall of the first church

Blessed Salomea
Stanisław Wyspiański's stained glass in the north window of the choir shows the foundress of the church who rejected the ducal coronet before taking the habit of a Poor Clare nun.

★ **Mater Dolorosa**
This late Gothic image by Master Jerzy, of Mary surrounded by angels holding instruments of Christ's Passion, is much venerated.

★ **Murals**
The polychrome decoration features flowers and conveys the Franciscan love of nature. This work illustrates the novel means of artistic expression employed by Wyspiański in sacred art.

Chapel of The Passion
The brothers of the Confraternity of The Passion have met in this chapel since the end of the 16th century to conduct their rituals (see p54). Their liturgy is theatrical and evokes the spirit of Baroque devotion.

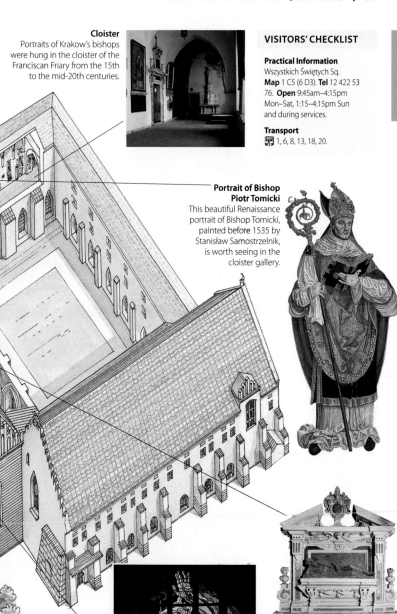

Cloister
Portraits of Krakow's bishops were hung in the cloister of the Franciscan Friary from the 15th to the mid-20th centuries.

VISITORS' CHECKLIST

Practical Information
Wszystkich Świętych Sq.
Map 1 C5 (6 D3). **Tel** 12 422 53 76. **Open** 9:45am–4:15pm Mon–Sat, 1:15–4:15pm Sun and during services.

Transport
1, 6, 8, 13, 18, 20.

Portrait of Bishop Piotr Tomicki
This beautiful Renaissance portrait of Bishop Tomicki, painted before 1535 by Stanisław Samostrzelnik, is worth seeing in the cloister gallery.

★ **Wyspiański's Stained-Glass Let It Be**
This expressive image of God the Father emerging from the cosmic chaos was rendered using bold colours and sinuous, flowing Art Nouveau forms.

Tomb of Giovanni Gemma (died 1608)
The monument to the Venetian physician to King Zygmunt III Vaza is one of the most interesting sepulchral sculptures of late Mannerism in Poland.

⓱ Statue of Józef Dietl
Pomnik Józefa Dietla

Plac Wszystkich Świętych. **Map** 1 C5 (6 D3). 🚊 1, 6, 8, 10, 13, 18, 20.

Józef Dietl (1804–78) was a medical professor who advocated treating the sick in spas. He was Rector of the Jagiellonian University, and became the first President (Mayor) of Krakow to be elected, in 1866, in the autonomous Galicia. He reformed the education system in Krakow, set up a project for the renovation of the city's heritage and was responsible for the restoration of the Cloth Hall.

The statue of Dietl was made between 1936 and 1938 by Xawery Dunikowski. The artist not only created the figure but also took a great deal of trouble to find it a prominent location. Using a model, he travelled all over Krakow and tried it out in various places before deciding on the present location in All Saints Square.

⓲ Church of the Bernardine Nuns
Kościół Bernardynek

ul. Poselska 21. **Map** 1 C5 (6 D4). **Tel** 12 422 22 46. 🚊 1, 6, 8, 10, 13, 18, 20. **Open** 9am–6:30pm daily and during services.

A small convent of the Bernardine Nuns was established in Poselska Street in 1646. The Church of St Joseph was built here between 1694 and 1703 for the nuns. Though small and modest the church interior displays splendid furnishings which include altars and a pulpit from the workshop of Jerzy Hankis. The miraculous image of St Joseph and Child in the high altar was a gift from Jakub Zadzik, Bishop of Krakow, who possibly received it from Pope Urban VIII.

A 17th-century statue of the child Jesus in the side altar is much venerated. It originally came from the Church of the Nuns of St Colette in Stradom and is therefore called the Koletański Christ.

Interior of the small Church of the Bernardine Nuns

⓳ Bernardine Church
Kościół Bernardynów

ul. Bernardyńska 2. **Map** 3 C1 (6 D5). **Tel** 12 422 16 50. 🚊 6, 8, 10, 13, 18. **Open** during services only.

Giovanni da Capistrano, the reformer of the Franciscan Order, later canonized, arrived in Krakow in 1453. For the next year he preached repentance and the renouncement of wealth and the immoral way of life. He also incited the people against the Jews. Influenced by his sermons, a few Krakovians took up the habit of the Reformed Franciscans, then called the Observants but known as the Bernardines in Poland. In 1453 Cardinal Zbigniew Oleśnicki built in Stradom a small timber church for this new monastic community, and soon after began building a large brick church. It was completed by Jan Długosz after Oleśnicki's death.

In 1655, while preparing to defend Krakow against the Swedes, Stefan Czarniecki gave orders to set fire to the Bernardine Church, which was located at the foot of Wawel Hill, so that the invaders could not use the church for their own protection. The beautiful statue of the Virgin and Child with St Anne, from Veit Stoss's workshop, and remnants of Mannerist tombs (now on the porch wall) are the only furnishings to have survived.

The new Baroque Church of the Bernardines was built between 1659 and 1680. Krzysztof Mieroszewski is believed to have been the architect. The marble shrine of Blessed Simon of Lipnica was erected in 1662 and the high altar between 1758 and 1766.

The 17th-century Baroque Bernardine Church

⓴ Częstochowa Seminary
Seminarium Częstochowskie

ul. Bernardyńska 3. **Map** 3 C1 (6 D5). 6, 8, 10, 13, 18.

In 1925 the Bishop of Częstochowa, Teodor Kubina, founded a seminary affiliated with the Faculty of Theology at the Jagiellonian University, for seminarists from his diocese. The monumental Modernist building was constructed between 1928 and 1930 to the designs of Zygmunt Gawlik and Franciszek Mączyński. The seminary is no longer in operation.

The façade is decorated with sculptures which were carved under the supervision of Xawery Dunikowski, one of the foremost Polish sculptors of the 20th century. The bas-relief at the top is particularly interesting. It shows Christ blessing the allegorical figure of Poland and the representatives of all social ranks, as well as the Virgin Mary accompanied by clergymen. The scene depicting a seminarist tempted by the devil, also on the façade, is worth noting.

Relief of a seminarist tempted by the devil, Częstochowa Seminary

㉑ Church of the Missionaries
Kościół Misjonarzy

ul. Stradomska 4. **Map** 3 C1 (6 E5). **Tel** 12 422 88 77. 504. 6, 8, 10, 13, 18. **Open** 2–7pm daily and during services.

The Missionaries were brought to Stradom in 1682 but built the Church of the Conversion of St Paul only in the years 1719 to 1728. The architect, Kacper Bażanka, was influenced in his design by two outstanding examples of Roman Baroque architecture. The interior of the Krakow church resembles that of Francesco Borromini's Church of the Magi at the Collegio di Propaganda Fide, and the exterior is close to Sant'Andrea

Baroque façade of the Church of the Missionaries

al Quirinale designed by Gianlorenzo Bernini. Some of the methods applied by Bażanka, such as the use of mirrors in the nave to direct reflected light onto the chapels, are characteristic of High Baroque. The church is regarded as one of the finest examples of 18th-century Baroque Polish architecture.

The same applies to the interior. Most altarpieces were painted by Tadeusz Kuntze and decorated with sculptures by Antoni Frączkiewicz.

㉒ Natural History Museum
Muzeum Przyrodnicze

ul. Św. Sebastiana 9/11. **Map** 3 D1 (6 E5). **Tel** 12 422 59 59. 6, 8, 10, 13, 18. **Open** 9am–3pm Mon–Fri, 11am–7pm Sat & Sun.

The core of the Natural History Museum was the collection of the Physiographic Commission of Krakow's Learned Society, established in 1865. It consisted mainly of stuffed birds and invertebrates. Today, the museum keeps live fish, reptiles and mammals; it also boasts a tropical rainforest display. A rhinoceros dating from the Pleistocene era, found in 1920 in Starunia, is a highlight of the collection.

㉓ Dietl Plantations
Planty Dietlowskie

Map 4 D1 (6 E5, F4). 184. 12, 22.

The old river bed of the Vistula, stretching from Stradom to Kazimierz, was filled in during the years 1878 to 1880 and transformed into a modern thoroughfare. Designed by Bolesław Malecki, it became a dual carriageway 1 km (0.6 mile) in length and 100 m (328 ft) wide, with a garden running through the middle. It was named Planty Dietlowskie, after Józef Dietl (*see p88*), President of Krakow and a keen advocate of the move, who saw the old Vistula bed as hindering the integration of central Krakow with Kazimierz. Both sides of the avenue are lined with high tenement blocks and elegant public buildings, one of which is the PKO Bank built between 1922 and 1924.

Tree-lined avenue separating Dietl's dual carriageway

Aerial view of Market Square and the Cloth Hall

Sights at a Glance

Churches

Historic Streets
and Squares

Historic Monuments
and Buildings

Museums and Galleries

OLD QUARTER

In 1257 Duke Bolesław the Chaste gave Krakow her charter. This law was of key importance to the city as it determined local government and trade privileges, thus stimulating the city's future development. The charter stipulated strict rules for this development: a large, centrally located square surrounded by a regular grid of streets was to become the city centre. The size of each plot determined the size of the houses. Although the architecture became ever more opulent, this urban scheme has survived almost intact. To this day the Old Quarter remains the heart of modern, fast-developing Krakow and is an area with a great concentration of important historic sights for visitors to enjoy.

☐ **Restaurants** *pp192–4*

1 Ambasada Śledzia
2 Aqua e Vino
3 Camelot
4 Chimera
5 Chłopskie Jadło
6 CK Dezerter
7 Cyrano de Bergerac
8 Czerwone Korale
9 Da Pietro
10 Del Papá
11 Farina
12 Gródek
13 Hawełka
14 Leonardo
15 Marmolada
16 Miód i Wino
17 Noworolski
18 La Petite France
19 Pimiento Argentino
20 Pod Różą
21 Przypiecek
22 Szara
23 Szara Gęś
24 Trzy Rybki
25 U Babci Maliny
26 Urara
27 Wentzl
28 Wierzynek

See also Street Finder maps 1, 5 & 6

0 metres 200
0 yards 200

Street-by-Street: Market Square

The Market Square (Rynek Główny) is located in the centre of Krakow's Old Quarter. Public, cultural and commercial activities have always concentrated around the Market Square. Museums and galleries of both classical and modern art can be found here. Antiquarian shops selling works of art, bookshops and the best restaurants, cafés and bars are located in the houses around the square. Each summer a number of street cafés open until the early hours. Flower stalls, street musicians, artists selling their works by the Cloth Hall, and the general hustle and bustle made by the vendors of souvenirs and their clients all contribute to the lively atmosphere of this area.

❹ Market Square
This is the largest town square anywhere in Europe. The life of medieval Krakow was centred around the square.

"The Magical Cab", the poem by K I Gałczyński, was inspired by a horse-drawn cab similar to one that you can hire here for a sightseeing trip.

❺ ★ Krzysztofory Palace
A branch of the Museum of Krakow is housed in this palace.

❼ ★ Cloth Hall (Sukiennice)
Originally a market hall, the Sukiennice houses shops, cafés and a renowned gallery of 19th-century Polish art.

❻ Town Hall Tower
The only remaining fragment of the Old Town Hall, the tower was remodelled after World War II.

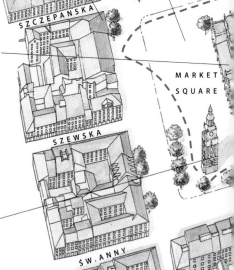

SŁAWKOWSKA

ŚW. JANA

SZCZEPAŃSKA

SZEWSKA

MARKET SQUARE

ŚW. ANNY

WIŚLNA

❶ ★ Church of St Mary
The main parish church in Krakow is renowned for its Gothic high altar, one of the largest in the world, carved by Veit Stoss.

❷ St Mary's Square
The parish cemetery was originally located on this site.

Locator Map
See Street Finder maps 1 & 6

OLD QUARTER

OKÓŁ AND STRADOM QUARTERS

❸ St Barbara's Church
The architecture of the church is medieval. Its furnishings are mainly Rococo but also include this 15th-century Pietà.

0 metres   50
0 yards   50

Statue of Adam Mickiewicz
This is a popular meeting point for Krakovians.

ADAMOWI
MICKIEWICZOWI
NARÓD

FLORIAŃSKA

SIENNA

GRODZKA

BRACKA

❾ St Adalbert's Church
This is one of the oldest churches in Krakow. The picturesque structure is at the end of the vista formed by Grodzka Street.

Key
— Suggested route

❶ Church of St Mary
Kościół Mariacki

St Mary's, or the Church of the Assumption of the Virgin, was the main parish church of Krakow's burghers. It is a Gothic basilica composed of nave, aisles and side chapels. There are two towers. The north tower was extended in the early 15th century and in 1478 topped with a spire by Matthias Heringk. It was the city's watch-tower. Inside the church there are many outstanding works of art, among which the magnificent high altar by Veit Stoss *(see pp96–7)* should be mentioned. Other furnishings include the Baroque pulpit, marble altars decorated with paintings by the Italian artist Giovanni Battista Pittoni and Renaissance tombs in the chapels.

Bugle-Call Tower
The spire is decorated with turrets and topped by a gilt crown. The famous bugle-call *(hejnał)* is played here at hourly intervals and broadcast at noon by the Polish radio.

The Porch (1750–52)
The late-Baroque porch was designed by Francesco Placidi. Carved busts of the Apostles and saints by Karol Hukan were added to the door panels in 1929.

Main entrance

1221–2 Building of the Romanesque church

1392–7 Nave and aisles built

1477–89 High altar completed

1585 Choir stalls completed

1200	1300	1400	1500	1600

End of the 13th century
Construction of the Gothic church begins

1355–65 New choir built

1478 North tower receives a spire

Detail of the main door

Choir Stalls
The stalls were made in 1585 but the biblical scenes in low relief which decorate the backs of the seats date from 1635.

VISITORS' CHECKLIST

Practical Information
Mariacki Sq 5. **Map** 1 C4 (6 D2).
Tel 12 422 05 21. **Open** 11:30am–6pm Mon–Fri, 2–6pm Sun.
w mariacki.com

The Montelupi Tomb
This Mannerist tomb of one of the richest Krakow families was made around 1600 in the workshop of Santi Gucci.

Visitors' entrance

★ The Ciborium
This Renaissance ciborium (receptacle for containing the Eucharist) at the entrance to the choir was made around 1552 to the design by Giovanni Maria Mosca.

KEY

① **The tracery of the Great West Window** was designed by Jan Matejko and the stained glass is by Józef Mehoffer and Stanisław Wyspiański.

② **South Bell Tower**

③ **High Altar** (see pp96–7)

④ **The murals** on the walls and vault were designed and executed by Jan Matejko between 1890 and 1892.

★ The Slacker Crucifix (1496)
The figure of the suffering Christ, carved in stone by Veit Stoss, is the most expressive sculpture ever made by the artist.

Exploring St Mary's: The High Altar

The high altar by Veit Stoss was made between 1477 and 1489. It is dedicated, like the church itself, to the Assumption of the Virgin Mary. The altar is a polyptych, some 11 m (36 ft) long and 12 m (39 ft) high – though it was even higher originally. The iconography determined its composition. The shutters were closed throughout the liturgical year but opened during important church feasts. The treatment of the human figure is naturalistic, dynamic and dramatically expressive. The low reliefs and figures of saints are masterpieces of late-Gothic art.

The Lamentation
The design of this particular panel was influenced by Netherlandish painting.

The Meeting of
St Anne and
St Joachim

The middle shutters
are opened every day
at 11:50am.

The Three Maries
at the Sepulchre

The Capture
of Christ

The Crucifixion

The Descent into Hell

The Birth of
the Virgin

The Presentation of the
Virgin in the Temple

The Risen Christ
appearing to Mary
Magdalene

The Entombment

**The Presentation of
Christ in the Temple**
In this scene the artist tries
to recreate the interior
of the temple.

Christ among the Doctors
This scene testifies to Stoss's
masterly depiction of the
diverse physiognomies.

Veit Stoss (Wit Stwosz)

Veit Stoss (1447–1533), one of the greatest wood-carvers of the late Gothic age, was born in Horb am Neckar in Germany. He lived in Krakow from 1477 to 1496, where he was exempted from paying taxes by the City Council. He created a number of sculptural works here.

The Coronation of the Virgin

St Stanisław

The Annunciation

The Nativity

St Adalbert

The Assumption
Mary and Christ are raised to Heaven by eight angels.

The Ascension

The Resurrection

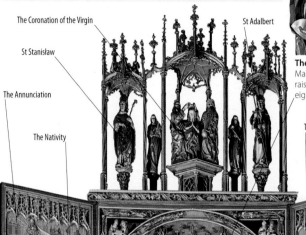

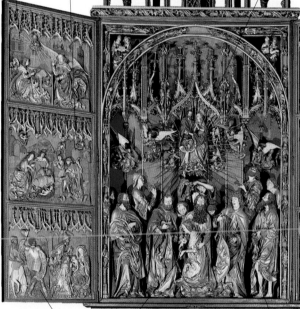

The Adoration of the Magi

Pentecost

Predella with the Tree of Jesse

The Death of the Virgin
The figure of the youthful Mary is one of the greatest sculptures ever made in Poland.

St John
Slightly hesitant, the saint is about to put a cape on the fainting Mary.

❷ St Mary's Square
Plac Mariacki

Map 1 C4 (6 D2).

St Mary's Square was once a parish graveyard. It was relocated between 1796 and 1804. The statue of the Virgin Mary that was here originally is now in the Planty by Jagiellońska Street. The bas-relief attributed to Veit Stoss, which once decorated the Calvary Porch, has survived and is now in the National Museum. A copy can be seen on the wall at No. 8 on the square. The prelate House and a Vicarage are among the houses in which original beamed ceilings and plasterwork have survived. St Barbara's Church is on the east side of the square, which also features a small water pump decorated with a figure of a student of medieval Krakow. It is a copy of a figure from the high altar in St Mary's (see pp96–7).

A student of medieval Krakow, St Mary's Square

❸ St Barbara's Church
Kościół św. Barbary

Mały Rynek 8. **Map** 1 C4 (6 D2). **Tel** 12 428 15 00. **Open** 9am–6pm Mon–Sat, 2–3:30pm Sun.

According to a legend St Barbara's Church was built using the bricks that were left over from the construction of the Church of St Mary. St Barbara's actually dates

The Gothic porch with Christ in Gethsemane, at St Barbara's

from 1394 to 1399, which coincides with one of the stages in the construction of St Mary's. Between 1415 and 1536 sermons were delivered in Polish in the former church, and in German in the latter. During this period the patricians of Krakow were mostly German and it was only much later that they became a minority among the Polish population. In 1586 the church was taken over by the Jesuits. Piotr Skarga preached here and Jakub Wujek, the translator of the Bible, is buried here. Added on the outside from 1488 to 1518 is a late Gothic chapel with a porch decorated with sculptures made by Veit Stoss's workshop. Furnishings date mostly from the 18th century but there is also an interesting early 15th-century Pietà in stone and a 15th-century crucifix on the high altar.

❹ Market Square
Rynek Główny

See pp100–103.

The Lajkonik

Every year, on the first Thursday after Corpus Christi, a parade led by a figure known as the *Lajkonik* proceeds from the Convent of the Premonstratensian Nuns in Zwierzyniec to the Market Square. The event commemorates the victory over the Tatars in 1287. On his way, the *Lajkonik* strikes some spectators with his mace, a sign which is thought to bring good luck, especially to girls. At the Market Square the *Lajkonik* receives a symbolic tribute. The original costume of the *Lajkonik*, designed in 1904 by Stanisław Wyspiański, is now in the Museum of Krakow.

The *Lajkonik*

❺ Krzysztofory Palace
Pałac Krzysztofory

Rynek Główny 35. **Map** 1 C4 (6 D2). Museum of Krakow: **Tel** 12 426 50 60. Cellars: **Open** 10am–5:30pm Tue–Sun. 🅿 🚾 mhk.pl

This is one of the oldest and most beautiful palaces in Krakow, with a magnificent arcaded courtyard. It was remodelled between 1682 and 1685 by Jacopo Solari for Kazimierz Wodzicki, one of the richest noblemen in Lesser Poland.

The palace is named after St Christopher, whose 14th-century statue decorates the building. Now belonging to the Museum of Krakow (which has several branches throughout the city), the building's top floor holds the Cyberteka: Krakow in Time and Space, which tells the history of the city through a combination of models and touch-screen computers. In the basement is a display devoted to the art of the *szopka* or nativity crib. The *szopka* has become an important expression of Krakow folk art, with locals competing to create the most ornate scene every year in the weeks leading up to Christmas.

❻ Town Hall Tower
Wieża Ratuszowa

Rynek Główny 1. **Map** 1 C4 (6 D2). Museum: **Tel** 12 426 43 34. **Open** Apr–Oct: 10:30am–5:30pm daily.

Until the early 19th century there were several public buildings on Market Square: the Town Hall, the Small Weigh-House, the Large Weigh-House and a pillory. The 70 m- (230 ft-) high Town Hall Tower is, unfortunately, the only structure to have survived. The Gothic Town Hall itself was remodelled many times and finally demolished in 1846. The present dome is Baroque. The tower houses a branch of the Museum of Krakow dedicated to the history of local government and is a venue for the Ludowy Theatre.

❼ Cloth Hall
Sukiennice

See pp104–5.

❽ Rynek Underground
Podziemia Rynku

Rynek Główny 1. **Map** 1 C4 (6 D2). **Tel** 12 426 50 60. **Open** Apr–Oct: 10am–10pm daily (to 8pm Mon, to 4pm Tue); Nov–Mar: 10am–8pm daily (to 4pm Tue). Book in advance via the website or by phone. **Closed** 2nd Mon of month. free Tue. **w** mhk.pl

This high-tech museum, tracing the story of the city, opened in September 2010 and is located under Market Square. The underground vaults contain displays on transport and trade

Church of St Adalbert on Market Square

as well as archaeological finds such as the remains of an 11th-century cemetery and ancient coins and clothing. The museum cleverly blends modern technology with interactive exhibits and more traditional museum displays.

❾ St Adalbert's Church
Kościół św. Wojciecha

Rynek Główny 3. **Map** 1 C4 (6 D3). **Open** 8:30am–5pm daily.

The small church of St Adalbert is one of the oldest in Krakow. A legend tells that St Adalbert preached here before leaving on his missionary journey to

try to convert the Prussians in 997. The architecture of the church amalgamates several styles, from Romanesque and Gothic, through Renaissance and Baroque, to the modern interior design. This mixture reflects various stages in the development of the Market Square, an exhibition on which is located in Rynek Underground. The display includes a cross-section of the ground beneath the square, as well as medieval water pipes and other objects found during the excavations carried out after World War II, which have also revealed the remnants of the building dating from the time of St Adalbert.

The iconic Cloth Hall in the middle of the Market Square

❹ Market Square: North and West Sides

The charter given to Krakow in 1257 determined the plan of the city. The square located in the middle of the medieval city has remained the centre of Krakow ever since. This square, some 200 m (656 ft) by 200 m (656 ft), is surrounded by a regular grid of streets, with three streets on each side. Only the off-the-grid location of the Church of St Mary, which pre-dates the charter, and Grodzka Street, with its funnel-like shape, vary the rigidity of the urban planning in this area. There were formerly many buildings in the square, but of those the Cloth Hall and the Town Hall Tower are the only ones to have survived. The square was a venue for many important events, including coronation ceremonies.

Deer House
This was once an inn. Johann Wolfgang von Goethe and Tsar Nicholas I both stayed here.

Horse House

Phoenix House

Kenc House

North Side

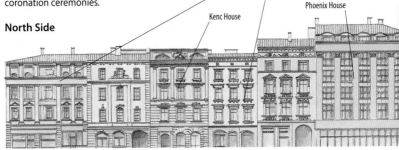

Palace of the Rams (Pałac Pod Baranami)
One of the most magnificent palaces owned by the Potocki family now houses a famous cabaret.

"Piwnica Pod Baranami" Cabaret

The cabaret which is housed in the Palace of the Rams was established in 1956. Although it was originally intended to exist no longer than "five years, possibly even less", the cabaret has been active for more than 50 years and is one of Krakow's top attractions. Piotr Skrzynecki (1930–97) was the founder and heart and soul of the cabaret. Wiesław Dymny, Ewa Demarczyk, Marek Grechuta, Krystyna Zachwatowicz, Zygmunt Konieczny, Leszek Wójtowicz, Anna Szałapak, Grzegorz Turnau and Zbigniew Preisner were among the best-known contributors and performers. The cabaret is a lively place full of poetry and music, joy and laughter.

Piotr Skrzynecki

West Side

Lamb House

House with a Tin Roof

Małachowski Palace

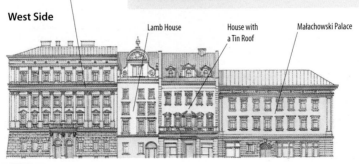

Betman House
This is also known as "Under the Beheaded" after a bas-relief which depicts the martyrdom of St John the Baptist.

Locator Map
Market Square: North and West sides

42 Market Square
belonged to the Boner family and in the 19th century to the renowned collector Feliks Manggha Jasieński.

Margrave's House
A former mint and presently a bank, the façade of this house features a splendid Rococo portal.

Red House

Eagle House (Dom Pod Orłem)
The basement of this fine Renaissance house formerly contained the Starmach Gallery of contemporary art.

Krzysztofory Palace (Pałac Krzysztofory)
This palace *(see p98)* houses the Museum of Krakow, among whose highlights is a gilded plaque, made in 1609, depicting St Eligius.

House under Three Stars

Spiš Palace (Pałac Spiski)
is home to the exclusive Hawełka Restaurant *(see p193)*.

❹ Market Square: South and East Sides

There are many stories about the Market Square. According to one of the legends, Krakow's pigeons are the enchanted knights of Duke Henryk Probus, who agreed to their metamorphosis in exchange for gold that he needed to secure papal acceptance for his coronation. The knights were supposed to regain their human form after the coronation but the duke lost the gold and his knights are still awaiting the promised transformation. The legend about the two brothers who built the St Mary's towers is more popular. When the older mason completed the taller tower he stabbed his younger brother to death in order to prevent him from surpassing his work but then, remorseful, killed himself.

Madonna House (Dom Pod Obrazem)
Formerly the palace of a wealthy burgher family called Cellari. The façade is decorated with the Madonna painted in 1718.

South Side

Wierzynek Restaurant

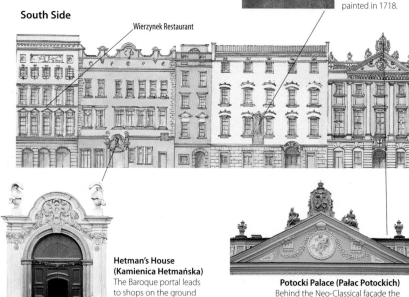

Hetman's House (Kamienica Hetmańska)
The Baroque portal leads to shops on the ground floor, in which Gothic vaults with carved keystones have survived.

Potocki Palace (Pałac Potockich)
Behind the Neo-Classical façade the original interiors and a small arcaded courtyard have survived.

East Side

Grey House (Kamienica Szara)

4 Market Square
This is one of a few houses with Art Nouveau decoration. It was added during the remodelling carried out in 1907–8 by Ludwik Wojtyczka.

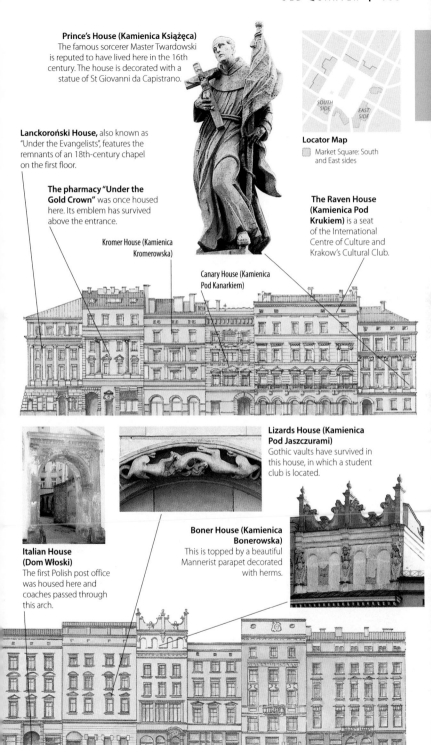

Prince's House (Kamienica Książęca)
The famous sorcerer Master Twardowski is reputed to have lived here in the 16th century. The house is decorated with a statue of St Giovanni da Capistrano.

Lanckoroński House, also known as "Under the Evangelists", features the remnants of an 18th-century chapel on the first floor.

The pharmacy "Under the Gold Crown" was once housed here. Its emblem has survived above the entrance.

Kromer House (Kamienica Kromerowska)

Canary House (Kamienica Pod Kanarkiem)

Locator Map
▢ Market Square: South and East sides

SOUTH SIDE
EAST SIDE

The Raven House (Kamienica Pod Krukiem) is a seat of the International Centre of Culture and Krakow's Cultural Club.

Lizards House (Kamienica Pod Jaszczurami)
Gothic vaults have survived in this house, in which a student club is located.

Boner House (Kamienica Bonerowska)
This is topped by a beautiful Mannerist parapet decorated with herms.

Italian House (Dom Włoski)
The first Polish post office was housed here and coaches passed through this arch.

❼ The Cloth Hall (Sukiennice)

Situated in the Market Square, this elaborate structure has evolved from simple stone trading stalls (dating to the time of Kazimierz the Great) to a pretty shopping arcade. Rebuilt to the design of Giovanni Maria Mosca following a fire in 1555, it was remodelled entirely in 1875 by Tomasz Pryliński. As well as stalls selling a variety of handicrafts and souvenirs, the Cloth Hall houses the Gallery of 19th Century Polish Art. The Noworolski Café, one of the best in Krakow, is a good place to relax after seeing the paintings and picking up a souvenir or two.

Frenzy of Exultations (1894) by Władysław Podkowiński
Originally considered daringly erotic, this Symbolist painting aroused much controversy when it was first displayed.

Four-in-hand (1881) by Józef Chełmoński
Paintings by Symbolists as well as Realists are exhibited alongside the *Four-in-hand*.

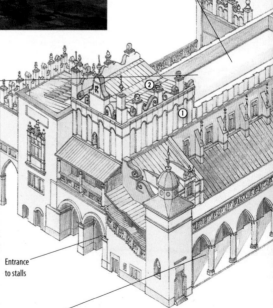

Entrance to stalls

Arcades
The side arcades and oriels were added during the rebuilding in 1875. The arcades echo the medieval architecture of Venice.

★ **Blue Hussars by Piotr Michałowski**
A separate room is dedicated to the work of Michałowski, the foremost Polish Romantic artist who lived between 1800 and 1855.

VISITORS' CHECKLIST

Practical Information
Market Square 1/3. **Map** 1 C4
(6 D2). **Tel** 12 433 54 00. **Open**
10am–6pm Tue–Sun. free
Sun (permanent exhibition only).
mnk.pl

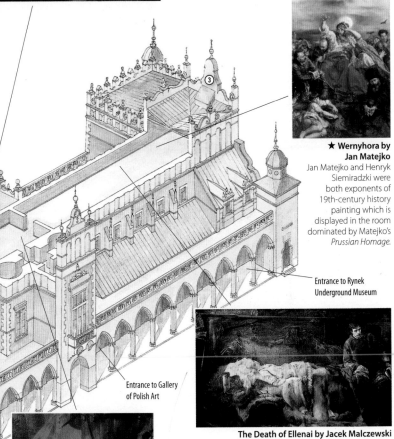

★ **Wernyhora by Jan Matejko**
Jan Matejko and Henryk Siemiradzki were both exponents of 19th-century history painting which is displayed in the room dominated by Matejko's *Prussian Homage*.

Entrance to Rynek Underground Museum

Entrance to Gallery of Polish Art

The Death of Ellenai by Jacek Malczewski
Characteristic of the artist's early work, which was permeated by the memories of people who had been imprisoned in Siberia, this painting was inspired by a poem by Juliusz Słowacki.

The Chocim Treaty by Marcello Bacciarelli
Late 18th- and early 19th-century Neo-Classical paintings are displayed in the same room.

KEY

① **The Renaissance parapet** is not only decorative but also offers protection from fire.

② **Roof with sunken rafters**

③ **Renaissance parapet**

John Paul II

Karol Wojtyła was born in 1920 in Wadowice *(see p162),* but lived in Krakow for many years. He arrived here in 1938 to read Polish philology at the Jagiellonian University. The outbreak of World War II put a stop to his studies. During the war he worked for the Solvay Chemical Plant and was active in the underground Rhapsody Theatre. In 1942 he entered the underground theological Seminary. As a devout priest and artists' friend, he became very popular. Despite his election to the Apostolic See in 1978 his links with Krakow remained as close as ever. He continued to return here with his apostolic missions on many different occasions, until his death in 2005.

Statue of John Paul II in the courtyard of the Episcopal Palace

❿ Episcopal Palace
Pałac Biskupi

ul. Franciszkańska 3. **Map** 1 C5 (5 C3). 🚋 1, 6, 8, 13, 18, 20. **Closed** to the public.

First recorded in the 13th century, this is one of the oldest buildings in Krakow. It was damaged by fire and remodelled several times. Giovanni Maria Mosca contributed to the decoration. The present palace dates from the times of Bishop Piotr Tomicki (16th century) and Bishop Piotr Gembicki (17th century). A fire in 1850 caused extensive damage but the splendid furnishings have partly survived.

John Paul II lived here between 1964 and 1978. He was then the Archbishop of Krakow. A statue of him, made in 1980 by Ione Sensi Croci, is in the courtyard.

⓫ Collegium Novum

ul. Gołębia 24. **Map** 1 B4 (5 C3). **Tel** 12 422 10 33. 🚋 2, 8, 13, 18. 🚌 504.

The Collegium Novum replaced the Jerusalem College after it was destroyed by fire in the 19th century. The ruins were demolished between 1883 and 1887 and the new building constructed. Its official opening turned into a patriotic demonstration

attended symbolically by delegations from all three parts of the partitioned Poland. According to the contemporary records, the architect of the new building, Feliks Księżarski, intended to emulate the vernacular architecture, especially the crystal vaults and decoration of the Collegium Maius, but in fact he imitated German and Austrian models. The magnificent staircase is similar to the one in the Town Hall in Vienna. The college is the seat of the Rector of the Jagiellonian University. It also houses departmental offices, the bursary and the Great Hall where inauguration and graduation ceremonies take place. The hall has a beamed and coffered ceiling, and is decorated with portraits by Jan Matejko.

⓬ Statue of Copernicus
Pomnik Mikołaja Kopernika

ul. Gołębia. **Map** 1 B4 (5 C3). 🚋 2, 8, 13, 18. 🚌 504.

The statue of Nicolaus Copernicus was made in 1900 by Cyprian Godebski. The astronomer is represented as a young scholar holding an astrolabe. The statue was originally in the courtyard of the Collegium Maius, but was moved to the present location in front of the Witkowski College in 1953. The statue was intended to function as a fountain.

⓭ Collegium Maius
See pp108–9.

⓮ Collegium Nowodvorianum

ul. Św. Anny 12. **Map** 1 B4 (5 C2). **Tel** 12 422 04 11. 🚋 2, 8, 13, 18. 🚌 504.

The Collegium Nowodvorianum was founded by Bartłomiej Nowodworski, a Knight Hospitaller of St John, Secretary to the King and a warrior in the Battle of Lepanto. This foundation was a result of his bequest of 1617 to the Classes, one of the university colleges and the first secular secondary school in Krakow, established in 1586. The Collegium was built between 1636 and 1643 by

The Neo-Gothic building of the Collegium Novum

Art Nouveau exterior of the Old Theatre

Jan Leitner. A beautiful courtyard with arcades and a grand stairway is one of the best preserved Baroque buildings in Krakow. The offices of the Collegium Medicum are housed here.

⓯ Church of St Anne
Kościół św. Anny

See pp110–11.

⓰ Old Theatre
Teatr Stary

ul. Jagiellońska 1. **Map** 1 C4 (5 C2). **Tel** 12 422 85 66. 🚋 2, 4, 14, 18, 24. 🚌 124, 152, 502.

The Old, or Modrzejewska, Theatre is named after the great actress Helena Modrzejewska. The oldest theatre building in Poland, it has been in use continuously since 1798. It was remodelled in the Neo-Renaissance style between 1830 and 1843 by Tomasz Majewski and Karol Kremer. The next major rebuilding was undertaken from 1903 to 1905 by Franciszek Mączyński and Tadeusz Stryjeński. The reinforced concrete construction applied to the interior, and the exterior Art Nouveau decoration, both date from this time. The stucco frieze was made in 1906 by Józef

Gardecki. The plaques on the Jagiellońska Street side commemorate the composer Władysław Żeleński, the director Konrad Swinarski and the actor Wiktor Sadecki.

The Old Theatre is regarded as one of the best in Poland. Many outstanding directors have worked here, including Zygmunt Hübner, Konrad Swinarski and Andrzej Wajda.

⓱ Palace of Art
Pałac Sztuki

Plac Szczepański 4. **Map** 1 C4 (5 C1). **Tel** 12 422 66 16. 🚋 2, 4, 14, 18, 24. 🚌 124, 152, 502. **Open** 8:15am–6pm Mon–Fri, 10am–6pm Sat & Sun. 📷

In 1854 the Friends of the Fine Arts Society was established in Krakow for the encouragement of Polish art. The society embarked upon the organization of exhibitions by living artists, the acquisition of paintings and sculptures, and the setting up of a comprehensive records office gathering documents of the history of Polish art in the 19th and early 20th centuries. The Art Nouveau building was designed by Franciszek Màcżyński and modelled on the famous Secession Pavilion in Vienna. The finest Krakow artists worked on the decoration. Jacek Malczewski designed the frieze depicting the vicissitudes of fortune and the struggle of artistic genius. The sculptors Antoni Madeyski, Konstanty Laszczka and Teodor Rygier contributed busts of great Polish artists. A portico attached to the façade is topped with a statue of Apollo crowned with a sun halo. Exhibitions of 19th-century and contemporary art are held here.

⓲ Bunker of Art
Bunkier Sztuki

Plac Szczepański 3a. **Map** 1 C4 (5 C2). **Tel** 12 422 10 52. 🚋 2, 4, 14, 18, 24. 🚌 124, 152, 502. **Open** 11am–7pm Tue–Sun. 📷 □ 📷 ⓦ bunkier.art.pl

This modern grey concrete building, facing the Planty, is one of the few examples of mid-1960s Brutalist architecture in Poland. It is the venue for some of the most interesting exhibitions of contemporary art, by both Polish and foreign artists. The Bunker of Art also features one of Krakow's most popular cafés.

Sculptural decoration on the Palace of Art

⓭ Collegium Maius

The Collegium Maius is the oldest building within the Academy of Krakow (now the Jagiellonian University). It was constructed in the 15th century by amalgamating a number of town houses. Lecture rooms and accommodation for professors were originally located here. In the 19th century the building housed the Jagiellonian Library. Between 1840 and 1870 the architects Karol Kremer, Feliks Księżarski and Hermann Bergman rebuilt the college in the Neo-Gothic style. After World War II the University Museum, established in 1867, was moved here.

★ Libraria
The Libraria was built in the 16th century as the College Library. Today it is a meeting place of the senate and is decorated with portraits of rectors and professors of the university.

Oriel
This oriel window projecting from the Stuba Communis enlivens the austere exterior wall.

★ Stuba Communis
The Stuba Communis, or Common Room, served as the professors' refectory. The hall features a 14th-century statue of Kazimierz the Great and a 17th-century staircase made in Danzig.

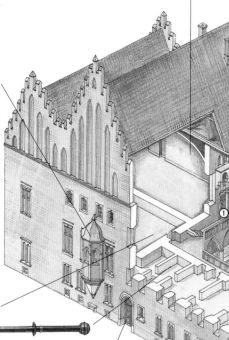

Entrance

University Treasury
The insignia of the rector, including a late 15th-century mace bequeathed by Bishop Zbigniew Oleśnicki and that of Queen Jadwiga from around 1405, are among the treasures.

Copernicus Room
This room is dedicated to the great astronomer, who studied here between 1491 and 1495, thus rendering the academy famous. The display features the so-called Jagiellonian armillary sphere made in 1510.

Cloister
The Gothic cloister, whose columns have a cut crystal-like decoration, is reminiscent of those in medieval Italian universities.

Green Hall
A collection of national memorabilia, including the piano that Frédéric Chopin played, can be visited by prior arrangement.

★ Great Hall
The Great Hall features stalls used by the senate during the ceremonies at which honorary degrees are conferred.

Chapel
The former apartment of John of Kęty, the professor of theology who became the patron saint of the Jagiellonian University, has been converted into a chapel, which is on the ground floor.

KEY

① **Porta Aurea (Golden Gate)**

② **A lavishly inlaid door** was originally in the Senior Room of the old Town Hall.

③ **Rector's Stairs**

⓯ Church of St Anne

A professor of the Krakow Academy, John of Kęty
(Jan Kanty) was already considered a saint at the time
of his death in 1473, when he was buried in the Gothic
Church of St Anne. Following his beatification, the senate
of the academy commissioned Tylman van Gameren
to build a new church. The construction began in 1689
under the supervision of Father Sebastian Piskorski.
The Italian architect and sculptor Baldassare Fontana
contributed the decoration and most of the furnishings,
including the altars, between 1695 and 1703. He was
assisted by the painters Carlo and Innocente Monti and
Karl Dankwart. St Anne's, with its sumptuous interior,
is considered to be a leading example of Baroque
ecclesiastical architecture in Poland.

Nave
The architecture, sculpture
and painting all contribute
to the decoration of the
nave and vault, and
exemplify particularly
well the wholeness
of the Baroque design.

**Procession Commemorating St John
of Kęty, 1767**
To mark the canonization of John of Kęty,
a procession with his holy relics was held
in Krakow. The saint's relics were carried
into the Church of St Anne with great
pomp and ceremony.

West Portal
The "scenographic" effect
of the main entrance to
the church is a result
of the superimposition
of three portals, one
within another.

Main entrance

Gloria Domini
The dome fresco by Carlo and Innocente Monti is an allegory of triumphant Catholicism, represented as the true Christian faith.

★ High Altar
The high altar is decorated with sculptures by Baldassare Fontana. The altarpiece, depicting the Virgin and Child with Anne, is by Jerzy Eleuter Siemiginowski, painter to Jan lll Sobieski.

Pulpit
The angel supporting the pulpit was carved in 1727 by the Krakow artist Antoni Frączkiewicz, who was influenced by the art of Baldassare Fontana.

★ Shrine of St John of Kęty
The relics of the saint rest in a sarcophagus supported by four figures personifying the faculties of the Academy of Krakow: Theology, Philosophy, Law and Medicine.

Choir Stalls
The stalls are decorated with paintings by Szymon Czechowicz, a leading Polish painter of the 18th century.

⑲ Szołayski House
Kamienica Szołayskich

Plac Szczepański 9. **Map** 1 C4 (5 D2).
Tel 12 433 54 50. 124, 152, 304,
424, 502. 2, 4, 14, 18, 24.
Open 10am–6pm Tue–Sat, 10am–
4pm Sun. free Sun. **mnk.pl**

The oldest parts of this building,
which house a branch of the
National Museum in Krakow,
date from the 15th century.
Since then, Szołayski House has
served as a private residence,
part of a monastery and a
newspaper office. Since 1934,
it has been an exhibition space,
except for a period during World
War II when it was occupied by
the Nazis. The house is now a
venue for visiting art exhibitions
from abroad, as well as themed
exhibitions celebrating prominent cultural figures from
Poland. There is also a display
of memorabilia relating to Felix
Jasieński (1861–1929), the art
collector who popularized
Japanese art in Poland.

Szołayski House sits on the historic
plac Szczepański

⑳ Church of
the Reformed
Franciscans
Kościół Reformatów

ul. Reformacka 4. **Map** 1 C4 (6 D1).
Tel 12 422 06 23. 124, 152, 502.
2, 4, 14, 18, 24. **Open** during
services only.

The Church of the Reformed
Franciscans was built between
1666 and 1672. The architecture
and modest furnishings conform
to the strict rule of the order.
The altarpiece on the left that

Crucifix on the altar in the Church of
St Mark

depicts St Kazimierz (Casimir)
is an outstanding example
of 17th-century work.
   The specific microclimate
within the crypt beneath the
church causes the reposing
corpses to undergo mummi-
fication. Those visitors seeking
a macabre experience may
request access to the crypt,
which is open on 2 and 3
November every year.

㉑ Church of
St Mark
Kościół św. Marka

ul. Św. Marka 10. **Map** 1 C4 (6 D1).
Tel 12 422 21 78. 124, 152, 502.
2, 4, 14, 18, 24. **Open** during
services only.

The early Gothic
church of the Monks
of St Mark was
founded in 1263
by Duke Bolesław
the Chaste. It has
been remodelled
a number of times
throughout its
history and the
interior acquired
an early Baroque
appearance in the
first half of the 17th
century. The high
altar, with its lavish
Mannerist ornamenta-
tion, was made in 1618
in the workshop of
Baltazar Kuncz. On
the left is the 17th-
century tomb of
Blessed Michał
Giedroyć (died 1485).

㉒ Polish Academy
of Skills
Gmach Polskiej Akademii
Umiejętności

ul. Sławkowska 17. **Map** 1 C4 (6 D1).
Tel 12 424 02 00. 124, 152, 502.
2, 4, 14, 18, 24. **Open** 9am–4pm
Mon–Fri. **pau.krakow.pl**

The building was constructed
between 1857 and 1866 as the
seat of the Academic Society of
Krakow, which in 1872 became
the Academy of Skills, the first
academic body to bring
together scholars from all three
parts of partitioned Poland. It
was designed by Filip Pokutyński
in the Neo-Renaissance style.
The exterior is decorated with
portrait medallions of people
in low relief who made
important contributions to
Polish academic and cultural life.
Inside, a small meeting room
features an impressive coffered
ceiling. The rich print collection
includes works by Albrecht
Dürer and Rembrandt.

㉓ St John Street
Ulica św. Jana

Map 1 C4 (6 D2). 124, 152, 502.
2, 4, 14, 18, 24.

This quiet street leading away
from the Market Square,
and closed off at its

Portal to the House of the Cistercian Abbots of Jędrzejów,
20 St John Street

north end by the façade of the Piarist Church, is lined with a selection of fine secular and ecclesiastic Baroque and Neo-Classical buildings.

The House of the Cistercian Abbots of Jędrzejów at No. 20 is of particular interest. Remodelled in 1744 by Francesco Placidi, the house is decorated with a magnificent late Baroque portal featuring atlantes.

The Wodzicki Palace at No. 11 was given a Neo-Classical façade by Ferdinand Nax after 1781. Around 1818 the Bernardine Friary was converted after a great deal of rebuilding.

❷ Church of St John
Kościół św. Jana

ul. Św. Jana 7. **Map** 1 C4 (6 D2). **Tel** 12 422 65 00. 124, 152, 502. 2, 4, 14, 18, 24. **Open** during services only.

The chronicler Jan Długosz records that this church was founded in the 12th century. The Romanesque architecture has been lost through much remodelling. The Gothic buttresses still project from the exterior side walls, but the façade and the interior are Baroque. The high altar of 1730 is decorated with sculptures by Antoni Frączkiewicz and the 16th-century miraculous Madonna, the Refuge of Prisoners.

❷ Czartoryski Museum
Muzeum Czartoryskich

See pp114–15.

❷ Piarist Church
Kościół Pijarów

ul. Pijarska 2. **Map** 1 C4 (6 D1). **Tel** 12 422 17 24. 124, 152, 502. 2, 4, 14, 18, 24. **Open** during services only.

This Baroque church was built between 1718 and 1728 probably to designs by Kacper Bażanka. The Rococo façade designed by Francesco Placidi was added in 1759 to 1761. Inside, the church is decorated with frescoes by a master of

St Florian's Gate at the end of Floriańska Street

illusion, Franz Eckstein. The high altar painted on the wall is by the same artist, as is the fresco in the nave vault that glorifies the name of the Virgin Mary. The altars in the aisles feature 18th-century paintings by Szymon Czechowicz.

The crypt under the church is renowned for the decoration of Christ's Tomb, which usually alludes symbolically to patriotic themes, and is set up here every year during Holy Week. The crypt is also a venue for theatre performances and various exhibitions.

The Rococo interior of the 18th-century Piarist Church

❷ St Florian's Gate and the Defensive Wall
Brama Floriańska i Mury Obronny

Map 2 D4 (6 E1). **Tel** 12 421 13 61. 124, 152, 502. 2, 4, 7, 14, 24. **Open** Apr–Oct: 10:30am–6pm daily. mhk.pl

In 1285 Duke Leszek the Black gave Krakow the right to have the city surrounded by walls. These fortifications developed during the following centuries, finally consisting of inner and outer moated walls and 47 towers. Eight fortified gates lead into the city. With the introduction of artillery, the defence system became redundant. Disused, it fell into disrepair by the end of the 18th century. The walls were dismantled early in the 19th century and later replaced by the Planty gardens *(see pp170–71)*. St Florian's Gate, dating possibly from the end of the 13th century, and a small stretch of the adjoining walls have been saved, largely through the efforts of Professor Feliks Radwański. East of St Florian's Gate is the Haberdashers' Tower, and the towers of the Joiners and Carpenters are to the west.

⑳ Czartoryski Museum

At the core of the Czartoryski Museum is the collection assembled late in the 18th century by Princess Izabella Czartoryska. It was initially at Puławy, but partly moved to Paris following the 1830 November Uprising. In 1876 the collection was brought to Krakow, thanks to the efforts of Prince Władysław Czartoryski. The Czartoryski Foundation sold the entire collection to the Polish government in December 2016, and the museum will be closed for extensive renovation until 2020.

Madonna and Child
By the Venetian Vincenzo Catena, this painting is a highlight of the Czartoryski's Italian collection.

Jesuit Saints
This fine bas-relief by the 17th-century Roman sculptor, Alessandro Algardi, depicts the Polish Jesuit, Stanisław Kostka, being admitted to the congregation of Jesuit saints.

Gallery Guide
There is no gallery space on the ground floor. The first-floor display is dedicated to Polish history of the 14th–18th centuries as well as Western European decorative arts. The picture gallery is on the second floor.

Porcelain Figures
These two figures of a Polish nobleman and noblewoman were made in Meissen.

Entrance

Nautilus Cup
The museum collection is rich in decorative arts and includes this 17th-century drinking vessel made in Danzig (now Gdańsk) from a large shell.

★ **Lady with an Ermine
by Leonardo da Vinci**
During renovations, this
late 15th-century portrait
is on display at the
National Museum in
Krakow *(see pp150–51)*.

VISITORS' CHECKLIST

Practical Information
ul. Św. Jana 19.
Map 1 C4 (6 E1).
Tel 12 370 54 60.
Closed for renovations
until 2020. ▨ ▨ Ⓦ mnk.pl

Transport
🚊 2, 4, 7, 14, 24.
🚌 124, 152, 424, 502, 512.

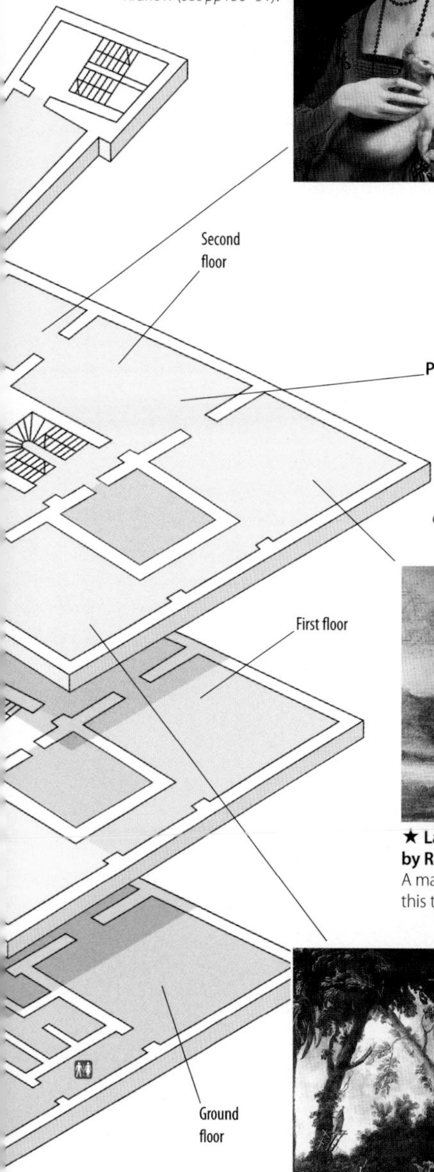

Second
floor

**Portrait of a Boy by
Caspar Netscher**
This sweet little
portrait is one of
several paintings in
the collection by
lesser Dutch artists
of the 17th century.

First floor

★ **Landscape with the Good Samaritan
by Rembrandt**
A masterpiece in the collection of Western painting,
this treatment of the natural world is breathtaking.

**Landscape by Alessandro
Magnasco**
This dramatic landscape is
characteristic of Italian painting
of the 18th century.

Ground
floor

Key

▨ Non-exhibition space

▨ History of Poland
1300–1900

▨ Decorative Arts of Western Europe

▨ Picture Gallery

The impressive exterior of the Barbican

㉘ Barbican
Barbakan

ul. Basztowa. **Map** 2 D3 (6 E1).
🚋 2, 4, 7, 14, 24. 🚌 124, 152,
304, 502. **Open** Apr–Oct: 10:30am–
6pm daily. 🎦

The Barbican, a round bastion,
was constructed in 1498–99 after
King Jan Olbracht was defeated
by the Turks in Bukowina, and
further Turkish incursions were
feared. It shows the changes that
had been introduced to military
architecture as a result of the
rapid development of artillery.
This relatively low structure
projecting from the city walls
with a considerable overhang
enabled the defenders to fire
with precision at the enemy
from the loop-holes, positioned
at different levels. The Barbican
was originally surrounded by a
moat and linked to St Florian's
Gate by a corridor. It is the best
preserved barbican in Europe.

㉙ Jama Michalika Café
Jama Michalika

ul. Floriańska 45. **Map** 2 D4 (6 E1).
Tel 12 422 15 61. 🚋 2, 4, 7, 14, 24.
🚌 124, 152, 304, 502. **Open** 9am–
10pm Mon–Thu & Sun, 9am–11pm
Fri & Sat. 🎦

In 1895 Jan Michalik opened
a patisserie near the Market
Square. It became very popular
with students of the Fine Arts
School who called the place
jama (grotto) for its lack of
windows. Poets, writers and
artists soon joined them and
in 1905 established the cabaret
Zielony Balonik (The Green
Balloon) here. The performances,
based on texts by Tadeusz Boy-
Żeleński, soon attracted a large
audience. Satirical Christmas
puppet shows, with mario-
nettes by Ludwik Puget and
Jan Szczepkowski, became
particularly popular.

In 1910 Michalik extended and
redecorated the premises to
designs by Franciszek Mączyński.
The main room received a glass
ceiling. Karol Frycz designed the
interior decoration, furniture
and most of the stained glass
in the Art Nouveau style.

The café is still an inviting place
where customers can go back in
time and enjoy the atmosphere
of the fin de siècle, as well as see
enduring folk shows.

㉚ Matejko House
Dom Matejki

ul. Floriańska 41. **Map** 2 D4 (6 E1).
Tel 12 433 59 60. 🚋 2, 4, 7, 14, 24.
🚌 124, 152, 304, 502. **Open** 10am–
6pm Tue–Sat, 10am–4pm Sun.
🎦 free on Sun. 🎥 W mnk.pl

The artist Jan Matejko was
born here in 1838, and in 1873
returned to live with his family.
He rebuilt the house and added
a new façade designed by
Tomasz Pryliński in the Neo-
Baroque style. After Matejko
died in 1893 the house was
transformed into a museum and
opened to the public five years
later. The statue of a hussar on
horseback, on the ground floor,
was part of Leon Wyczółkowski's
design for the Matejko Monument. The private rooms on
the first floor have remained
unchanged, while the second
floor is used for a display of the
artist's works, which include
cartoons for the murals that are
in the Church of St Mary. His
studio on the third floor is full
of the props and curiosities he
collected. Pieces of old armour
and instruments of torture excavated on the site of the old Town
Hall are of particular interest.

㉛ Floriańska Street
Ulica Floriańska

Map 1 C4, 2 D4 (6 D2–E1, 2).
🚋 2, 4, 7, 14, 24. 🚌 124, 152,
304, 502.

This street, leading from
St Florian's Gate to the Market
Square, formed part of the
Royal Route which became
fully established after the court
moved from Krakow to Warsaw.

The interior of the Jama Michalika Café

The historic Floriańska Street, leading to the Church of St Mary and Market Square

The Royal Route was often used by a sovereign arriving for a coronation, and again when his body was taken in procession for the funeral at Wawel. In the 19th century Floriańska was the busiest street in Krakow, with trams introduced in 1881. Medieval walls have survived in most houses, but the original architecture has been lost through later remodelling. More storeys and new eclectic façades were added to most buildings early in the 20th century, when Floriańska gained its present appearance.

㉜ Słowacki Theatre
Teatr im. Juliusza Słowackiego

Pl. Świętego Ducha 1. **Map** 2 D4 (6 E2). **Tel** 12 424 45 28. 🚋 2, 4, 7, 14, 24. 🚌 124, 152, 502.

The proposal for a new theatre in Krakow, one which would replace the small and dilapidated Old Theatre, was put forward in 1872. Jan Zawiejski submitted the design and was put in charge of the works which were to be financed entirely through donations. The foundation stone was laid in 1891, and the theatre opened in 1893. Zawiejski designed an opulent building in which vernacular elements, such as the parapet inspired by the Cloth Hall, and foreign influences were blended into an eclectic whole. Allegorical sculptures decorate the exterior of the theatre.

The opulent interior features a grand staircase decorated with stuccowork by Alfred Putz. The four-tiered auditorium can seat up to 900 people. The stage curtain, one of the major attractions, was painted by Henryk Siemiradzki. It depicts Apollo striking an accord between Beauty and Love, surrounded by muses as well as other allegorical figures which represent Art drawing inspiration from man's fate.

㉝ Church of the Holy Cross
Kościół św. Krzyża

ul. Świętego Krzyża 23. **Map** 2 D4 (6 E3). **Tel** 12 429 20 56. 🚋 2, 4, 7, 14, 24. 🚌 124, 152, 502. **Open** during services only.

The Gothic church of the Order of the Holy Cross was built in two stages. The construction of the choir began immediately after 1300. The main nave and tower date from the first half of the 14th century. The interior is extremely well preserved and the nave impresses with its intricate pattern of vaulting ribs, supported on a single, round pillar. Among its furnishings, the Gothic font made in 1423 by Jan Freudenthal and the late Renaissance triptych in the Węgrzyn Chapel (next to the porch) are of particular interest. There are also various Baroque altars and stalls, as well as a number of memorial plaques of famous sculptors, active at the end of the 19th century, which are worth seeing.

The Church of the Holy Cross

㉞ Church of the Dominican Nuns
Kościół Dominikanek

ul. Mikołajska 21. **Map** 2 D4 (6 E3). **Tel** 12 422 79 25. 🚋 3, 10, 20, 24, 52. **Open** during services only.

The church, dedicated to the Virgin Mary, Queen of Snow, was founded in 1632–34 by Anna Lubomirska. Prior to the church, a fortified manor of Albert, Krakow's *wójt* (chief officer), was on this site in the 14th century. As a result of Albert's revolt against King Władysław the Short, a new building for the local government was erected. The latter was converted in the 1620s into a convent for the Dominican nuns. The church contains a miraculous 17th-century icon of the Virgin.

The eclectic façade of the Słowacki Theatre

㉟ Dominican Church

The Dominicans began the construction of a new church in 1250. It contained the shrine of St Jacek, a place of mass pilgrimage. Opulent mausolea, modelled on the Zygmunt Chapel at Wawel, were added in the 17th century by noble families, and in the 18th century the church was furnished with late Baroque altars. The fire of Krakow in 1850 destroyed the church almost completely. It was rebuilt by 1872 and today is an important evangelical centre which attracts masses of the faithful.

Cloister
The Gothic cloister was a burial place of burghers whose memorial plaques and tombs can still be seen here.

★ Zbaraski Chapel
The fine decoration of the chapel, built in 1627 to 1633 by the Castelli artists, is in sharp contrast with the monumental forms of the altar and tombs in black marble.

Tomb of General Jan Skrzynecki
This beautiful monument carved by Władysław Oleszczyński commemorates the hero of the November Uprising of 1830 (died 1860).

★ **Shrine of St Jacek**
The Renaissance Chapel of St Jacek was rebuilt around 1700 by Baldassare Fontana, who also designed this magnificent monument. The chapel is decorated with paintings by Tommaso Dolabella.

VISITORS' CHECKLIST

Practical Information
ul. Stolarska 12. **Map** 1 C5 (6 D3).
Tel 12 423 16 13.
Open 6:30am–8pm daily
🆆 **krakow.dominikanie.pl**

Transport
🚋 1, 3, 6, 8, 10, 13, 18, 20, 24, 52.

Chapel of the Virgin Mary of the Rosary
In 1621 the Virgin of the Rosary icon was carried in a procession to secure, through prayers, victory over the Turks at Chocim.

The Myszkowski Chapel
This was built between 1603 and 1614 by masters from Santi Gucci's circle, using marble from the Świętokrzyskie (Holy Cross) Mountains. Portrait busts of the Myszkowskis form part of the splendid decoration of the dome.

KEY

① **The Lubomirski Chapel** displays lovely paintings and sculptures.

② **Crowstep gable**

③ **The memorial plaque of Filippo Buonacorsi (Callimachus)** (died 1496) honours the great humanist at the Polish royal court *(see p47)*.

④ **Choir stalls**, pulpit and confessionals, all in the Neo-Gothic style, date from the second half of the 19th century.

Tomb of Prospero Provano
The monument of this salt magnate (died 1584) is one of the finest Polish sculptural works of circa 1600. It is located next to the Myszkowski Chapel.

KAZIMIERZ QUARTER

South of the Old Town, nestled on the banks of the Vistula, is Kazimierz, once the home to a thriving Jewish population and now an exciting district frequented by Krakovians and visitors alike. The centre of the city's Jewish community for over 500 years, the area was all but destroyed during World War II, its inhabitants moved first to the ghetto and then to the camps. It was left to fall into disrepair until the 1990s but, despite the ravages of war and time, many of the district's synagogues and cemeteries still stand, attracting those eager to explore the area's Jewish legacy. Revitalized in the 21st century, Kazimierz not only commemorates its past but embraces its future. Kooky cafés and bohemian bars lining the atmospheric narrow streets, together with antiques shops and trendy art galleries, feed a burgeoning arts and entertainment scene, cementing Kazimierz as Krakow's most alternative district.

Sights at a Glance

Churches
- 9 Corpus Christi Church
- 11 Church of St Catherine
- 12 Paulite Church "On the Rock"

Museums
- 7 Galicia Jewish Museum
- 8 Museum of Municipal Engineering
- 10 Ethnographic Museum

Historic Cemeteries
- 6 New Jewish Cemetery

Synagogues
- 1 Tempel Synagogue
- 2 Isaak's Synagogue
- 3 High Synagogue
- 4 Old Synagogue
- 5 Remu'h Synagogue and Cemetery

Restaurants see p194
1. Dawno temu na Kazimierzu
2. Fabryka Pizzy
3. Genji Sushi Premium
4. Horai
5. Klezmer Hois
6. Nolio
7. Pierożki u Wincenta
8. Polakowski
9. Studio Qulinarne
10. Trezo
11. Zazie Bistro

See also Street Finder maps 3 & 4

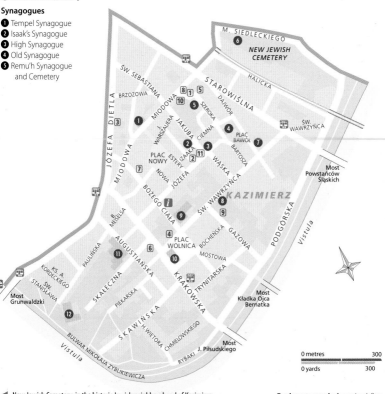

◄ New Jewish Cemetery, in the historic Jewish neighbourhood of Kazimierz

For keys to symbols see back flap

Street-by-Street: Szeroka Street Area

The Jewish quarter was located in the east part of Kazimierz and concentrated first around Szeroka Street, then Libusza Square, which was later known as New Square. As well as the Jews displaced here in the late 15th century from Krakow, Czech and German refugees also came to live in Kazimierz. Many synagogues, baths, schools and cemeteries were established, and the area became an active centre of Judaic culture and learning. During the Nazi occupation of Krakow, however, all this was dismantled. The Jewish community was forced into the ghetto and much of its legacy eradicated. Several synagogues in the area, together with two cemeteries, help visitors to explore the past.

❶ Tempel Synagogue
The decoration of this synagogue, built in the Neo-Renaissance style, was influenced by Moorish art.

Jewish Tombs

The signs carved on tombs convey symbolic meanings. The grave of a rabbi is indicated by hands joined in prayer. Basins and jugs for the ritual ablution of hands can be found on graves of the Levites. Three interlaced snakes feature on the grave of a physician, and a crown of knowledge on that of a learned man. A lion or a six-pointed star of David signifies a descendant of Judah.

0 metres 50
0 yards 50

Key

— Suggested route

The Kupa Synagogue
This was built in the 17th century and financed by the Kahal of Kazimierz. It was remodelled many times and was also used for non-religious purposes.

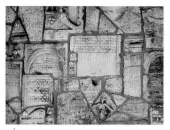

⑤ ★ Remu'h Cemetery
The Wailing Wall commemorates the tragic fate of the Jews from Krakow during World War II.

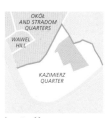

Locator Map
See Street Finder maps 4

Bath (mikvah)   Poper Synagogue

⑤ Remu'h Synagogue
This synagogue is dedicated to the rabbi Remu'h, who was reputed to be a miracle worker. His grave is still venerated by pious Jewish pilgrims.

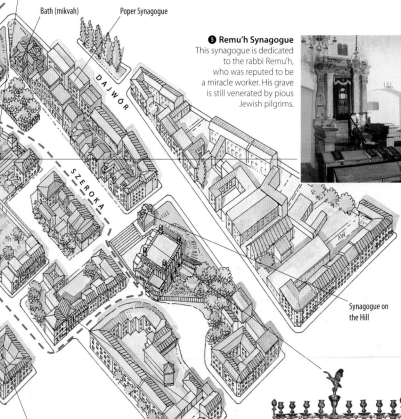

DAJWÓR

SZEROKA

Synagogue on the Hill

❷ Isaak's Synagogue
The stuccowork in this Baroque synagogue is of great interest.

❸ High Synagogue
With its late Gothic architecture and Renaissance decoration, this is one of Krakow's most picturesque synagogues.

❹ ★ Old Synagogue
This menorah is among the treasures in Poland's oldest synagogue. The building was destroyed by the Nazis, and later restored.

❶ Tempel Synagogue
Synagoga Tempel

ul. Miodowa 24. **Map** 4 D1 (6 F5). **Tel** 12 430 54 11. 3, 9, 12, 22, 24, 52. 184. **Open** 10am–4pm Sun–Thu, 10am–dusk Fri.

The most recent of the synagogues in Kazimierz, the Tempel was built in the Neo-Renaissance style between 1860 and 1862. It is used by non-Orthodox Jews. Inside note the stained glass and period decoration.

Façade of Isaak's Synagogue, the home of the Jewish Education Centre

❷ Isaak's Synagogue
Bożnica Izaaka

ul. Kupa 18. **Map** 4 D1. **Tel** 12 430 22 22. 6, 8, 10, 13. 504. **Open** 8am–6pm Sun–Thu, 8:30am–4:30pm Fri. .

This synagogue was built between 1638 and 1644 as a foundation of Izaak Jakubowicz, an elder of the Jewish community. Inside, the plaster work by Giovanni Battista Falconi has survived in a large nave with a barrel vault. The Jewish Education Centre is housed here.

❸ High Synagogue
Bożnica Wysoka

ul. Józefa 38. **Map** 4 D1. **Tel** 12 430 68 69. 19, 24. **Open** 10am–7pm daily.

This synagogue dates from 1556 to 1563. It is a picturesque structure supported by buttresses. A Renaissance portal is worth noting. Only a few furnishings

have survived, including a money box and the remains of an altar. There is a fascinating bookshop on the ground floor.

❹ Old Synagogue
Stara Synagoga

ul. Szeroka 24. **Map** 4 D1. **Tel** 12 431 05 45. 19, 24. **Open** Apr–Oct: 10am–2pm Mon, 9am–5pm Tue–Sat, 10am–4pm Sun; Nov–Mar: 10am– 2pm Mon, 10am–4pm Tue, Thu, Sat & Sun, 10am–5pm Fri. **Closed** first Sat & Sun of each month; Nov–Mar: Wed. free Mon. **mhk.pl**

The Old Synagogue was used in the past as a temple and was also a seat of the Kahal and other offices of the Jewish community. Religious and social life was concentrated here. The synagogue now houses a museum dedicated to the history and culture of Krakow's Jews.

The brick building dates back to the mid-15th or beginning of the 16th century. Its present appearance is the result of a remodelling in 1557–70. The parapet, and Gothic interior with ribbed vaulting supported by slender columns, all date from then.

The hall used for prayer is almost bare, in accordance with the rule of the Jewish religion. The *bimah*, an elevated platform with an iron balustrade used for readings from the Torah, is the only piece of furnishing.

The east wall features the *aron hakodesh*, an ornamental shrine for the Torah Scrolls.

❺ Remu'h Synagogue and Cemetery
Bożnica i Cmentarz Remuh

ul. Szeroka 40. **Map** 4 D1. **Tel** 12 429 57 35. 19, 24. **Open** 9am–4pm Sun–Fri (May–Sep: to 6pm).

One of the two still active synagogues, the Remu'h temple is used by Orthodox Jews. It was founded by Israel Isserles Auerbach around 1553 and named after his son, the great author and philosopher Rabbi Moses Remu'h. Inside, the *bimah* and an ornamental *aron hakodesh* are worth noting.

Accessed via the synagogue, the Remu'h Cemetery, established in 1533, is one of the very few Jewish

Hall of Prayers in the Old Synagogue

Entrance to the Remu'h Synagogue and Cemetery

cemeteries in the whole of Europe with so many tombs, both gravestones (matzeva) and sarcophagi. Their rich floral and animal decoration is of particular interest.

The cemetery was almost entirely destroyed during World War II. However, the tomb of Remu'h, which still attracts pilgrims from all over the world, was spared from Nazi destruction. Over 700 tombs have been excavated since World War II. They were probably buried during the Swedish invasion in the early 18th century. The Wailing Wall by the entrance was made using fragments of tombstones destroyed during the war.

❻ New Jewish Cemetery
Nowy Cmentarz Żydowski

ul. Miodowa 55. **Map** 4 E1. ▦ 3, 19, 24. **Open** 10am–4pm Sun–Fri.

Established in the early 19th century, this cemetery is a burial place of the great Jews of Krakow of the 19th and 20th centuries. All Kazimierz's rabbis and many of the great benefactors of Krakow rest here. They include Józef Oettinger and Józef Rosenblatt (professors of the Jagiellonian University), Józef Sare (the city President), and Maurycy Gotlieb (one of the foremost Polish artists of the 19th century).

❼ Galicia Jewish Museum
Żydowskie Muzeum Galicja

ul. Dajwór 18. **Map** 4 E2. **Tel** 12 421 68 42. ▦ 3, 19, 24. **Open** 10am–6pm daily. 🅿 ☒ **galiciajewish museum.org**

Housed in a restored former mill, the Galicia Jewish Museum was founded in 2004 by photographer Chris Schwartz to commemorate the once-thriving Jewish culture of southeastern Poland. Schwartz's evocative photographs of synagogues and graveyards fill the exhibition halls. The museum also hosts changing exhibitions dedicated to Jewish historical themes.

❽ Museum of Municipal Engineering
Muzeum Inżynierii Miejskiej

ul. Św. Wawrzyńca 15. **Map** 4 D2. **Tel** 12 421 12 42. ▦ 3, 19, 24. **Open** Jun–Sep: 10am–6pm Tue, Thu & Sun, 10am–4pm Wed, Fri & Sat; Oct–May: 10am–4pm Tue–Sun. 🅿 free Tue. ☒ **mimk.com.pl**

Set in a former tram depot, this museum holds a fascinating collection of motor cars through the ages, including many Polish-made vehicles that are no longer around. There are hands-on displays of science and technology for kids, and a large collection of trams parked in the tram shed.

❾ Corpus Christi Church
Kościół Bożego Ciała

ul. Bożego Ciała 26. **Map** 4 D2. ▦ 504. ▦ 3, 6, 10, 13. **Open** 9am–noon, 1:30–7pm Mon–Sat and during services.

Corpus Christi Church was built on marshland where, according to legend, a monstrance (religious container) with the Eucharist stolen from the Collegiate Church of All Saints had been found. A mysterious light shining in the darkness indicated the site where the profaned monstrance had been abandoned. The construction of the church, founded by King Kazimierz the Great, began in 1340 and was completed in the early 15th century. As a parish church it was bestowed by local burghers with sumptuous furnishings, most of which have survived.

In 1634 to 1637 the high altar was decorated with a painting of The Nativity by Tommaso Dolabella, court artist to Zygmunt III Vaza. The large stalls for monks, matching the altar, were made in 1632. A 17th-century gilded altarpiece with the relics of Blessed Stanisław Kazimierczyk is located in the north aisle.

The altar of Christ the Redeemer, decorated with sculptures by Anton Gegen-baur, is also worth noting. A slab in the north aisle indicates the burial place of the architect Bartolomeo Berecci, who was assassinated in 1537.

Image of the Madonna in the Church of Corpus Christi

Krakow's Jewish Community

Before it was all but annihilated in the Holocaust, Krakow had one of the most vibrant, wealthy and prominent Jewish communities in Europe. An important trading post between Prussia, Prague and Vienna, it has been home to Jews since the 14th century. Anti-semitic protests date to 1369 and in 1495 Jews were expelled from Krakow to Kazimierz *(see p121)*. In 1938, the Jewish population was over 60,000, one quarter of the total population. In 1948, the post-Holocaust Jewish population was 5,900 and by 1978, a mere 600. Today, Krakow's Jewish community is slowly being revived.

King Kazimierz the Great founded the city that took his name in 1335. Originally a separate town, it became a leading centre of Jewish culture.

Rabbi Moses ben Isserles (1525–72) was one of the greatest rabbis of the 16th century, and lived and taught in Kazimierz. He is revered by Jews for his learned additions to the Shulkhan Arukh (the code for everyday life). He was also a keen historian, astronomer, geometrician and philosopher.

Gottlieb's Day of Atonement

This famous painting by Maurycy Gottlieb, a Polish Jew, was executed in 1878. It portrays the artist (the figure in the middle resting on his arm) attending synagogue on the holiest day of the Jewish year, Yom Kippur (the Day of Atonement). Beset with woes, the painter's pose reflects the conflict that faced Polish Jewry as a whole in the late 19th-century: whether they were in the first place Jews or Poles.

Jewish diversity in Krakow is shown in these three professional portraits from the late 1870s: on the left is an Orthodox Jew and the two on the right are Hassidic Jews. Krakow was long considered to be one of the primary centres of Jewish debate, as all parts of the religious and political spectrum were represented in the city's wide-ranging Jewish population.

Jewish theatre was a crucial part of Jewish life in Krakow until the late 1930s. Besides entertainment, it also provided one of the last bastions of the Yiddish language.

The Nazis ordered large numbers of Jews to move from Kazimierz and enter the ghetto; often, homes were swapped with Polish families going the other way. The Krakow Jewish ghetto was centred on plac Bohaterow Getta on the south side of the river (*see p158*).

Identity documents were issued even before the creation of the Krakow ghetto in 1941. All Poles had to carry a card that clearly stated their ethnic provenance in order to limit the civil rights and entitlements of the holder. The card shown here belonged to Cyrla Rosenzweig, a Polish Jew who was rescued from the Holocaust by Oskar Schindler.

Modern-day Jewish Krakow has become a thriving centre of Jewish tradition and culture since the reintroduction of democracy to Poland in 1989. The growing population comprises former residents who have returned to their birthplace as well as many young descendants of those who later died in the ghetto and at Auschwitz. Many have found success as entrepreneurs, opening hotels and kosher restaurants.

Schindler's Krakow

Oskar Schindler (1908–78), immortalized in Steven Spielberg film *Schindler's List*, was a German businessman who saved over 1,000 Jews from the gas chambers during World War II, by employing them at his factories. The original Schindler factory at ul. Lipowa 4 has now been transformed into a museum (*see p158*). Schindler lived at ul. Straszewskiego 7, in the upstairs flat.

Oskar Schindler with Holocaust survivors in Tel-Aviv

Town Hall in Kazimierz, housing the Ethnographic Museum

⑩ Ethnographic Museum
Muzeum Etnograficzn

Plac Wolnica 1. **Map** 4 D2. **Tel** 12 379 60 23. 🚌 504. 🚊 6, 8, 10, 13. **Open** 10am–7pm Tue–Sun. **Closed** public hols. 🅿️ free on Sun. 🚻 📷

Kazimierz's Renaissance Town Hall is now home to the Ethnographic Museum. It displays a rich collection of exhibits, including costumes from all over Poland, traditional Krakow Christmas cribs, folk art and musical instruments. There is also a section covering the seasonal folk festivals once celebrated by both Christians and Jews, and a fantastic display of recreated house interiors on the ground floor.

⑪ Church of St Catherine
Kościół św. Katarzyny

ul. Augustiańska 7. **Map** 4 D2. **Tel** 12 430 62 42. 🚌 504. 🚊 6, 8, 10, 13. **Open** during services only.

According to the chronicler Jan Długosz, the Church of St Catherine was built by King Kazimierz the Great as a penance for murdering Father Marcin Baryczka in 1349. Baryczka delivered a document issued by bishops excommunicating the king. The king repaid the messenger with the order to have Baryczka drowned in the Vistula. However, the construction of the church possibly began in 1343 and continued until the early 16th century. Regarded as one of the most beautiful Gothic churches in Krakow, its furnishings were lost in the 19th century when it was briefly transformed into a warehouse. The Baroque high altar, decorated with the *Mystical Marriage of St Catherine* by Andrea Venesta, 1634, has survived. Worth visiting is the Gothic cloister which dates from the time of Kazimierz the Great. It features late Gothic murals and large 17th-century paintings. Two chapels adjoin

Fresco in the cloister in the Church of St Catherine

the cloister: one houses the miraculous *Madonna of Consolation* and the other the relics of Blessed Isaiah Boner.

⑫ Paulite Church "On the Rock"
Kościół Paulinów Na Skałce

ul. Skałeczna 15. **Map** 3 C2. **Tel** 12 619 09 00. 🚌 504. 🚊 6, 8, 10, 13. **Open** 9am–5pm Mon–Sat, 1–5pm Sun. Crypt: **Open** Apr–Oct: 9am–5pm daily; Nov–Mar: on request. 📷

A small church of St Michael "On the Rock" was recorded back in the 11th century. This was the site where Bishop Stanisław of Szczepanów, later canonized, was murdered *(see pp24–5)*. In the 14th century this Romanesque church was replaced by a large Gothic church founded by Kazimierz the Great. Four hundred years later it was in danger of collapsing. It was rebuilt in the late Baroque style, between 1733 and 1742. The design by Anton Gerhard Müntzer was modified by Antonio Solari and the uniform furnishings all date from the 1740s. A small font by the church is decorated with a statue of St Stanisław, made in 1731. The tormentors of the saint, who are said to have quartered his body, threw his cut-off finger into the font. The water is reputed to have had healing properties ever since.

Paulite Church "On the Rock"

The Crypt in the Church "On the Rock"

Jan Długosz, the great Polish historian of the Middle Ages, was buried in the crypt beneath the Church "On the Rock" in 1480. In 1876 it was decided to transform the crypt into a national pantheon for the burial of those who had made important contributions to Polish culture. The architect Teofil Żebrawski remodelled the crypt, transforming it into a gallery with a separate chapel housing the altar. Recesses were designed to house the sarcophagi. The stained-glass window above the altar depicts the Madonna of Częstochowa, the Queen of Poland. Coats of arms of provinces of the Polish-Lithuanian Commonwealth were painted on the vault.

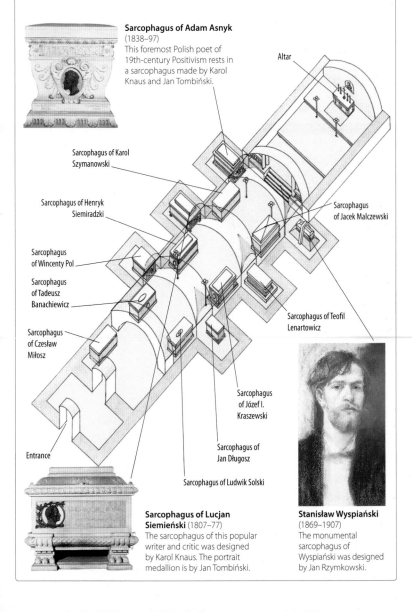

Sarcophagus of Adam Asnyk
(1838–97)
This foremost Polish poet of 19th-century Positivism rests in a sarcophagus made by Karol Knaus and Jan Tombiński.

Altar

Sarcophagus of Karol Szymanowski

Sarcophagus of Henryk Siemiradzki

Sarcophagus of Jacek Malczewski

Sarcophagus of Wincenty Pol

Sarcophagus of Tadeusz Banachiewicz

Sarcophagus of Czesław Miłosz

Sarcophagus of Teofil Lenartowicz

Sarcophagus of Józef I. Kraszewski

Entrance

Sarcophagus of Jan Długosz

Sarcophagus of Ludwik Solski

Sarcophagus of Lucjan Siemieński (1807–77)
The sarcophagus of this popular writer and critic was designed by Karol Knaus. The portrait medallion is by Jan Tombiński.

Stanisław Wyspiański
(1869–1907)
The monumental sarcophagus of Wyspiański was designed by Jan Rzymkowski.

WESOŁA, KLEPARZ AND BISKUPIE

A number of settlements developed around Krakow over the centuries. They were linked culturally and economically with Krakow but were independently administered. As there were no specific boundaries between them and land ownership often changed, the settlements north and east of the city walls developed to constitute a complex urban mosaic, and included Przedmieście Mikołajskie, the royal town of Kleparz, and the privately owned Wesoła, Lubicz and Biskupie. They all looked like small towns. Imposing churches and a few palaces were surrounded by irregularly scattered residential timber buildings. Merchants and craftsmen who were active here avoided paying taxes to the Town Hall, thus contributing to the economic decline of Krakow. As a result, in 1791 the City Council decided to incorporate these quarters into Krakow. This part of the city saw the greatest surge in building activity during the great development of Krakow in the second half of the 19th century.

Sights at a Glance

Historic Monuments and Buildings

2 Society of Physicians
6 Astronomical Observatory
8 Former Main Railway Station
10 Grunwald Monument
11 National Bank of Poland
12 Academy of Fine Arts
13 Polish State Railways Headquarters
15 Globe House

Churches and Monasteries

1 Church of St Nicholas
3 Church of the Sacred Heart of Jesus pp136–7
4 Church of the Immaculate Conception of the Virgin Mary
5 Church of the Discalced Carmelite Nuns
9 St Florian's Church
14 Church of St Vincent de Paul
16 Church of the Nuns of the Visitation

Historic Parks

7 Jagiellonian University Botanical Gardens

☐ **Restaurants** see p194

1 Glonojad
2 Jarema

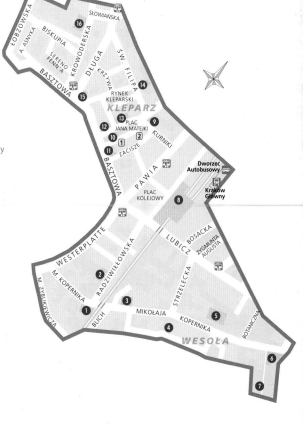

See also Street Finder maps 1, 2 & 3

Street-by-Street: Along Kopernika Street

Wesoła Quarter, originally a small settlement by the Romanesque Church of St Nicholas, developed along the old route to Mogiła, which is today Kopernika Street (ulica Mikołaja Kopernika). Its skyline was dominated by churches, monasteries and suburban residences of the nobility, set in well-kept gardens. In the 19th century a number of university buildings, mostly hospitals belonging to the Medical School, were built here. Some of these buildings display interesting architectural forms.

❸ ★ **Church of the Sacred Heart of Jesus**
This is one of the most interesting examples of modern ecclesiastical architecture.

❷ ★ **Society of Physicians**
The metal bannisters were designed by Stanisław Wyspiański in the Art Nouveau style, featuring sinuous floral ornaments.

A medieval stone pillar to the dead
by the Church of St Nicholas is unique. It was originally located in the courtyard of St Valentine's Hospital in Kleparz.

❶ **Church of St Nicholas**
For centuries this church was a landmark of the settlement which developed along the Krakow-Mogiła route.

Kopernika Street
lined densely with trees, is one of the most beautiful streets in Krakow.

Locator Map
See Street Finder maps 1 & 3

❺ Church of the Discalced Carmelite Nuns
The Baroque façade, one of the most beautiful in Krakow, is worth seeing.

❻ Astronomical Observatory
Belonging to the Jagiellonian University, with its elegant architecture and location next to the Botanical Gardens, this observatory looks more like a Neo-Classical villa than a university building.

❼ Jagiellonian University Botanical Gardens
Exotic and local flora make the gardens a favourite place for days out.

Key

 Suggested route

❹ Church of the Immaculate Conception of the Virgin Mary
The entrance to the Baroque interior is through this monumental portal.

0 metres   50
0 yards   50

Madonna and Child with Saints Adalbert and Stanisław

❶ Church of St Nicholas
Kościół św. Mikołaja

ul. Kopernika 9. **Map** 2 D4 (6 F3). **Tel** 12 431 22 77. 🚊 3, 10, 20, 24, 52. **Open** during services only.

Recorded in the first half of the 13th century, this is one of the oldest churches in Krakow. The remnants of the Romanesque church and a Gothic portal have survived in the chancel. During Swedish occupation, in 1665, the church was plundered and burned and the present building is the result of a Baroque remodelling undertaken between 1677 and 1682. Furnishings were commissioned by the Academy of Krakow, whose patronage over this collegiate foundation goes back to 1465. A coat of arms of the academy (a shield with crossed maces) decorates the backs of the stalls. The high altar, featuring an effigy of St Nicholas and architectural decoration forming coulisses, was probably designed by Francesco Placidi. It. The church also houses a late Gothic triptych, depicting the Coronation of the Virgin, and a Renaissance Madonna and Child with Saints Adalbert and Stanisław, patron saints of Poland. A bronze font, dating from 1536, is worth noting.

It is also of interest that Feliks Dzierżyński, who was to become the founder of the *Cheka* (Bolshevik secret police) and a Bolshevik revolutionary, was married in this church in 1910.

❷ Society of Physicians
Gmach Towarzystwa Lekarskiego

ul. Radziwiłłowska 4. **Map** 2 D4 (6 F2). **Tel** 12 422 75 47. 🚊 3, 10, 20, 24, 52. **Open** by prior telephone arrangement only.

This building was constructed in 1904 to designs by the architects Władysław Kaczmarski and Józef Sowiński. A rather modest Neo-Classical exterior is in contrast to the sumptuous interior decoration designed by Stanisław Wyspiański. This multi-talented artist created complex decoration in which, typically for the Art Nouveau movement, the arts and crafts complement each other. Wyspiański chose colour schemes for the walls and designed the exquisite stained-glass showing *Apollo, The Solar System*, as well as the metal balusters and furniture.

Apollo, The Solar System, by Wyspiański in the Society of Physicians building

❸ Church of the Sacred Heart of Jesus
Kościół Najświętszego Serca Pana Jezusa

See pp136–7.

Façade of the Baroque Church of the Immaculate Conception

❹ Church of the Immaculate Conception of the Virgin Mary
Kościół Niepokalanego Poczęcia NMP

ul. Kopernika 19. **Map** 2 E4. 🚊 2, 4, 7, 10, 14, 20, 52. **Open** 8am–4pm daily and during services.

This church, also known as the Church of St Lazarus, was used in the past by novices of the order of the Discalced Carmelites. The rigidity of the Baroque architecture of this church, built between 1634 and 1680, reflects the strict building regulations of the Carmelite order. Large and complex, the high altar dominates the small interior. Modelled on the high altar in the Carmelite Church of Santa Maria della Scala in Rome, it was made in 1681 of black marble from the Dębnik quarry, which was owned by the Carmelites.

❺ Church of the Discalced Carmelite Nuns
Kościół Karmelitanek Bosych

ul. Kopernika 44. **Map** 2 E4. **Tel** 12 421 41 18. 🚌 124, 152, 502. 🚊 2, 4, 7, 10, 14, 20, 52. **Open** during services only.

A large convent was built in the neighbourhood of the friary of the same order between 1720 and 1732.

The church is small and has a Greek cross groundplan. The interior with its many columns is impressive. The sumptuous façade has elegant decoration in the late Baroque style.

The architect of the church is unknown but Karol Antoni Bay of Warsaw and Kacper Bażanka are considered likely to have designed it. Due to the strict rule of the order, the church is open to the public only during services. The painting on the high altar depicts Saint Theresa of Avila, to whom the church is dedicated.

Portal in the Church of the Discalced Carmelite Nuns

❻ Astronomical Observatory

Obserwatorium Astronomiczne UJ

ul. Kopernika 27. **Map** 2 F4. **Tel** 12 425 14 57. 124, 152, 424, 502. 2, 4, 7, 10, 14, 20, 52. **Closed** to the public.

The establishment of the observatory in Wesoła was directly linked to the reform of the Academy of Krakow carried out in the 1770s by Hugo Kołłątaj, a task he was given by the Commission for National Education. As a result,

experimental sciences gained a more prominent role in the curriculum. The suburban Jesuit residence, taken over by the commission after the abolition of the order, was rebuilt to house the observatory. Stanisław Zawadzki, the architect to King Stanisław Augustus, redesigned the building in an austere Neo-Classical style. He decorated the façade with astronomical signs.

The building is now occupied by the Jagiellonian Botanical Institute. A modern astronomical observatory is located in the former Skała fortress in Bielany.

❼ Jagiellonian University Botanical Gardens

Ogród botaniczny UJ

ul. Kopernika 27a. **Map** 2 F4. **Tel** 12 663 36 35. 124, 152, 424, 502. 2, 4, 7, 10, 14, 20, 52. **Open** mid-Apr–Oct: 9am–7pm daily. Greenhouses: **Open** 10am–6pm Sat–Thu. Museum of Botanical Gardens: **Open** 10am–2pm Wed & Fri, 11am–3pm Sun.

Next to the observatory, the Botanical Gardens of the Jagiellonian University are located on the former grounds and lodge of the Czartoryski family. The gardens were established in 1780 by Jan Jaśkiewicz and designed by the Viennese gardener Franz Kaiser. A 500-year-old oak tree in the depths of the garden, as well as exotic and native plants, are particularly worth seeing. Also of interest are late-Gothic pillars, originally from the Collegium Maius, used here as plinths supporting plant pots.

Two of the gardens' palm houses are interesting examples of 19th-century architectural structures. They are complemented by a third, 20th-century

Vibrant flowers in the Jagiellonian University Botanical Gardens

palm house designed by Stanisław Juszczyk and built in 1964 to mark the 6th centenary of the Jagiellonian University. Busts of celebrated botanists decorate the gardens.

❽ Former Main Railway Station

Budynek dawnego dworca głównego

Plac Kolejowy 1. **Map** 2 D3 (6 F1). 2, 4, 7, 10, 14, 20, 24, 52.

A railway link was established in 1847 between Krakow and Silesia, known as the Northern, or Franz Joseph Railway. Between 1844 and 1847 a new station was built north of the city. Designed by Piotr Rosenbaum, it was considered to be one of the most elegant stations in Europe, though it was later rebuilt. In 1898 Teodor Talowski constructed a viaduct next to the station, in the Romanesque Revival style. The building is no longer in use as a station, and ticket offices are now under the platforms nearby.

Krakow's Former Main Railway Station

❸ Church of the Sacred Heart of Jesus

This monumental church was built between 1909 and 1921 to designs by the architect Franciszek Mączyński. He applied a number of historic styles which he modified and combined in new ways. What he created is one of the most interesting ecclesiastical buildings of the first quarter of the 20th century in Poland. Leading artists worked on the interior. Karol Hukan carved sculptures for the altars, while Jan Bukowski painted murals of striking beauty and designed unusual confessionals. The mosaic above the high altar is by Piotr Stachiewicz, and the south portal facing Kopernika Street was designed by Xawery Dunikowski. A small statue of Mączyński on the exterior of the east wall is also by Dunikowski.

★ South Portal
The main entrance to the church is through this monumental portal. Note the exquisite ornaments and figures which are both regarded as outstanding examples of Polish sculpture of the early 20th century.

Mosaic in the Porch
Made of mosaic pieces in vivid colours and set against a shiny background, the figures of Mary and Child have an almost unreal, mystical appearance.

Entrance

Murals decorating the Nave Vaulting
These murals contribute to the rich and monumental character of the interior. They were painted by Jan Bukowski, who also executed decoration in other churches in Krakow, including St Mary's and the Church of the Bernardine Nuns, as well as the Loretto Chapel by the Capuchin Church.

★ Altar of St Joseph
Altars in the aisles were made by the sculptor Karol Hukan. Of particular interest is the altar of St Joseph, made in 1922 to 1923. It features this figurative group, which is rich in dynamic and wavy forms.

Confessional
The confessionals were designed by Jan Bukowski, Professor of the Industrial School of Art, in the style of the Baroque Revival and are freely decorated with ornaments.

High Altar
The design of the high altar, featuring a half-dome supported by a free-standing colonnade, was influenced by Italian Renaissance architecture. The statues above the altar portray Christ and Jesuit saints.

KEY

① **Side porch and tower**

② **Mosaic above the high altar**

Statue of Franciszek Mączyński
The church was Mączyński's most important design. His statue, outside the east wall, is by Xawery Dunikowski.

Street-by-Street: Matejko Square

Kleparz, an independent settlement north of Krakow, was granted a municipal charter in 1366. It was incorporated into Krakow in 1791. After the introduction of the railway, Kleparz developed rapidly around the railway station. In the heart of the quarter, the empty space in front of the Barbican was transformed into an elegant square welcoming visitors to Krakow, arriving here by rail or approaching the city from the north, via Warszawska Street.

❿ ★ **Grunwald Monument**
The making of this monument helped to stimulate patriotic feelings in the late 19th century. It commemorates the Lithuanian-Polish victory over the Teutonic Knights at Grunwald in 1410.

⓬ **Academy of Fine Arts**
The academy houses a collection of works by its leading professors and students, including *Self-Portrait* by Jacek Malczewski.

BASZTOWA

A bust of Jan Matejko, carved by Jan Tombiński, can be found above the main entrance to the Academy of Fine Arts. Another monument to the artist is located near the Barbican.

Monument to Jan Matejko

Barbican

Tomb of the Unknown Soldier

⓫ **National Bank of Poland**
The Allegories of Industry and Agriculture, carved by Karol Hukan, decorate the façade of this bank.

| 0 metres | 50 |
| 0 yards | 50 |

Key

— Suggested route

⓮ Church of St Vincent de Paul
This church was built from 1875 to 1887 to designs by Filip Pokutyński. The façade was inspired by Italian medieval architecture.

Locator Map
See Street Finder maps 1 & 3

The Church of the Sisters of Charity was built by Filip Pokutyński from 1869 to 1871.

❾ ★ St Florian's Church
In days gone by life in Kleparz centred around this collegiate church. The effigy of St Florian by Jan Tricius decorates the high altar.

⓭ Polish State Railways Headquarters
This was the most opulent building erected in Krakow at the end of the 19th century.

Elegant town houses at Matejko Square show a range of different architectural styles of the early 20th century.

The Baroque altar of St John of Kęty in St Florian's Church

9 St Florian's Church
Kościół św. Floriana

ul. Warszawska 1B. **Map** 2 D3. **Tel** 12 422 48 42. 304. 2, 4, 7, 14, 24. **Open** during services only.

In 1184 Duke Kazimierz the Just received the relics of St Florian from Pope Lucius III and decided to deposit them in Krakow. The horses which drew the carriage carrying the relics of the martyr stopped suddenly in Kleparz, before reaching the city's gate, and refused to move forward. This was interpreted as a miraculous sign indicating where the relics should be placed. The church was, therefore, built on this spot between 1185 and 1212. After the capital was transferred to Warsaw, the church came to prominence as it was used to receive the deceased royalty brought from Warsaw for burial at Wawel. The funeral processions started here.

The church was damaged by frequent invasions and no trace of the medieval architecture has remained. The present interior and its decoration date from 1677 to 1684. The high altar with an effigy of St Florian, painted by Jan Tricius in the late 17th century, as well as an incomplete late-Gothic altar of St John the Baptist are of interest. The exterior was entirely remodelled by Franciszek Mączyński in the early 20th century.

10 Grunwald Monument
Pomnik Grunwaldzki

Plac J Matejki. **Map** 2 D3 (6 E1). 154, 192, 304. 2, 4, 7, 13, 15, 20, 24.

The monument, featuring King Władysław Jagiełło on horseback, was raised to mark the 500th anniversary of the 1410 victory at Grunwald (Tannenberg in German) over the Teutonic Knights. It was commissioned by the statesman, composer and pianist, Ignacy Jan Paderewski, from the sculptor Antoni Wiwulski.

The monument was inspired by grandiose German monuments of the second half of the 19th century. It was generally well received but some critics mocked the theatrical treatment of the figures. Some even suggested that the only lifelike figure was that of the dead Grand Master Ulrich von Jungingen. The monument was destroyed by the Nazis in 1939 and only reconstructed in 1975 by the sculptor Marian Konieczny.

11 National Bank of Poland

ul. Basztowa 20. **Map** 2 D3 (6 E1). **Tel** 12 181 26 00. 304. 2, 4, 7, 14, 24. **Open** 7am–5pm Mon–Fri.

The bank, built between 1921 and 1925 by the architects Teodor Hoffman and Kazimierz Wyczyński, exemplifies the Neo-Classical style which became popular during the inter-war years. Neo-Classicism was then applied to important public buildings housing administrative and financial institutions, and was in sharp contrast to the Functionalism favoured in left-wing circles. The exterior sculptural decoration is by Karol Hukan and Stanisław Popławski. Inside, the domed banking hall is worth a visit.

The Academy of Fine Arts in Renaissance Revival style

12 Academy of Fine Arts

Plac J Matejki 13. **Map** 2 D3 (6 E1). **Tel** 12 299 20 00. 304. 2, 4, 7, 14, 24.

The school of Fine Arts in Krakow gained independent status in 1873 through the efforts of the artist Jan Matejko. Three years later the school was allocated a plot in Kleparz by the city's authorities. The building was constructed in 1879 to 1880 to designs by Maciej Moraczewski. The architect adopted the Renaissance Revival style for

The imposing building of the National Bank of Poland

this building, in accordance with the spirit of 19th-century Historicism which favoured such forms for school architecture. On the first floor is a studio where Matejko painted his *Kościuszko at Racławice* and *The Vows of King Jan Kazimierz*.

In 1900 the school gained university status, becoming the Academy of Fine Arts. Some of the best Polish artists were among its students. The building in Kleparz is currently the seat of the academy's governing body and houses the faculties of painting, printmaking and sculpture.

⓭ Polish State Railways Headquarters

Plac J Matejki 12. **Map** 2 D3 (6 E1).
🚌 304. 🚋 2, 4, 7, 14, 24.
Closed to the public.

This imposing building was constructed in 1888 by an unknown Viennese architect who combined the forms of both Romanesque and Baroque Revival into an eclectic whole. It is possibly the only building in Krakow to have been directly influenced by the 19th-century monumental architecture of its Austrian neighbour, Vienna.

⓮ Church of St Vincent de Paul
Kościół św. Wincentego de Paul

ul. Św. Filipa 19. **Map** 2 D3. **Tel** 12 429 25 33. 🚌 304. 🚋 2, 4, 7, 14, 24.
Open during services only.

The present church was built between 1875 and 1877 and replaced the medieval Church of Saints Philip and James which had been dismantled by the Austrian authorities in 1801. The architect, Filip Pokutyński, was inspired by Italian late-Romanesque architecture. Although modest in design, the church differs from other 19th-century ecclesiastical

The ornate interior of the Church of St Vincent de Paul

architecture in Krakow because of its clear, compact and monumental forms.

The side altar features a miraculous icon depicting Christ Crucified. This much venerated image was brought after World War II from Milatyn near L'viv.

⓯ Globe House
Dom pod Globusem

ul. Długa 1. **Map** 1 C3. 🚌 304.
🚋 2, 4, 7, 14, 24.

This house was built in 1904 to 1906 for the Chamber of Commerce and Industry. It was designed by the architects Franciszek Mączyński and Tadeusz Stryjeński. The building is considered to be one of the best examples of the Art Nouveau style in Polish architecture. It is an interesting asymmetrical structure dominated by a pyramidal tower topped by a globe. The interior decoration, including murals in the great hall, is mainly

The Globe House, a prime example of Art Nouveau architecture

the work of Józef Mehoffer. Stained-glass windows above the stairs depict allegorical subjects such as the progress of mankind through industry and commerce, thus reflecting the function of the building. The several cast-iron decorations are also of interest. Today, the building houses the publishers Wydawnictwo Literackie.

The façade of the Church of the Nuns of the Visitation

⓰ Church of the Nuns of the Visitation
Kościół Wizytek

ul. Krowoderska 16. **Map** 1 C3.
Tel 12 632 16 28. 🚋 2, 4, 7, 14, 24.
Open during services only.

The convent was founded by Bishop Jan Małachowski as a votive offering after he was miraculously saved from drowning in the Vistula. The church is an interesting example of Krakow's Baroque ecclesiastical architecture. It was built from 1686 to 1695 by Giovanni Solari.

The façade is richly decorated with sculptures and ornaments. Some lavish decoration is also characteristic of the interior which, although small, is very elegant. The unusual high altar was made in 1695 by the sculptor Jerzy Golonka. The plasterwork is by Jan Liskowicz. The 18th-century murals decorating the vault have been much altered.

PIASEK AND NOWY ŚWIAT

Piasek, known as Garbary until the 19th century, is located west of the Old Quarter. Its development was hindered in the past by frequent invasions and a lack of fortifications to prevent them. A number of settlements with independent jurisdictions were located between Garbary and Wawel. They included Groble, Smoleńsko, Wielkorządowa, Wygoda, Retoryka and Rybaki, as well as Nowy Świat which remained under Krakow's

jurisdiction. All these settlements were integrated by the Austrian authorities. By the end of the 19th century Piasek (Sand) and Nowy Świat (New World) began to flourish; wealthy residents moved in, drawn by the pleasant and tranquil atmosphere away from the noisy town centre. As a result, some of the best residential architecture can be found here. It is mostly eclectic in style, dating from the start of the 20th century.

Sights at a Glance

Historic Monuments and Buildings
1 Philharmonic Hall
2 Former Museum of Industry and Technology
6 House of the Singing Frog
7 Europeum
8 Małopolska Garden of Arts
15 Wyspiański Monument
17 School of Chemistry
18 Jagiellonian Library
19 Academy of Mines and Metallurgy, Main Building
22 Spider House

Museums and Galleries
10 Emeryk Hutten-Czapski Museum
11 The Józef Czapski Pavilion
13 Józef Mehoffer House Museum
16 National Museum in Krakow, Main Building pp150–51

Churches
3 Church of the Felician Nuns
4 Church of the Merciful God
9 Church of the Sisters of the Sacred Heart of Jesus
12 Capuchin Church
23 Carmelite Church

Historic Streets
5 Retoryka Street
20 Avenue of Three Poets
21 Karmelicka Street

Open Space
14 Błonia Fields

See also Street Finder maps 1 & 5

Restaurants see p195
1 Biała Róża
2 CK Browar
3 Dynia Resto-Bar
4 Green Way
5 Mamma Mia
6 Międzymiastowa
7 The Olive
8 Pod Norenami
9 Smakołyki
10 Someplace Else
11 Veganic
12 Zielona Kuchnia

◀ The statue of St Barbara on the roof of the Academy of Mines and Metallurgy   For keys to symbols see back flap

Street-by-Street: Piłsudski Street

Józefa Piłsudskiego (formerly Wolska) Street formed part of the route connecting Krakow with Wola Justowska, a route first recorded in the 16th century. After Nowy Świat and the neighbouring jurisdictions were incorporated into Krakow, it became one of the main avenues in this part of town. Elegant residential and public architecture developed here by the end of the 19th century and some of the buildings show Polish architecture at its best. A stroll down the street is also rewarded by great views of the vast Błonia Fields with Kościuszko Mound in the distance, behind which Piłsudski Mound can also be seen.

⑨ Church of the Sisters of the Sacred Heart of Jesus
The square in front of this church was once a flood plain of the Rudawa river which was filled in prior to the construction of the convent buildings.

⑥ House of the Singing Frog
This house was designed by Teodor Talowski and is decorated with some exquisite, though somewhat overdone, sculptures of fantastic creatures.

0 metres 50
0 yards 50

JÓZEFA PIŁSUDSKIEGO

RETORYKA

Key

— Suggested route

⑤ ★ Retoryka Street
The houses designed by Teodor Talowski have a unique "antiquarian" look and contribute to the picturesque character of the street.

⑩ Emeryk Hutten-Czapski Museum
This monster decorates the exhibition pavilion in which Emeryk Hutten-Czapski housed the numismatic collection he brought to Krakow.

Locator Map
See Street Finder maps 1 & 5

❶ Philharmonic Hall
The hall received a state-of-the-art organ following refurbishment after a fire in 1991.

❷ Former Museum of Industry and Technology
This is one of the most interesting examples of Modernist architecture in Poland.

⑪ The Józef Czapski Pavilion
Personal effects of artist Józef Czapski plus archive footage help to celebrate his life and works at this modern museum.

❸ Church of the Felician Nuns
The church was designed by Feliks Księżarski. Its interior is one of the few examples of Romanesque Revival ecclesiastical architecture in Krakow.

❹ Church of the Merciful God
This memorial plaque of an unknown knight is an exceptional Gothic work surrounded by 19th-century architecture.

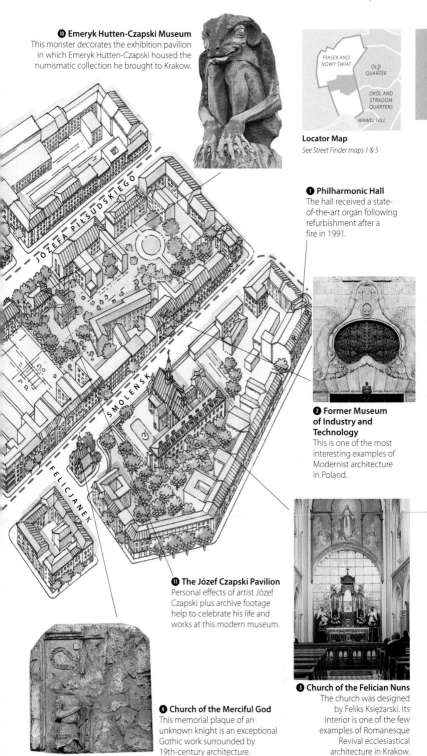

The exterior of the Neo-Classical Philharmonic Hall

❶ Philharmonic Hall
Filharmonia

ul. Zwierzyniecka 1. **Map** 1 B5 (5 C3).
Tel 12 619 87 21. 🚊 1, 2, 6, 8, 13, 18, 20.

The Society of Friends of Music, which was active in Krakow between 1817 and 1884, was regarded as the first philharmonic organization in occupied Poland. The Szymanowski State Philharmonia was established in Krakow in 1945. Walery Bierdiajew, Andrzej Panufnik and Krzysztof Penderecki were among the principal conductors. The orchestra and choir are complemented by the renowned chamber orchestra, Capella Cracoviensis. The hall is housed in the former Catholic Cultural Institution. It was built between 1928 and 1930 by Pokutyński and Filipkiewicz in the Neo-Classical style which was popular with Polish architects around 1930.

❷ Former Museum of Industry and Technology
Gmach dawnego Muzeum Techniczno - Przemysłowego

ul. Smoleńsk 9. **Map** 1 B5 (5 B3).
🚊 2, 8, 13, 18, 20.

This museum was established in 1868 by Andrzej Baraniecki who presented the city with his library and large collection of decorative arts. The museum

ran courses in fine art, as well as a school of painting for women, and workshops on crafts. Collaboration with other institutions at the forefront of modern design was established. The museum published a number of titles, including journals such as *Przegląd Techniczny* (Technical Revue) and *Architekt* (The Architect). It also played an important role in the development of Polish applied art.

The museum was initially housed in the west wing of the Franciscan friary. The new building was constructed in 1908–14 to designs by Tadeusz Stryjeński. Józef Czajkowski designed the elegant façade, which is rich in geometrical forms. The structure of the building, which uses reinforced concrete, was novel at the time and the layout of the rooms was unusual. It is a leading example of Modernist architecture in Poland. The Museum of Industry and Technology was closed down in 1952 and today the Faculty of Industrial Design of the Academy of Fine Arts is housed here.

Façade detail, former Museum of Industry and Technology

❸ Church of the Felician Nuns
Kościół Felicjanek

ul. Smoleńsk 4/6. **Map** 1 B5 (5 B3).
Tel 12 422 08 37. 🚊 2, 8, 13, 18, 20.
Open 8:30am–6pm daily and during services.

The church of the Felician Nuns is one of the largest churches built in Krakow in the 19th century. This basilica in the Romanesque Revival style was built between 1882 and 1884 to designs by Feliks Księżarski, but modified by Sebastian Jaworzyński. The monumental and austere forms are striking, but softened inside through lavish decoration of the altars. The church houses relics of Blessed Maria Angela Truszkowska, the foundress of the Order, who died in 1899.

Altar of Blessed Maria Angela, Church of the Felician Nuns

❹ Church of the Merciful God
Kościół Miłosierdzia Bożego

ul. Bożego Miłosierdzia 1.
Map 1 B5 (5 B3). 🚊 2, 8, 13, 18, 20.
Open during services only.

In 1555 Jan Żukowski established in Nowy Świat a home for the destitute and a small church. The church was consecrated in 1665. Located outside the city wall, both buildings were badly damaged during a number of invasions. The church has survived. On the outside wall facing Smoleńsk Street, remnants of a Gothic sepulchre, with a kneeling figure of a knight, can be seen.

Among the rather modest Baroque furnishings, the one of most interest is the image of the *Misericordia Domini* (The Suffering Christ and Sorrowful Mary) of 1650, hanging in the chancel.

Adjacent to the church is a presbytery, built in the eclectic style in 1905–6 by Jan Zubrzycki.

❺ Retoryka Street
Ulica Retoryka

Map 1 B5 (5 B3, 4). 1, 2, 6, 20.

The name of this street comes from the Retoryka jurisdiction, which was established in this area by the Ossolińskis in the first half of the 18th century. In the late 19th century the construction of boulevards began along the Rudawa river, which ran here. They were lined with houses whose architecture was marked by imaginative forms and unusual decoration. In 1910 the river was enclosed in a tunnel beneath street level. The houses designed by Teodor Talowski are most interesting. He used pseudo-antiquarian, intentionally damaged motifs such as mosaics and plaques bearing popular Latin inscriptions for the external decoration. The plaque on his own house reads *festina lente* (hasten slowly) and that on the Ass House, *faber est suae quisque fortunae* (one makes one's own destiny).

The houses in Retoryka Street, designed by Talowski and other leading architects active in Krakow around 1900, are interesting examples of Polish architecture at the dawn of the modern age.

❻ House of the Singing Frog
Dom Pod Śpiewającą żabą

ul. Retoryka 1. **Map** 1 B5 (5 B3). 1, 2, 6.

The corner house at No. 1 Retoryka Street, built in 1889–90,

Decorative façade of the House of the Singing Frog

is considered to be the most interesting of Talowski's designs. The unusual structure consists of a number of segments varing in height and decoration, so that it could be viewed at an angle from the adjacent street corner. The name of the house is a joke which refers to both the function and location of the building: it used to house a music school whose singing students were often accompanied by croaking frogs in the nearby Rudawa river.

❼ Europeum

Plac Sikorskiego 6. **Map** 1 B4 (5 B2). **Tel** 12 433 57 60. 124, 152, 292. 2, 8, 13 18, 20. **Open** 10am–6pm Tue–Sat, 10am–4pm Sun. free on Sun. **mnk.pl**

The Europeum is home to the most important assemblage of non-Polish European works of art in the National Museum in Krakow collection. Notable exhibits include works by

Lorenzo Lotto, Pieter Brueghel the Younger and Paolo Veneziano.

The gallery is housed in a renovated 17th-century granary set on a quiet, tree-lined square. At the back of the museum is an intriguing collection of masonry fragments from historic buildings all over the city.

❽ Małopolska Garden of Arts
Małopolski Ogród Sztuki

ul. Rajska 12. **Map** 1 B4 (5 B1). **Tel** 12 375 21 50. 114, 139, 159, 164, 169, 192. 4, 8, 13, 14, 24. **Open** from 9am; closing times vary. **mos.art.pl**

This multifunctional arts complex features several exhibition spaces, a concert hall, a small cinema and a delightful café, all wrapped up in a strikingly contemporary building that consists of a slatted clay façade, glass frame, industrial beams and a garden courtyard. Opened in 2012, the Małopolska Garden of Arts was built on and around buildings belonging to the Juliusz Słowacki Theatre as a joint project by the theatre and the regional government. The semi-enclosed spaces at the front and side of the building are wonderfully peaceful areas in which to sit and relax, and there are always events or exhibitions taking place inside. Many of Krakow's biggest cultural festivals now use the centre as their main venue.

The striking exterior of the Małopolska Garden of Arts

❾ Church of the Sisters of the Sacred Heart of Jesus
Kościół Sercanek

ul. Garncarska 26. **Map** 1 B5 (5 B3).
Tel 12 422 57 66. 🚊 15, 18.
Open during services only.

The Convent of the Sisters of the Sacred Heart of Jesus was built between 1895 and 1900 to designs by Władysław Kaczmarski and Sławomir Odrzywolski. The architects designed the building along Garncarska Street so as to close one side of a square located here. They adjusted the façade of the church and the adjoining buildings of the convent to fit the slight bend in the street. This explains the irregularity of the plan.

The church is eclectic in style. The exterior walls show bare brickwork, ornamented in the Romanesque Revival style, as well as pseudo-Renaissance *sgraffiti* and Neo-Classical sculptures by Jan Tombiński. Furnishings display Neo-Romanesque forms.

Detail from the Church of the Sisters of the Sacred Heart of Jesus

❿ Emeryk Hutten-Czapski Museum
Muzeum im Emeryka Hutten-Czapskiego

ul. Piłsudskiego 12. **Map** 1 B5 (5 B3).
Tel 12 433 58 40. 🚊 2, 8, 13, 18, 20.
Open 10am–6pm Tue–Sat, 10am–4pm Sun. 🅿 free Sun. **w** mnk.pl

This small palace in the Renaissance Revival style was built in 1884 by the architect Antoni Siedek for Hubert Krasiński. A few years later the property was purchased by

The Emeryk Hutten-Czapski Museum, in the Renaissance Revival style

Emeryk Hutten-Czapski who moved from the Vilnius area, bringing with him an exquisite collection of coins, prints and manuscripts. A pavilion, purpose-built to house this collection, was added in 1896. It was designed by Tadeusz Stryjeński and Zygmunt Hendel. The inscription decorating the pavilion reads *Monumentis Patriae naufragio ereptis* (To the national heritage salvaged from destruction). In 1903 the Czapskis bequeathed the palace and collection to the city of Krakow.

⓫ The Józef Czapski Pavilion
Pawilon Józefa Czapskiego

ul. Piłsudskiego 12. **Map** 1 B5 (5 B3).
Tel 12 433 58 40. 🚊 2, 8, 13, 18, 20.
Open 10am–6pm Tue–Sat, 10am–4pm Sun. 🅿 free Sun. 🅰 🅿
w mnk.pl

Set in an elegant cube-shaped building in the garden behind the Emeryk Hutten-Czapski Museum, the Czapski Pavilion celebrates the life of Emeryk's grandson Józef (1896–1993). An accomplished painter as well as an outstanding writer and patriotic activist, Józef Czapski was instrumental in uncovering the truth about the nearly 20,000 Polish officers who were murdered by the Soviet secret police at Katyń and other locations during World War II. Czapski himself had narrowly avoided the massacre. He went into exile after World War II and became an influential member of the émigré cultural community built around the Paris-based monthly *Kultura*. The exhibition in the small pavilion displays the

artist's paintings, personal diaries and photos and uses archival film and interview footage to tell the story of this remarkable man.

⓬ Capuchin Church
Kościół Kapucynów

ul. Loretańska 11. **Map** 1 B4 (5 B2).
Tel 12 422 48 03. 🚊 124, 152, 192, 502. 🚊 2, 4, 8, 13, 14, 15, 18.
Open 9:30am–4:30pm and 5–7pm daily as well as during services.

The Capuchin friars arrived in Krakow in 1695. They began constructing the church and friary a year later. The work was supervised at first by Carlo Ceroni, who was later succeeded by Martino Pellegrini. The simple interior reflects the strict rule of the Order which espouses extreme poverty. The altars, however, feature good paintings. They include *The Annunciation* by Pietro Dandini, *St Erasmus and St Cajetan*, two 18th-century effigies by Łukasz Orłowski, and *St Francis of Assisi* by Szymon Czechowicz. A wooden crucifix in front of the church indicates

The interior of the Loreto Chapel by the Capuchin Church

the tomb of the Confederates of Bar who fell in a rebellion against the Russians in 1768.

Between 1712 and 1719 an external Loreto Chapel was built to a design by Kacper Bażanka; this is linked to the church through a cloister. It houses a Neo-Classical altar with a miraculous statue of the Madonna of Loreto and a beautiful tabernacle, also designed by Bażanka. An animated Christmas crib is erected here every year, featuring historic Polish characters.

Portrait of Mrs Mehoffer by the Modernist artist Józef Mehoffer

⓭ Józef Mehoffer House Museum
Muzeum Józefa Mehoffera

ul. Krupnicza 26. **Map** 1 B4 (5 B2). **Tel** 12 433 58 80. 4, 8, 13, 14, 24. **Open** 10am–4pm Tue, Wed, Fri–Sun, 10am–6pm Thu. free Sun.

Stanisław Wyspiański was born in this house in 1869. In 1930 it was bought by Józef Mehoffer (1869–1946), one of the foremost Modernist artists in Poland. In 1968 the house was acquired by the National Museum and the Józef Mehoffer House Museum was established. The interiors have been preserved in the tasteful way they were arranged by the artist himself. Many of his works, including paintings, stained glass and murals, are on display. Behind the house is the delightful Meho Café *(see p196)*.

⓮ Błonia Fields

Map 1 A5. 114, 134, 152, 164, 173, 179, 192, 292. 15, 18, 20.

The Błonia Fields formed part of the grounds owned by the Convent of Premonstratensian (Norbertine) Nuns in Zwierzyniec and were originally used as pastures. In 1366 the nuns made a rather bad deal with the city's authorities and exchanged Błonia for a house in Floriańska Street. The house proved to be unprofitable and was eventually destroyed by fire. This gave rise to a joke about the nuns who had exchanged pastures for a bonfire. For centuries the nuns tried in vain to regain the land but the Błonia Fields remain the property of the City of Krakow.

Błonia were used in the past as a venue for mass religious and national celebrations: the first football match in Krakow took place here in 1894 and Pope John Paul II said a Holy Mass here on four occasions. Today it is a wildlife sanctuary in the centre of Krakow and a popular place for recreation.

⓯ Wyspiański Monument
Pomnik S. Wyspiańskiego

al. 3 Maja (in front of the National Museum). **Map** 1 A5 (5 A3). 144, 164, 173, 179, 503. 20.

The monument was unveiled in 1982 to mark the 75th anniversary of the death of the great artist and playwright of the so-called Young Poland movement (Polish Modernism). The sculptor, Marian Konieczny, depicted Stanisław Wyspiański surrounded by the characters from two of his plays, *The Wedding* and *November Night*. The monument was badly received and prompted unfavourable interpretations.

⓰ National Museum in Krakow, Main Building

See pp150–51.

⓱ School of Chemistry
Zespół Szkół Chemicznych

ul. Krupnicza 44. **Map** 1 A4 (5 A2). **Tel** 12 422 32 20. 114, 164, 169, 173, 179. **Closed** to the public.

In 1834 the Institute of Technology was established in Krakow, funded by the bequest of the architect Szczepan Humbert. It was later transformed into the State School of Industry. This irregular brick structure, decorated with Art Nouveau ornaments, now houses the School of Chemistry.

Wyspiański Monument

⑯ National Museum in Krakow, Main Building

The modern building of the National Museum in Krakow was designed by Czesław Boratyński, Edward Kreisler and Bolesław Schmidt in 1934 but the building was not completed until 1989. Permanent galleries display Polish painting and sculpture of the 20th century, decorative arts, and arms and other mementos of the Polish Army. Temporary shows are also organized here. The art collection is one of the largest in Poland and includes works by leading Modernist artists, as well as some outstanding works from the period between the two World Wars. While the Czartoryski Museum undergoes renovation, Leonardo da Vinci's *Lady with an Ermine* is on display here.

★ Polonia, a Cartoon for Stained Glass
Stanisław Wyspiański's cartoons for stained-glass windows in the Cathedral symbolically depict visions of the past but also relate to modern issues.

First floor

Nike of the Legions
This is one of Jacek Malczewski's symbolic *tours de force*. Nike, the goddess of victory, is sitting by the body of a legionary whose face resembles Józef Piłsudski.

The Uniform of Józef Piłsudski
"The uniform of the grey rifleman" reminds one of the tragic but nevertheless victorious history of the Polish Legions between 1914 and 1917.

Audiovisual room

Ground floor

Library and Reading Room

Mace
This gilded "buzdygan" mace belonged to Grand Hetman Stanisław Jabłonowski, who fought in the Battle of Vienna in 1683.

Main entrance

Education Room

Second floor

Emballage (1975)
This work by Tadeusz Kantor is an artistic interpretation of Jan Matejko's great history piece depicting *The Prussian Homage*.

Execution (1949)
The art of Andrzej Wróblewski (1927–1957), who died prematurely, is a personal analysis of the tragic war years.

Self-Portrait with Masks
This self-portrait by Wojciech Weiss (1875–1950) dates from the early years when the artist remained under the influence of Symbolism.

★ **A Design for Mickiewicz's Statue in Vilnius**
This monumental statue by the Cubist artist Zbigniew Pronaszko (1885–1958) was never executed and exists only as a model.

Key

Temporary exhibitions

Arms and Uniforms in Poland

Gallery of Polish Art of the 20th Century

Gallery of Decorative Arts

Non-exhibition space

Gallery Guide

Temporary displays and the exhibition "Arms and Uniforms in Poland" are located on the ground floor. The display on the first floor is dedicated to decorative arts and temporary exhibitions. The Gallery of Polish Art of the 20th Century is housed on the second floor.

⓲ Jagiellonian Library
Biblioteka Jagiellońska

ul. Oleandry 3. **Map** 1 A4 (5 A2).
Tel 12 633 09 03. 🚋 15, 18. 🚌 144,
164, 169, 173, 179, 194, 292, 503.
🚋 20. **Open** 8:15am–8:50pm
Mon–Fri, 9am–4pm Sat.

For many centuries the Library of the Jagiellonian University was housed in the Collegium Maius *(see pp108–9)*. This new building was constructed between 1931 and 1939 to designs by Wacław Krzyżanowski. It has impressive modern forms and a spacious and functional interior. It is not only the success of the design but also the high quality of craftsmanship and the use of luxurious materials that make this building an outstanding example of Krakow's architecture in the interwar years.

A new wing of the library, designed by Romuald Loegler, was completed in 2001, when the university celebrated the 6th centenary of its re-establishment. The additional wing matches the forms of the old building and is one of the most interesting examples of architecture of the 1990s.

Themed exhibitions of books and manuscripts are held in the lobby. Entrance to the reading rooms is with a membership card only.

⓳ Academy of Mines and Metallurgy, Main Building

Al. Mickiewicza 30. **Map** 1 A3, 4 (5 A1).
Tel 12 617 33 33. 🚌 144, 164, 169,
173, 179, 194, 292, 503. 🚋 20.
Open 7:30am–8pm daily.

The Academy of Mines was established in Krakow in 1919. In 1922 the Faculty of Metallurgy was added. After 1945 the academy was transformed into a large and well-equipped technological university. It has its own nuclear reactor and modern acoustic laboratory. The enormous main building, with 110,000 sq m (1,183,600 sq ft) of floor space, was built between 1923 and 1935. It was designed by Sławomir Odrzywolski and Wacław Krzyżanowski in a Neo-Classical style that is particularly prominent in the façade and portico. The statues of miners and steel workers in front of the building are by Jan Raszka.

Statues in front of the Academy of Mines and Metallurgy

In German-occupied Poland the building became the seat of the Governor-General. A museum housed in Building C-1 is dedicated to the history of the academy.

⓴ Avenue of Three Poets
Aleje Trzech Wieszczów

Map 1 A3, 1 A4, 1 B2, 1 C2. 🚌 144,
164, 169, 173, 179, 194, 292, 503.

In the mid-19th century an earthen embankment was constructed along what is today this avenue, and in 1887 to 1888 a railway line was laid for trains connecting Krakow to Płaszów. East of the embankment, new streets were laid out and new houses constructed in the eclectic and Art Nouveau styles. When in 1910 the borders of Krakow were extended, the railway and the embankment were dismantled. Their site was replaced by a wide avenue comprising a dual carriageway with a belt of greenery in the middle. Each of the sections of the avenue was named after a Romantic poet: Krasiński, Mickiewicz and Słowacki. The intention was to transform the avenue into Krakow's Champs Elysées.

An illuminated page in the Behem Codex, Jagiellonian Library

Looking down Karmelicka Street

㉑ Karmelicka Street
Ulica Karmelicka

Map 1 B3, 5 (B1, C1). 🚌 169, 179. 🚋 4, 8, 13, 14, 24.

Karmelicka Street formed part of the old route connecting Krakow to Czarna Wieś and Łobzów. Formerly known as Czarna, Karmelicka was always the main street in the Garbary quarter. The Carmelite Church and, at No. 12, the Town Hall of Garbary were built here. Initially the street was divided into two parts: the wider part stretched from the Cobblers' Gate to a small bridge, beyond which the street narrowed considerably. This explains why the Carmelite friary building projects into the present-day street.

By the end of the 19th century Karmelicka became one of the most elegant streets in Krakow. Splendid houses were built to designs by Maksymilian Nitsch, Teodor Talowski and Filip Pokutyński. The writers Stanisław Przybyszewski and Tadeusz Boy-Żeleński were among the celebrated residents.

㉒ Spider House
Dom pod Pająkiem

ul. Karmelicka 35. **Map** 1 B3 (5 B1). 🚋 4, 8, 13, 14, 24. **Closed** to the public.

This house was built in 1889 by Teodor Talowski, one of the leading architects in Krakow in the late 19th century. His intention was to give this irregular structure "an ancient appearance" by adding a "Gothic" round corner tower and a high gable in the style of Netherlandish Mannerism. By using different architectural styles of the past he wanted to pretend that the house had been rebuilt many times. He inserted, for example, a parapet modelled on the Renaissance Cloth Hall into the crenellated "Gothic" frieze. The decoration is rich in inventive detail.

㉓ Carmelite Church
Kościół Karmelitów

ul. Karmelicka 19. **Map** 1 B3 (5 C1). **Tel** 12 632 67 52. 🚌 169, 179. 🚋 4, 8, 13, 14, 24. **Open** 9:30am–4:30pm and 5–7pm daily and during services.

According to a legend, Duke Władysław Herman cured his skin disease by rubbing sand on the infected areas. He took the sand from a site miraculously indicated by the Virgin Mary.

This site was therefore named Piasek (sand), and a votive church founded by the duke was built in 1087. Thus was born the legend of the Madonna of the Sand.

The church was actually founded by Queen Jadwiga in 1395. It was almost entirely destroyed during the Swedish invasion in the 17th century and its remnants were incorporated into the new Baroque church which was consecrated in 1679. The magnificent high altar, made in 1698 to 1699, and lavishly decorated with acanthus leaves, is worth noting. The splendid stalls and the balcony with the organ, both by Jan Hankis, are also of interest. An icon of the Madonna of the Sand, painted directly on the wall, is much venerated.

The Calvary Chapel in the side wall of the Carmelite Church

Queen Jadwiga (Hedwig)

Queen Jadwiga (c. 1374–99) was famous for her piety and charity. She contributed to the development of the Academy of Krakow. Venerated since the Middle Ages, she was finally canonized in 1997. A touching legend links Jadwiga to the Carmelite Church. It tells the story of a mason employed at the construction of the church who lamented to Jadwiga about his poverty and lack of money to buy medicine for his wife. The Queen removed a gold brooch from her shoe and offered it to the man. The imprint of her foot can still be seen today.

The imprint of Queen Jadwiga's foot

The Socialist Realist architecture of Nowa Huta

❶ Nowa Huta

502. 🚊 4, 10, 22.

Krakow was widely considered an anti-Communist town in the aftermath of World War II due to its patriotic, intellectual and clerical traditions. In order to change this, the Communists undertook a programme of quick industrialization of the Krakow region to increase the working-class population. In 1948 a contract was signed between Poland and the Soviet Union for a giant steelworks named after Lenin, which has since been renamed Sendzimir. The construction of a new town named Nowa Huta (New Steelworks) began in 1949. It was designed by Tadeusz Ptaszycki in the Socialist Realist style.

The housing estate, Centre, built between 1949 and 1955, is a bold exercise in urban planning. In this "model Communist town" there was no room for churches. After years of campaigning by the people of Nowa Huta, however, the construction of churches finally began in the 1970s. Among these, the well-known Ark of God (see p39) is an outstanding piece of modern sacral Polish architecture. The Maximilian Kolbe Church in the Mistrzejowice district of Nowa Huta is another outstanding modern church. During the period of Martial Law (1981–3), the workers residing in Nowa Huta clearly demonstrated that

they were not the best allies of the Communists, and the town became notorious for anti-regime protest.

The **Nowa Huta Museum**, on a central alley known as the Alley of Roses (Aleja Róż) due to its many blooms, hosts themed exhibitions on the new town's history. Fascinating exhibitions about life during the Communist period are also held at the **PRL Museum** (Polish Peoples' Republic, Polska Rzeczpospolita Ludowa in Polish), which documents the history of the Marxist state that officially existed from 1952 to 1990. The museum is housed in the former Światowid cinema (Kino Światowid), an imposing example of Socialist-Realist architecture.

Ⅲ Nowa Huta Museum
os. Słonecznie 16. **Tel** 425 97 75.
Open Apr–Oct: 9:30am–5pm Tue–Sun; Nov–Mar: 9am–4pm Tue, Thu & Sat, 10am–5pm Wed. 🖼 free on Wed. 🆆 **mhk.pl**

Ⅲ PRL Museum
os. Centrum E1. **Tel** 12 446 7821.
Open 10am–5pm Tue–Sun. 🖼 free on Tue. 📷 🆆 **mprl.pl**

❷ Mogiła

7 km (4 miles) east of Krakow.
123, 153, 163. 🚊 15.

Mogiła village developed around the Cistercian Abbey. The Cistercians were brought to Poland in 1222, or 1225, by Iwo Odrowąż, the Bishop

of Krakow. The new monastery was named *Clara Tumba* ("Bright Tomb", Jasna Mogiła, in Polish) because of the proximity of the reputed burial place of the legendary princess Wanda.

This Romanesque **Cistercian Church** followed the strict building regulations of the Cistercian order. The chancel ended with a flat perpendicular wall, and pairs of chapels with a square ground-plan were added to the transept. In 1447 the church was destroyed by fire. Gothic forms were introduced during its rebuilding. Stanisław Samostrzelnik decorated the interior with murals in the first half of the 16th century. These Renaissance paintings are complemented by 18th-century furnishings. The Baroque façade was added by Franz Moser as late as 1779–80. Other wall paintings in the church were made by Jan Bukowski in the early 20th century.

The Gothic cloister built in the time of Kazimierz the Great is the most beautiful part of the abbey. It leads to the Chapter House, which features murals painted in the 19th century by Michał Stachowicz. These illustrate scenes from the life of Wanda. Not far from the abbey is the Church of St Bartholomew. Built in 1466, it is one of the oldest timber churches in Poland.

⚑ Cistercian Church
Klasztorna 11. **Tel** 12 644 23 31.
Open 6am–7pm daily.

❸ Polish Aviation Museum

Al. Jana Pawła II 39. 🚌 502.
🚊 4, 5, 9, 10, 52. **Tel** 12 640 99 60.
Open 9am–5pm Tue–Sun. 🖼 free Tue. 📷 🆆 **muzeumlotnictwa.pl**

This museum is located on the historic Rakowice-Czyżyny airfield, one of the oldest military airfields in Europe (established in 1912) and the second largest in Poland prior to World War II. The museum has a modern central pavilion which features one of the best collections of early 20th-century aircraft. The collection consists of more than 200 aircraft, including pre-war Polish fighter planes, Spitfires, German Albatrosses and Soviet Kakaruzniks. Also in the museum are 22 rare aeroplanes that were once part of Hermann Göring's personal collection. In addition, there are several displays in neighbouring hangars and a large open-air section.

❹ Branice

12 km (7.5 miles) east from Krakow.
🚌 131. 🚆 10 to Pleszów terminus, then bus. Manor: Branice 131.

Branice is situated not far from Niepołomice and is worth visiting for its two manors which exemplify the small-scale residential architecture of the gentry of Lesser Poland. The Old Manor, later converted into a store, was built around 1603 for the Castellan of Żarnów, Jan Branicki, by an architect from the circle of Santi Gucci. The exterior of the manor is decorated with *sgraffiti* and topped with a parapet. The doors and fireplace inside are lavishly decorated with imaginative Mannerist ornaments carved in stone.

The New Manor was built in the early 19th century in Classical style. Its high hipped roof, and the entrance marked

The Renaissance Old Manor in Branice, one of two in the area

by a small portico supported by columns, make this building characteristic of Polish architecture of this type. Both manors are set in a picturesquely landscaped park, laid out in the 19th century.

Next to Branice is the village of Ruszcza with the Church of St George. The church was built around 1420 by the Royal Master of the Pantry, Wierzbięta of Branice. His Gothic memorial plaque and the Baroque high altar are both of interest.

❺ Niepołomice

24 km (15 miles) southeast of Krakow.
🚐 minibus from ul. Worcella opposite Galeria Krakowska.
Church: **Open** 7am–6pm daily.
Castle: **Tel** 12 281 30 11. **Open** May–Sep: 10am–6pm; Oct–Apr 10am–5pm. 🎟

The royal grounds in Niepołomice, situated on the outskirts of a vast woodland, were much favoured by Polish kings. They came here to rest and hunt, and developed magnificent buildings in the town they owned. The Gothic church in Niepołomice was founded by King Kazimierz the Great between 1350 and 1358. Like other sacred buildings founded by this sovereign, this church had two aisles separated by pillars.

It was later rebuilt in the Baroque style. Fragments of the rich stone decoration from the interior of the medieval church have survived and are displayed in the Old Sacristy. Outstanding Gothic paintings made between 1370 and 1375 by an Italian master, commissioned by Princess Elżbieta (daughter of Władysław the Short), are also in the Old Sacristy.

Next to the church are two mausolea of noble families, both in the form of chapels covered by domes. Built in 1596, the Branicki Chapel is the earlier of the two. It features an ornamental tomb made by the Italian architect

Façade of the castle in Niepołomice, a residence of Polish kings

and sculptor Santi Gucci in the Mannerist style. In the Chapel of the Lubomirski family, built in 1640, wall paintings depicting scenes from the life of St Carlo Borromeo are of interest. Late-Baroque altars were added in the 18th century.

The hunting lodge in Niepołomice was originally built by Kazimierz the Great. It was transformed by Zygmunt August into a magnificent residence. The new castle was constructed between 1550 and 1571. Its regular plan and the central, square courtyard differ from other royal Renaissance houses in Poland. In 1637 massive stone arcades were added to the courtyard. Part of the castle is used to house the Museum of Hunting.

The dense forest (Puszcza Niepołomicka), a favourite hunting ground of Polish kings, stretches right behind the town. Brown bears, bison, lynx, wildcat and deer are known to have inhabited it. The forest is not so magnificent as it used to be, though wild areas have been preserved, including the bison sanctuary in the Proszowo forest.

⑥ Podgórze

Immediately south of Kazimierz, on the opposite shore of the Vistula river, the gritty post-industrial suburb of Podgórze is a compelling destination for visitors. It was the site of a Jewish ghetto during World War II, and Jews from all over Krakow were crowded into its cramped streets before being transported to Auschwitz-Birkenau and elsewhere. Several sites in Podgórze and neighbouring Plaszów recall this period in Kraków's history, most notably the celebrated Schindler Factory (now a major museum), where Oskar Schindler saved over 1,000 Jews from inevitable death.

Part of an exhibition of life in Krakow during World War II, at the Schindler Factory

Oversized chair sculptures on plac Bohaterów Getta

☷ Plac Bohaterów Getta
Map 4 E2. 🚋 3, 19, 24.

This former market square was where Krakow's Jews unloaded their belongings and waited to be allocated accommodation in the Podgórze ghetto, which was established in March 1941. Two years later, they assembled here again, prior to their deportation to the camps. This history of traumatic arrivals and departures is marked in Piotr Lewicki and Kazimierz Łatak's installation of oversized iron chairs scattered across the square. The chairs serve as a reminder that when the ghetto was cleared in March 1943, bits of abandoned furniture were all that was left of Krakow's Jewish community.

🏛 Pharmacy Under the Eagle
Apteka pod Orłem
Plac Bohaterów Getta 18. **Map** 4 E3.
Tel 12 656 56 25. 🚋 3, 19, 24.
Open 10am–2pm Mon, 9am–5pm Tues–Sun. 🎟 (free Mon) 📷 🌐 mhk.pl

As the ghetto rose up around their pharmacy, gentiles Dr Tadeusz Pankiewicz and his

three assistants opted to stay behind; the pharmacy became a social hub and source of aid for the Jewish community. Now a small but fascinating museum, the pharmacy has been recreated to look as it did during the war. Multimedia displays, as well as photographs and personal effects hidden in drawers and cupboards, tell the devastating stories of those forced to live in the ghetto.

The façade of the Pharmacy Under the Eagle, on plac Bohaterów Getta

🏛 Schindler Factory
Fabryka Schindlera
ul. Lipowa 4. **Map** 4 F2. **Tel** 12 257 00 95. 🚋 3, 19, 24. **Open** Apr–Oct: 10am–4pm Mon, 9am–8pm Tues–Sun; Nov–Mar: 10am–2pm Mon, 10am–6pm Tue–Sun. 🎟 (free Mon) 📷 💻 🌐 mhk.pl

The Schindler Factory, located in the former industrial district of Zabłocie, will forever be associated with Oskar Schindler *(see p127)*. A German wartime industrialist, he protected local Jews by employing them in his factory, arguing that they were essential to his business. His story was popularized by Thomas Keneally's Booker Prize-winning novel *Schindler's Ark* and Steven Spielberg's 1993 film *Schindler's List*.

Part of the Historical Museum of Krakow, the factory hosts an exhibition entitled "Krakow Under Nazi Occupation 1939–45". Everyday life for Krakow's Jewish and Polish inhabitants – from the last pre-war summer of 1939 through the Nazi occupation until the arrival of the Red Army in January 1945 – is illustrated using original documents, radio and film recordings, photographs and multimedia installations. The fate of the Jewish population – incarcerated in the ghetto, exploited as slave labour, then transported to the death camps – is a major theme, though lives of other citizens are also covered in detail, notably the arrest and murder of prominent members of the city's intellectual and political elite. Poignant exhibits include Schindler's desk and a wall of photographs of those that Schindler saved.

🏛 Museum of Contemporary Art in Krakow (MOCAK)
Muzeum Sztuki Współczesnej Krakowie (MOCAK)
ul. Lipowa 4. **Map** 4 F2. **Tel** 12 263 40 00. 🚊 3, 19, 24. **Open** 11am–7pm Tues–Sun. 🅿 🔌 📷 **w** mocak.pl.

This energetic and constantly evolving institution has carved out an important place for itself in the city's cultural landscape since its opening in 2011. The building is a result of a remodelling of the Schindler Factory and features both intimate spaces and open galleries. The main exhibition halls display the cream of Polish contemporary art in minimalist, grey-concrete surroundings. Adjacent spaces host changing exhibitions by international artists.

🏛 Cricoteka
ul. Nadwiślańska 2–4. **Map** 4 E2. **Tel** 12 442 77 70. 🚊 3, 19, 24. **Open** 11am–7pm Tue–Sun. 🅿 ✏ 📷 **w** cricoteka.pl

Opened in 2014, this museum and research centre is dedicated to the work of Tadeusz Kantor (1915–1990), the artist and theatre director who founded the Cricot 2 theatre in 1955 *(see p85)*. Kantor created drama that was absurd, subversive, socially profound and hilariously funny, and went on to enjoy critical success at home and abroad. Stage props, costumes and a video archive of classic Cricot 2

performances are highlights of the museum.

The building is an attraction in itself, with a shimmering V-shaped structure hovering on stilts above a nineteenth-century electricity plant.

The foyer of the striking Cricoteka, located on the bank of the Vistula

Father Bernatek Bridge
Kładka Ojca Bernatka
ul. Mostowa to ul. Nadwiślańska. **Map** 4 D3. 🚊 3, 6, 8, 10, 13, 19, 24.

This graceful cycle- and foot-bridge, connecting the popular Kazimierz quarter with the less-visited south bank, opened in 2010. The bridge is named after Father Laetus Bernatek (1847–1927), a member of the order of Hospitallers of St John, who campaigned to build the first modern hospital in Kazimierz.

The bridge is popular with couples who celebrate their love by attaching a padlock to the railings and throwing the key into the river.

🏔 Krakus Mound
Kopiec Krakusa
ul. Franciszka Maryewskiego. **Map** 4 F4. 🚊 3, 6, 11, 13, 23, 24.

The southern limits of Podgórze are marked by the grassy, man-made hill known as Krakus Mound. Archaeologists believe it was raised in the 2nd–1st century BC for religious purposes, although popular folklore maintains that it is the burial mound of Krakow's legendary founder, King Krakus. There is an excellent view of central Krakow from the summit.

🏕 Płaszów Concentration Camp
Płaszów obóz koncentracyjny
ul. Jerozolimska. 🚊 3, 6, 11, 13, 23, 24.

Two kilometres southeast of plac Bohaterów Getta, an area of untended open parkland marks the spot of Płaszów concentration camp. Many of Krakow's Jews were subjected to forced labour here in 1942–4, and it was also the site of mass executions. Unlike other Holocaust sites, there are few memorials or markings for visitors. However, it is a deeply evocative site suited to quiet contemplation.

Sights at a Glance

0 metres   500
0 yards   500

For keys to symbols *see back flap*

The Chapel of St Kinga in Wieliczka salt mine

❼ Wieliczka

12 km (7.5 miles) southeast of Krakow. 🚐 Minibus from Krakow's Main Railway Station. 🚆 from Krakow's Main Railway Station and Krakow-Płaszów.

Southeast of Krakow is the town of Wieliczka, home to one of the region's most remarkable sights. The Wieliczka Salt Mine, a UNESCO-World Heritage Site, has been active as early as the 11th century, its salt regarded for years as a major natural asset of the Kingdom of Poland. Inside the mine is a vast network of underground galleries, tunnels, chambers and pits that have been carved into the salt blocks over the centuries. Salt was also used as a building material in the carving of vast underground chapels and altars in front of which the miners prayed for God's protection against accidents. Look out too for statues, also sculpted from the mine's salt blocks.

Visitors can descend to depths of 65–135 m (210–440 ft) and explore sections of the mines. Highlights include the Saltworks Museum, which is housed inside the mine, and a gallery of fascinating salt crystals. The exhibits on display in the museum illustrate old mining methods and the tools that were used. There is also a unique underground health resort, offering a range of subterranean therapies and physiotherapy activities.

Wieliczka Salt Mine

ul. Daniłowicza 10. **Tel** 12 278 73 02.
Open Apr–Oct: 7:30am–7:30pm daily;
Nov–Mar: 8am–5pm daily. **Closed**
1 Jan, Easter, 1 Nov, 24–25 & 31 Dec.
🏛️ 🚻 🏠 🖥️ 🆒 **kopalnia.pl**

The small chapel overhanging the mountain river in Ojców

❽ Ojców

24 km (15 miles) northwest of Krakow. 🚐 from Krakow's Main Coach Station.

The valley of the Prądnik river is the most beautiful part of the local uplands. The river eroded a deep gorge through the limestone. The steep cliffs are overgrown with trees through which stunning rock formations can be seen.

Kazimierz the Great had a number of hill-top castles built in the area to guard the western border of his Kingdom. The one in Ojców was one of the most important fortresses in Poland,

but only remnants have survived. The late 14th-century **Castle Tower** has been renovated and now houses a museum dedicated to the castle. In 1956 part of the Prądnik valley was transformed into the Ojców National Park.

After the discovery of the healing properties of the local springs in the mid-1800s, the village at the foot of the castle was transformed into a spa: therapy clinics were set up and luxurious hotels built. The Łokietek Hotel, once the most sumptuous of all the buildings, now houses the **Ojców National Park Museum**. During the Partition era, the Tsarist authorities denied planning permission for a church; as a result only a small timber chapel was built in 1901–2, overhanging the Prądnik river.

🏛️ Castle Tower

Open 13 Apr–11 Nov: from 10am; closing times vary.

🏛️ Ojców National Park Museum

Tel 12 389 20 40. **Open** May–Oct: 9am–4:30pm daily; Nov–Apr: 8am–2:45pm Mon–Fri.

❾ Grodzisko

28 km (17 miles) northwest of Krakow. 🚆 from Krakow's Main Railway Station.

Grodzisko is situated on the opposite bank of the Prądnik river from Ojców. The Convent of the Poor Clares was established here in 1262. Blessed Salomea, the sister of Duke Bolesław the Chaste, was the first Mother Superior. The nuns moved to Krakow

The altar of the Church of the Blessed Salomea in Grodzisko

in 1320 and the convent fell into ruin. The cult of the Blessed Salomea developed over time, and in 1677 Canon Sebastian Piskorski transformed Grodzisko into a sanctuary devoted to this pious nun. He designed a complex hermitage consisting of the small **Church of the Blessed Salomea** and a number of chapels enclosed within a wall. There are several charming Baroque touches, like the elephant bearing an obelisk, an idea borrowed from the Italian architect Bernini.

The beautiful maze garden in Pieskowa Skala Castle

🏛 **Church of the Blessed Salomea**
Open 9–10am Sun.

⑩ Pieskowa Skała

35 km (22 miles) northwest of Krakow. 🚌 from Krakow's Main Coach Station.

The **Pieskowa Skała Castle** was built by King Kazimierz the Great in the 14th century as part of the defence system on the Krakow-Częstochowa Uplands. It became private property in 1377.

Between 1542 and 1544, enlargement of the castle was undertaken by Stanisław Szafraniec and his wife, Anna Dębińska. The commission was probably given to the Italian architect Nicolo da Castiglione.

The castle houses a museum of the history of Polish interiors from medieval times to the 19th century. Some pieces of furniture, tapestries and decorative objects, as well as works of art, are on display.

🏛 **Pieskowa Skała Castle**
Tel 12 389 60 04. **Open** May–Sep: 9am–5pm Tue–Thu, 9am–1pm Fri, 10am–6pm Sat & Sun; Oct & Apr: 10am–4pm Fri, 9am–1pm Sat & Sun; Nov–Mar: pre-booked groups only. 🎟 free Wed. 🚻 📷 🚗
🌐 **pieskowaskala.eu**

⑪ Tyniec

10 km (6 miles) west of Krakow. 🚌 112. 🚊 12, 18, 22, 52 to Rondo Grunwaldzkie, then bus.

The picturesque **Benedictine Abbey** at Tyniec is situated on a rocky escarpment by the Vistula, west of Wawel. The monks were brought to Krakow in 1044, probably by King Kazimierz the Restorer. A Romanesque basilica was built here soon after. Only parts of the walls and a few architectural fragments of this basilica have survived. The new church and monastery were built in the 15th century. The church was remodelled in the early 17th century in the Baroque style, and magnificent stalls were added to the chancel. Large altars in black marble were made in the 18th century.

In the 12th and 13th centuries, during the period when Poland was fragmented into principal-ities, Tyniec was transformed into a fortress and played an important role during the struggles for the crown of the suzerain province of Krakow. By the end of the 16th century the fortifications were extended. A number of gates linked through an angled corridor were introduced as part of a defence system modelled on Wawel. Tyniec was a strategic site and as a result often came under attack.

🏛 **Benedictine Abbey**
Tel 12 688 54 50. **Open** May–Oct: 10am–6pm daily; Nov–Apr: 10am–4pm daily. 🚻 📷 🌐 **tyniec. benedyktyni.pl**

Benedictine Abbey in Tyniec on the Vistula

The Church of the Presentation of the Virgin Mary in Wadowice

⑫ Wadowice

40 km (25 miles) southwest of Krakow.
🚌 from Krakow's Main Coach Station.
Family House of John Paul II: **Tel** 033
823 2662. **Open** daily. May–Sep:
9am–7pm; Nov–Mar: 9am– 2:30pm;
Apr & Oct: 9am–6pm.

Wadowice was first recorded
in 1327, but the town came to
international attention in 1978
when Karol Wojtyła, born here
on 18 May 1920, was elected
Pope. Almost immediately the
town became a place of mass
pilgrimage and the local sites
associated with the Pope include
the Baroque Church of the
Presentation of the Virgin Mary
in Market Square, where he was
baptised, and his family home,
which now houses a museum
dedicated to the pontiff.
Another site associated with
John Paul II is the monumental
votive Church of St Peter the
Arch-shepherd which was built
on the outskirts of Wadowice
in thanksgiving for the Pope's

survival of an assassination
attempt on 13 May 1981.
Designed by Ewa Węcławowicz-
Gyurkovich and Jacek
Gyurkovich, the walls of its
nave seem to give way under
the power of light, symbolizing
the triumph of good over evil.
The town has had a chequered
history, especially in the last
century. While under German
occupation during World War II,
it was renamed Frauenstadt and
the entire Jewish population
was either executed on the
spot or sent to nearby
Auschwitz (see below).
Wadowice has since been
growing as a tourist centre,
replacing the local industries,
which collapsed in the newly
free-market economy during
the 1990s.

⑬ Auschwitz
(Oświęcim)

See pp164–7.

⑭ Kalwaria
Zebrzydowska

30 km (19 miles) sw of Krakow.
🚌 from Main Coach Station.
🚆 from Krakow's Main Railway
Station, change at Krakow-Płaszów.
Bernardine Church: **Open** 6am–
7pm daily.

Calavaries, or Ways of the
Cross, were introduced in
the 16th century and were
built throughout Europe to
commemorate the Passion
and Death of Christ. The land-
scaping of Calvary grounds
had to imitate the topography
of Jerusalem. They consisted
of structures commemorating
the "tragedy of Salvation" and
imitations of holy sites connected to the Virgin Mary.
Poland's first Calvary was
built by Mikołaj Zebrzydowski
from 1600 onwards. He located
the chapels representing the
Stations of the Cross along
Christ's route to Golgotha
on the Żary Hill near his
residence in Zebrzydowice.
Mystery plays enacting
Christ's Passion are staged in
Kalwaria during Holy Week.
The "funeral of the Virgin"
takes place on the feast of
the Assumption. Crowds of
pilgrims arrive to venerate the
miraculous icon of the Mother
of God, whose cult in the
Bernardine Church goes back
to the 17th century. Kalwaria
is one of the main religious
centres in Lesser Poland.

The Baroque façade of the early
17th-century Bernardine Church in
Kalwaria Zebrzydowska

Kalwaria Zebrzydowska

The most interesting chapels in the Kalwaria Zebrzydowska are those designed by Paulus Baudarth, a Flemish architect and goldsmith. He was commissioned to design many chapels, and avoiding repetition must have been a difficult task. He applied many different ground-plans, including a Greek cross, a circle and even a triangle. In some chapels he resorted to truly Baroque ideas, and based the plans on the shape of a heart or rose.

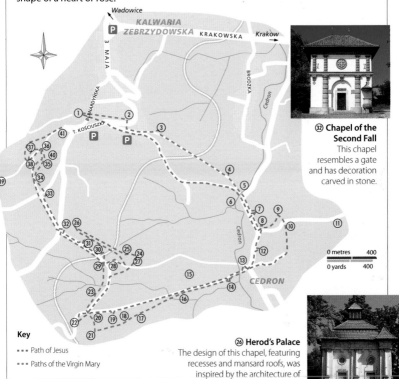

㉜ Chapel of the Second Fall
This chapel resembles a gate and has decoration carved in stone.

㉖ Herod's Palace
The design of this chapel, featuring recesses and mansard roofs, was inspired by the architecture of old Polish manors.

Key
- - - Path of Jesus
- - - Paths of the Virgin Mary

Sights on the Way of the Cross

① St Raphael's Chapel
② Chapel of the Throne
③ Chapel of the Joyful Patriarchs
④ Chapel of the Triumphant Apostles
⑤ Chapel of St John Nepomuk
⑥ Bridge of Angels
⑦ Chapel of Farewell
⑧ Church of the Sepulchre of the Virgin Mary
⑨ Gethsemane
⑩ Chapel of the Arrest of Christ
⑪ Church of the Ascension
⑫ Jewish Chapel
⑬ Bridge over the Cedron
⑭ East Gate
⑮ Bethsaida
⑯ Apostles' Chapel
⑰ Chapel of the Veneration of the Soul of the Virgin
⑱ Angels' Chapel
⑲ House of Annas
⑳ The Cenacle
㉑ House of Mary
㉒ House of Caiaphas
㉓ Chapel of the Fainting Virgin
㉔ Pilate's Town Hall
㉕ The Holy Steps
㉖ Herod's Palace
㉗ Chapel of the Taking up of the Cross
㉘ Chapel of the First Fall
㉙ Chapel of the Heart of Mary
㉚ Chapel of Simon of Cyrene
㉛ St Veronica's Chapel
㉜ Chapel of the Second Fall
㉝ Chapel of the Sorrowful Women
㉞ Chapel of the Third Fall
㉟ Chapel of the Stripping of Christ
㊱ Church of the Crucifixion
㊲ Chapel of the Anointment
㊳ Chapel of the Holy Sepulchre
㊴ Hermitage of St Mary Magdalene
㊵ Hermitage of St Helen
㊶ Chapel of the Madonna of Sorrows

⑬ Auschwitz I

For most people, Auschwitz represents the ultimate horror of Hitler's war. Over 1.1 million people died here between 1940 and 1945, 90 percent of whom were Jews. Auschwitz began as a camp for Polish political prisoners, many of whom died of malnourishment, overwork or torture. It subsequently became a camp for Soviet prisoners of war, who were similarly mistreated. From 1942 onwards, the subsidiary Auschwitz-Birkenau camp was built to deal with the vast numbers of Jews brought to be murdered as part of the Nazi's Final Solution. Auschwitz is now a UNESCO World Heritage site.

Exhibitions
The daily horrors of life in the camp are today displayed in some of the barracks.

The Camp

Auschwitz I opened in 1940 on the site of former Polish army barracks. Originally built to incarcerate Polish political prisoners, further buildings were added in the spring of 1941 as the number of prisoners dramatically increased. Camp administration was also based at Auschwitz I.

0 metres   100
0 yards   100

Gas Chambers and Crematoria
The entire Auschwitz complex had seven gas chambers and five crematoria. Six of the gas chambers were in Birkenau but the first was at Auschwitz, operating from 1941.

The Two Camps

Though part of the same camp complex, Auschwitz and Birkenau are in fact 3 km (2 miles) apart, on the western suburbs of the bustling town of Oświęcim (Auschwitz in German). Birkenau was opened in March 1942 in the village of Brzezinka, where the residents were evicted to make way for the camp. There were an additional 47 sub-camps in the surrounding area.

Aerial view of the complex taken by the Allies in 1944. The yellow dotted line marks Birkenau; the blue shows Auschwitz I.

KEY

① **SS Guard house and office of the camp supervisor**

② **"Arbeit Macht Frei" entrance**: the words above the infamous entrance to Auschwitz translate as "Work makes you free". This was certainly not the case for the prisoners transported here, who were often worked to death.

③ **Block 11 was the central jail** that housed prisoners from all over the camp complex.

④ **Store containing the poison, Zyklon B**, first used at Auschwitz to kill prisoners.

⑤ **Camp kitchen**

⑥ **Present-day Information Centre for visitors**

The "Wall of Death"
This is a reconstruction of the wall near Block 11 used for the summary executions by shooting. Usually covered in flowers, it now serves as a place of remembrance.

VISITORS' CHECKLIST

Practical Information
Oświęcim. **Road map** D5. **Tel** 33 844 81 00. W **auschwitz.org**
Open Feb: 7:30am–4pm; Mar & Oct: 7:30am–5pm; Apr, May, Sep: 7:30am–6pm; Jun, Jul, Aug: 7:30am–7pm; Nov & Jan: 7:30am–3pm; Dec: 7:30am–2pm. **Closed** 1 Jan, Easter Day, 25 Dec. Call to arrange, or check website for details.

Transport
Bus to Auschwitz from Krakow Bus Station; bus to Birkenau from Information Centre.

Maksymilian Kolbe
The camp jail, in Block 11, was used for those who broke camp rules. Few emerged alive. Father Kolbe *(see p37)* died here after sacrificing his life for another inmate's.

Roll Call Square
Roll call took place up to three times a day and could last for hours. Eventually, due to the increasing numbers of prisoners, roll call was taken in front of individual barracks.

1939 1 Sep, Hitler invades Poland.	**1940** First deportation of German Jews into Nazi-occupied Poland.	**1941** First gas chamber goes into operation.	**1942** The implementation of the Final Solution is agreed at the Wannsee Conference and mass deportation to Auschwitz begins.		**1944** As the Soviet Army closes in, the SS begin destroying all evidence of the camp.	**1945** 27 Jan, Soviet soldiers liberate the few remaining prisoners at Auschwitz.
1939	**1940**	**1941**	**1942**	**1943**	**1944**	**1945**
	1940 Oświęcim chosen as the site of the Nazis' new concentration camp.	**1941** Himmler makes first visit to Auschwitz and orders its expansion.	**1942** First section of Birkenau camp completed.	**1943** Four gas chambers built for mass murder.	**1945** 18 Jan, 56,000 prisoners evacuated on "Death March".	**1945** 7 May, Germany surrenders to the Allies.

Auschwitz II–Birkenau

Birkenau was primarily a place of execution. Most of Auschwitz's machinery of murder was housed here. In the six gas chambers in use at different stages of the camp's construction, over one million people were killed, 98% of whom were Jewish. Victims included people from over 20 nations. Birkenau was also an enormous concentration camp, housing 90,000 slave labourers by mid-1944 and providing labour for many of the factories and farms of southwestern, Nazi-occupied Poland. The gas chambers were quickly destroyed by the Nazis shortly before the Soviet Army arrived in January 1945.

Hell's Gate
In 1944 the numbers arriving began to increase dramatically. A rail line was extended into the camp. The entrance gate through which the trains passed was known as "Hell's Gate".

Visiting Birkenau
There is little left of the camp's buildings today; its main purpose is for remembrance. Most visitors come to pay their respects at the Monument to the Victims of the Camp, near the site of the gas chambers.

The Unloading Ramp
Arriving at the ramp was a terrifying experience It was here that SS officers separated the men from the women and children, and the SS doctors declared who was fit for work. Those declared unfit (as many as 70 or 80 per cent) were taken immediately to their death.

The Camp

Birkenau was the largest camp in Nazi-occupied Europe. In 1944 it had more than 90,000 prisoners, the majority of whom were murdered or taken on forced marches to other camps. From the unloading ramp to the gas chambers, the crematoria to the ash dumping grounds, the whole process of murder was carried out systematically and on an enormous scale. This reconstruction shows the camp at its peak in 1944, when as many as 5,000 people could be killed every day.

The Liberation of the Camps

With the war all but lost, in mid-January 1945 the Nazi authorities gave the order for all the camps to be destroyed. Such was the speed of the collapse of the German army, however, that only part of Birkenau was destroyed. Between 17–21 January more than 56,000 inmates were evacuated by the Nazis and forced to march west; many died en route. When the Soviet army entered the camps on 27 January 1945, they found just 7,000 survivors.

Survivors of Auschwitz II-Birkenau, filmed by Soviet troops

Kanada

"Kanada" was the nickname of the barracks where property stolen from prisoners was stored. It was the preferred place to work at Auschwitz II-Birkenau as it offered opportunities to inmates to pilfer items to barter for food or medicine later.

The Sauna

New arrivals selected for work were deloused and disinfected in this building, which became known as the "sauna". Periodic disinfections of existing prisoners were also carried out here.

| 0 metres | | 200 |
| 0 yards | | 200 |

The Ash Pond

Tons of ash – the remains of hundreds of thousands of Auschwitz victims – were dumped in ponds and troughs dug around the outskirts of the camp.

KEY

① **Towers and barbed wire** isolated the camps from the outside world.

② **Large gas chambers and crematoria** (from 1943)

③ **Area of expansion**, nicknamed "Mexico", never completed.

④ **Wooden barracks**, with 500–600 people living in each.

⑤ **Hell's Gate**

Barracks

The conditions of the living quarters at the camps were terrible. With little or no sanitation, poor nutrition and no medical care, diseases such as typhus spread rapidly. This image shows a typical wooden barracks at Birkenau shortly after liberation.

A Two-Hour Walk around Planty

The Planty green belt in Krakow has replaced the city's medieval fortifications, built between the late 13th and 15th centuries. They were demolished early in the 19th century and the small stretch of wall by Floriańska Street is the only fragment to have survived. The gardens of Planty were landscaped to include a network of radiating lanes and beautiful vistas. In the second half of the 19th century the well-kept Planty became a popular venue for socializing. After a period of regeneration the Planty now features period fencing, benches and street lamps.

Wawel to the University

The walk begins by the Coat of Arms Gate at Wawel. Walk downhill and cross the street to enter the so-called Wawel gardens. The Gothic Revival Seminary building will be on your right, and a sculpture depicting an owl can be seen on your left ①.

Continue down through the park some 40 m (130 ft) towards a little square decorated with a statue of the renowned translator of French literature into Polish, Tadeusz Boy-Żeleński, carved by Edward Krzak ②. Turn right and after some 50 m (165 ft) you will reach the wall enclosing the gardens of the Archaeological Museum (see p85). Mounted in the wall are small plaques, overrun with greenery, commemorating the contributions made by the honorary Committee for the Renovation of Krakow's Monuments.

Carry straight on and cross Poselska Street. Those interested in archaeology may turn right to visit the museum. On the other side of the street is a plinth indicating the site of one of many medieval towers that formed part of the defence wall. The outline of the wall is marked by sandstones which you can see positioned along the lanes. Take a sharp left turn and walk

down 20 m (65 ft) to a little square where, hidden behind trees, is a statue made in 1884 of Grażyna and Litawor ③, two characters from a poem by Adam Mickiewicz.

From this statue, take a right turn to return to the main lane. You will notice the buildings of the Franciscan Church (see pp86–7) and the Episcopal Palace (see p106). Go straight ahead and cross Franciszkańska Street to enter the University Gardens. Walk down the main lane along the wall of the Episcopal Palace, passing by the end of Wiślna Street. Some 150 m (492 ft) further down, by Jagiellońska Street, is an 18th-century statue of the Virgin Mary of Grace ④, which originally was in the graveyard of the Church of St Mary. After another 40 m (130 ft), you may choose to rest, looking at the Kościuszko Mound which can be seen through Józefa Piłsudskiego Street in the distance. Then carry on, passing by the façade of the Collegium Novum, the main university building. An oak planted in 1918, known as the Oak of Liberty, can be seen in front of the college. A red-brick paved

One of many fountains in the Planty gardens

① Owl (1964) by Bronisław Chromy

0 metres 300
0 yards 300

pattern in the square imitates the curves of Copernicus's astrolabe. The statue of the astronomer ⑤ *(see p106)*, surrounded by trees, is to the left of Collegium Novum and in front of the Witkowski College. Further down, you will pass by the Collegium Nowodvorianum *(see pp106–7)* and after some 50 m (165 ft) cross St Anne's Street. The university Church of St Anne *(see pp110–11)* will be on your right.

Planty in autumn, with visitors strolling along a path

beautiful statue of Artur Grottger ⑥ made in 1901 by Wacław Szymanowski. Cross St Thomas's Street (ulica św. Tomasza) and after some 300 m (985 ft) turn left. In this "corner" of the Planty is the statue of Lilla Veneda ⑦, the leading character in a play by Juliusz Słowacki. Walk some 200 m (655 ft) down one of the lanes which run alongside Basztowa Street. The next monument you will notice is that of Queen Jadwiga and King Władysław Jagiełło ⑧. It was raised to commemorate the fifth centenary of the union between Poland and Lithuania in 1386. After crossing Sławkowska Street, you will find on your left a large pond where in summer swans can be seen. You can cross a little bridge over the pond and this will lead you to a statue of the Harpist ⑨. Continue down the main lane. Pass by the remains of the defence wall with St Florian's Gate *(see p113)* to finally reach the Barbican *(see p116)*.

⑦ Statue of Lilla Veneda by Alfred Daun

Krakow's Main Railway Station to Stradom

Walk some 300 m (985 ft) through the so-called Station Gardens. The major attractions here are the Słowacki Theatre *(see p117)* and the Church of the Holy Cross *(see p117)*.

Continue to the subway entrance by which the Straszewski Obelisk ⑩ is located. Florian Straszewski was the man who laid out Planty. Behind the Church of the Holy Cross is a statue of the playwright Michał Bałucki ⑪. Walk another 300 m (985 ft) cross Mikołajska Street to enter the "Na gródku" Gardens. The Church of the Dominican Nuns *(see p117)* will be on your right. Continue down the lane and cross Sienna Street. The Dominican Church *(see pp118–19)* will be on your right. You will pass by an unusual statue of Colonel Narcyz Wiatr-Zawojny ⑫, who was shot dead in 1946 by the secret police (UB). The statue was made in 1992 by Bronisław Chromy. Stroll another 500 m (0.3 mile) downhill to enter the so-called Stradom Gardens and the end of the walk.

Tips for Walkers

Starting point: At the foot of Wawel, by Kanonicza Street.
Length: approx. 5 km (3 miles).
Getting there: Bus No. 504 (the nearest stop is by Straszewskiego Street), or tram Nos. 6, 8, 10, 13 and 18 to Wawel.
Stopping-off points: Café at the Bunker of Art near the Collegium Novum. There are benches throughout the park.

KEY TO MAP LABELS:
⑨
BASZTOWA
PIJARSKA
SZPITALNA
ⓘ ⑩
PLAC ŚW. DUCHA
⑪
FLORIAŃSKA
SZPITALNA
ŚW. MARKA
ŚW. TOMASZA
ŚW. KRZYŻA
Planty
WESTERPLATTE
MIKOŁAJSKA
MAŁY RYNEK
SIENNA
NA GRÓDKU
⑫
DOMINIKAŃSKA
ŚW. GERTRUDY

Key

••• Walk route

Palace of Art to the Barbican

Continue some 100 m (330 ft) and cross Szewska Street. The Bunker of Art *(see p107)* will be on your right. A little further down, some 20 m (65 ft) after crossing Szczepańska Street, continue to walk down the Planty's main lane. You will pass a little square where you will see the Palace of Art *(see p107)* on the right, while on your left will be a most

A One-Hour Walk around Zwierzyniec

In the 12th century Zwierzyniec was a small village, founded as the endowment to the Premonstratensian nuns, whose convent was located by the Rudawa river, a tributary of the Vistula. Polish sovereigns used to take a rest in the royal gardens located in this village. Henri de Valois is reputed to have organized orgies here to the outrage of his subjects. The richest Krakovians followed in the kings' footsteps by establishing their country residences in Zwierzyniec. Despite being incorporated into Krakow in the early 20th century, Zwierzyniec has managed to retain its original village character.

⑤ Salwator Cemetery

② Altar in St Margaret's Chapel

Salwator

After arriving at the tram terminus, walk to the Church of the Premonstratensian Nuns ①. The church was founded in the second half of the 12th century but its appearance today is a result of a remodelling undertaken between 1595 and 1638. The Neo-Classical decoration of the choir is most interesting. It was created between 1775 and 1779 to designs by Sebastian Sierakowski. The convent building next to the church is one of the largest in Poland. It is worth visiting for its courtyard. After leaving the church, go up

the chapel. The Church of the Holy Redeemer ③ is further uphill. According to Polish chroniclers, it was built immediately after

the steep Św. Bronisławy Street. The Chapel of St Margaret ②, built in 1690, will be on your left. Those who died of the plague were buried by

0 metres 300
0 yards 300

Key

••• Walk route

The Kościuszko Mound, a monument to Tadeusz Kościuszko

Poland had accepted Christianity in 966, by Duke Mieszko I. The duke presented the church with a miraculous crucifix. Evidence shows, however, that the church was actually constructed later and consecrated in 1148. Despite extensive remodelling, the church has retained much of its Romanesque character. An interesting painting of 1605 by Kasper Kurch depicts a most unusual scene of the crucified Christ shaking off his shoe in order to pass it to a poor fiddler playing under the Cross. A 17th-century pulpit has also survived by the church, as well as a number of interesting tombs from the first half of the 19th century.

A residential estate ④ established in the early 20th century is located near the church. Its Art Nouveau architecture is worth seeing.

Salwator Cemetery

Walk down Anczyca Street and turn right into Aleja Jerzego Waszyngtona

(Washington Avenue). The small Salwator Cemetery ⑤ consecrated in 1865 is located on the outskirts of the Salwator estate. A chapel, built in 1888 to 1889 in the Neo-Gothic style to a design by architect Sebastian Jaworzyński can be seen in the middle of the cemetery. A great number of tombs of those who made important contributions to Polish culture can be found here.

Kościuszko Mound

The tree-lined Aleja Jerzego Waszyngtona will lead you to the Kościuszko Mound on Sikornik Hill. At its foot, the Chapel of St Bronisława ⑥ marks the site of the hermitage of the eponymous nun. The chapel was built between 1856 and 1861 by Feliks Księżarski in the Neo-Gothic style. The Kościuszko Mound ⑦ was

⑥ Chapel of the St Bronisława at the foot of the Kościuszko Mound

erected between 1820 and 1823 to commemorate the leader of the insurrection of 1794. This monument to the hero in the struggle for Polish independence was inspired by the mounds of two mythical Polish rulers, Krak and Wanda, which are located in the environs of Krakow. The construction of the mound became a patriotic endeavour and the monument itself a destination for national pilgrimages arriving in Krakow. Fortifications ⑧ at the foot of the Kościuszko Mound were constructed after 1850 by the Austrians as part of a project which aimed to transform Krakow into a massive fortress. The fortress is currently used as a café-restaurant and houses the popular RMF FM radio station. A bus stop, which serves the city centre, is situated by the entrance to the hotel.

KRÓLOWEJ JADWIGI
PANORAMICZNA
EMAUS
SALWATORSKA
MIAKOWÓW
KASZTELANSKA
SENATORSKA
JERZEGO WASZYNGTONA
L. ANCZYCA
④
③
ŚW. BRONISŁAWY
②
GONTYNA
①
UKRYTA
KSIĘCIA JÓZEFA
Vistula

① Church and Convent of the Premonstratensian Nuns at Salwator

Tips for Walkers

Starting point: The Salwator tram terminus.

Length: 2.5 km (1.6 miles). Getting there: The walk starts from the tram depot in Salwator. You can get there by tram Nos. 1, 2 and 6. Return by bus No. 100 which stops at the foot of the Kościuszko Mound.

Stopping-off points: Benches to relax can be found on Aleja Jerzego Waszyngtona. Pod Kopcem restaurant, near the foot of the mound, has a terrace café.

For keys to symbols *see back flap*

A Walk in Las Wolski

Las Wolski (the Wolski Wood) is the largest green area in Krakow. It has partly retained its original character as a forest, while the remaining ground is maintained as a park. Paths and lanes wind up and down this hilly terrain, leading to many spots of outstanding beauty, both natural and man-made. The lovely architecture of the Camaldolese Monastery and Decius Villa, both on the outskirts of the park, are worth exploring. The walk route described below includes sights in the Wolski Wood and the surrounding neighbourhood.

The park by the Decius Villa

① Entrance to the Camaldolese Monastery

Srebrna Góra (Silver Mount)
The walk begins at the bus stop at the intersection of Aleja Wędrowników (Wędrowników Avenue) and Księcia Józefa Street. Walk some 500 m (0.3 mile) down Aleja Wędrowników then turn right into Aleja Konarowa (Konarowa Avenue).

Climb up the Silver Mount to visit the Camaldolese Monastery ①. The monastery of this strict Reformed Benedictine order was built between 1605 and 1642 by two outstanding architects, Valentin of Säbisch and Andrea Spezza, among others. The stone-clad façade of the church is particularly impressive. The austerity of the interior is in striking contrast with the lavishness of the decoration of the chapels, which feature stuccowork by Giovanni Falconi. The so-called Royal Chapel, dating from 1633 to 1636, is very beautiful. The stairs on either side of the high altar lead down to the crypt which houses a catacomb. This subterranean gallery has recesses excavated in the sides for tombs of the deceased monks. Next to the catacomb is the *ossuarium*, a common grave containing bones removed from the recesses in the catacomb. The hermitages are closed to visitors but can be seen from the ossuary chapel.

Women are allowed into the church on a few festive days only.

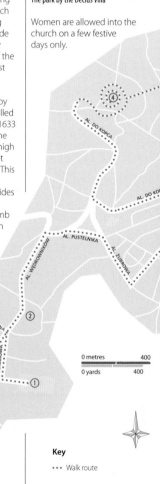

② The Wolski Wood, a favourite place for walks

Key

••• Walk route

0 metres 400
0 yards 400

Wolski Wood (Las Wolski)

Leave the monastery by Aleja Konarowa (Konarowa Avenue), the same route by which you arrived, then turn right into Wędrowników Avenue which is the main lane of Wolski Wood ②. This wood was transformed into a public park in 1917 through the efforts of Juliusz Leo, the President of the City of Krakow. Turn right again into a path which leads to Aleja Żubrowa (Bison Avenue). After a few minutes' walk the entrance to the zoo ③ will be in front of you. The zoo was established in 1929. It differs from other zoological gardens owing to its location in the middle of a forest. Leave the zoo via Al Do Kopca (Towards the Mound Avenue) which will take you to the Marshal Piłsudski Mound ④ on top of Sowiniec Mount. The mound was constructed between 1934 and 1936 as a monument commemorating the Poles who fell during the long struggle for independence from the three powers that partitioned Poland between 1772 and 1918. The mound is called "a Tomb of Tombs" and contains ashes from many battlefields. Walk down the mound and continue along Aleja Panieńskich Skał (Virgin Rocks Avenue) toward the Sanctuary of the Virgin Rocks ⑤ where you will find picturesque limestone formations. According to a legend, this was the place where the Premonstratensian nuns of Zwierzyniec took refuge and hid from the Tatars. A 16th-century timber church ⑥ at the end of the avenue was moved here from Komorowice.

Wola Justowska

Continue walking along Aleja Panieńskich Skał and turn right at the T-junction into Aleja Kasztanowa (Chestnut Avenue).

⑤ A statue of the Virgin in Panieńskich Skał

Wola Justowska, a fashionable district of Krakow, begins here. Carry on until you see the Decius Villa (Willa Decjusza) ⑦ ahead. Justus Decius was Secretary to King Zygmunt the Old. In 1530 he transformed a late-Gothic manor, dating from the 15th century, into a Renaissance residence. The villa was extended in the first half of the 17th century and a loggia added, offering a view over the area. The villa houses the European Academy, which is dedicated to the study of European cultural heritage. A nearby bus stop serves the city centre.

Tips for Walkers

Starting point: The bus stop at the intersection of Księcia Józefa Street with Wędrowników Street.
Getting there: Bus routes 109, 209, 229, 239 and 269 will take you to Srebrna Góra. Take bus 134 by the entrance to the zoo or bus routes 102, 134, 152 and 192 from Wola Justowska to return to the city centre.
Stopping-off points: There are benches to relax on throughout the Wolski Wood. Restaurants are at the foot of Srebrna Góra and near the zoo and there is a café in the Villa of Decius.
Note: Women are only permitted into the Camaldolese Church on 7 Feb, 25 Mar, Easter Sun, Whit Sun; Whit Mon, Corpus Christi; 19 Jun, Sun after 19 Jun, 15 Aug, 8 Sep, 8 Dec and 25 Dec.

⑦ A suburban residence known as the Villa of Decius

For keys to symbols *see back flap*

TRAVELLERS' NEEDS

WHERE TO STAY

Krakow is home to some of Poland's best hotels. Besides the big international names, such as Radisson Blu and Sheraton, visitors will also find many independent hotels famed for their architecture, for traditions extending back to the 19th century, and for their *fin-de-siècle* atmosphere. The best of these have managed to recapture the magnificence that was lost during the period of Communist rule. Many of the hotels in the older parts of the city have been renovated, and new establishments have sprung up on the city's fringes and around the river. The number of backpacker hostels has also mushroomed, ensuring that there is a broad choice of accommodation for all budgets. Visitors can still expect to pay a premium for an Old Quarter location, but the competition helps keep prices in check. From all the hotels in Krakow, this section highlights some of the best; they have been listed according to theme, location and price on pages 182–5.

Where to Look

Most of Krakow's hotels are located in the Old Quarter, near the main Market Square; in the former Jewish district of Kazimierz; and in the city-centre districts that surround these two areas. All of these districts are within walking distance of each other, and finding accommodation that is close to the action is never too difficult. Accommodation located outside these central areas is usually linked to the centre by reasonably swift bus or tram services; there are no parts of Krakow where visitors will feel isolated or cut off.

Elegant, flower-filled room at the Polski Hotel Pod Białym Orłem *(see p182)*

Hotels

Krakow is one of the most atmospheric places to stay in the whole of Central Europe. The city boasts an impressive number of historic, mostly 19th-century hotels, especially grand old establishments like Pod Różą, Pollera and Elektor *(see p182)*, which have preserved the decor and atmosphere of the belle époque. There are also many luxury hotels – notably Copernicus *(see p184)*, Stary *(see p185)* and Pałac Bonerowski *(see p184)* – that have made good use of old buildings, adapting medieval and Renaissance town houses to the needs of the modern hospitality industry, while leaving much of the original exposed-brick and stone features intact. Modern five-star chains such as Radisson Blu and Sheraton are also present in Krakow, alongside many of the more budget-oriented chains such as Ibis, Best Western, Novotel and Campanile. Recent years have seen the emergence of a breed of boutique and design hotels, such as Pugetów and andel's *(see p184)*, that aim to make best use of the local artistic traditions; and there is also a healthy quantity of B&Bs, offering charming, characterful and informal accommodation in the heart of the city.

Making a Reservation

Most of Krakow's hotels, apartments and hostels are featured on international booking sites such as **Booking.com, Airbnb**

Neo-Classical building housing the Fortuna B&B *(see p183)*

◄ The lively Main Market Square (Rynek Glowny) in Krakow

and **Hostelworld**. Reservations can also be made by contacting the establishment directly by phone or email. Early booking is advisable for most of Krakow's hotels, especially during high summer, when finding vacancies may be quite a challenge. Peak times are July and August, the period around the May Day public holiday and New Year's Eve. However, it is worth noting that the tourist season lasts all year round, and only autumn and winter see a decline in the number of tourists. Krakow also sees a constant flow of international conferences, meetings and festivals. Finding a hotel on arrival may prove difficult at any time.

Communal lounge area at the Metropolitan Boutique Hotel *(see p185)*

Facilities

Most hotels offer ensuite rooms with satellite or cable television. Many international channels come with their Polish-dubbed versions, although with a bit of channel-surfing you will be able to find a couple of international alternatives. Usually a selection of English-language news channels are available, along with German and a few other major languages. The provision of Wi-Fi Internet access is also pretty standard throughout the Polish hotel industry. Even in the better hotels, bathrooms may feature a shower rather than a bathtub, so if you specifically want a bathtub, you should enquire about this when booking. Many hotels in Krakow supply an electric kettle in the room, together with modest supplies of tea, coffee and sugar. Rooms in the more expensive hotels may have a mini-bar, 24-hour room service and laundry service; some hotels have facilities such as business centres with computers and printers. Fitness facilities are increasingly common, but only a handful of hotels in the luxury bracket offer spas or swimming pools. Tourist information is sometimes available at the reception desk, as well as ticket booking facilities for various events.

Check-out time is generally noon, but luggage can usually be left at reception. Hotel personnel frequently speak both English and German.

Discounts

Hotels often advertise rate cuts and budget specials on Internet booking sites. In general, prices tend to fluctuate according to the season, and most hotels in Krakow reduce their prices in autumn and winter. Throughout the year, business and conference hotels, which are often full on weekdays, usually reduce their prices at weekends. You can use Internet booking sites to compare prices and look for special offers. There are not many single-bed hotel rooms available for solo travellers, so negotiate a discount when offered a double room for single use.

Swimming pool at the contemporary Galaxy hotel *(see p183)*

Wherever you are thinking of staying, it is always worth asking for a discount, and you stand a good chance of getting one if you are planning a longer stay.

Hidden Extras

In accordance with Polish law, the prices quoted or displayed in hotels have to include tax and service. In most places, they also include breakfast, but this is not always the case, so check in advance. Telephone calls from hotel rooms are never included, and they are far more expensive than elsewhere.

Although free Wi-Fi Internet access is increasingly standard in the hospitality industry, some hotels (mostly in the business category) may charge for this service; again, it is wise to ask in advance.

Despite these hidden extra costs, Polish hospitality almost always extends to providing guests with a free supply of mineral water. Regardless of the standard of hotel, a fresh bottle of sparkling water is usually left in your room every day. As a rule, if it is not in the mini-bar, it is free.

Tips are not offered to hotel staff, except at the most exclusive hotels where it is customary to offer 10 per cent. You may, however, choose to give less depending on the service you have received. Be aware that saying "thank you" when paying a bill is automatically taken to mean "keep the change".

Travelling with Children

Children are welcome everywhere in Poland. Most hotels offer additional beds for children, and usually no extra charge is made for this as long as the child is under the age of seven or eight. However, check that this is the case when making your reservation.

In hotel restaurants there should be no problem in ordering children's portions, and most places also have high chairs. Only the very best hotels offer baby-sitting facilities as part of their service.

Disabled Travellers

As a general rule, all newly built hotels and guesthouses in Krakow include one or two rooms for disabled travellers. A lot of older hotels, especially those in the luxury bracket, have also updated their facilities for disabled guests. However, be aware that many older hotels, especially those in the Old Quarter, which have no space for lifts, remain devoid of any facilities for the disabled. It is advisable to contact the hotel beforehand to check which facilities for the disabled they have. Also, bear in mind that hotels only have a small number of rooms for disabled travellers and they usually sell out much faster than the regular rooms, so advance booking is recommended.

Brightly coloured room at the Secret Garden Hostel *(see p185)*

Cheerful decor in the communal lounge at the Flamingo Hostel *(see p185)*

Rooms and Apartments to Let

Many rooms and apartments in Krakow are rented out to tourists for short- or long-term stays. Accommodation of this type can be found in all areas of the city. Apartments in the Old Quarter are often located in beautifully renovated old buildings and are usually more expensive than those further out. Apartments tend to have a fully equipped kitchenette and a TV; most also have Wi-Fi access. Some of the more expensive apartments are cleaned daily or every few days.

Rooms and apartments are often rented out directly by the owner via accommodation websites such as Booking.com or Airbnb. A number of agents, such as **Krakow Apartments**, **Old City Apartments** and **Sodispar**, rent out holiday apartments in central locations.

B&Bs

There is a small but growing number of bed-and-breakfasts in Krakow, catering for travellers who want something a bit more informal than the average hotel, with the added benefit of friendly and helpful hosts. Krakow's B&Bs tend to have a bit more character than contemporary hotels, frequently featuring homely decor that is in keeping with the often very old buildings in which they are situated. Some of the more characterful B&Bs in Krakow include La Fontaine, Tango House, Wielopole, Klezmer-Hois

and Kolory *(see p183)*. Be aware that rooms might be on the small side. While most B&Bs offer rooms with ensuite bathrooms, some will offer a mixture of ensuite rooms and rooms with shared facilities. Some B&Bs will have someone at reception 24 hours a day, while others may be staffed only at specific daytime hours. Always confirm your arrival time by email or phone to make sure somebody will be there to meet you.

Hostels

There is a huge number of backpacker hostels in Krakow, most of which offer cheap, simple dorm accommodation in fun, informal surroundings. Beds in hostels can be booked via the hostels' own websites or on specialist websites such as Hostelworld. Many hostels offer doubles, triples and quads as well as dorms, and they are increasingly popular with couples and families who enjoy the social aspects of backpacker culture but who want a private room.

Hostels in Krakow vary a great deal in terms of character: some have a bar on site and encourage late-night socializing, while others offer a bit more peace and quiet. The type of atmosphere favoured will be clear from the description on each hostel's website. Many hostels have invested a lot of money in contemporary design and comforts, and are similar in style to small boutique hotels.

Breakfast is available at some Krakow hostels, but not all – this can be checked when making your booking. Due to their popularity, it is advisable to book hostels at least a week or two in advance.

Camping

There is a modest handful of suburban campsites in Krakow, and although they are a fair way from the centre, all are well served by public transport. **Krakowianka** (open from May to September) is a tranquil suburban site next to the wooded Solvay Park, just off the Zakopane road, 6 km (4 miles) south of town. During the summer months there is an open-air swimming pool for the use of the campers, and the Solvay shopping mall is a short walk away; however, there's nothing else of sightseeing or recreational interest in this part of town. **Smok** (open all year) is a privately run site 4 km (2.5 miles) west of town, on the main Oświęcim road, in a pleasant suburban setting with plenty of greenery around.

Recommended Hotels

The places listed on pages 182–5 have been picked from a range of accommodation

A room in the moden Wyspiański hotel *(see p184)*

types, from charming B&Bs and backpacker hostels to luxury establishments, chains, boutique hotels and the grand, historic hotels for which Krakow is renowned. They are listed by price within each area, be that the narrow alleys of the Old Quarter, bohemian Kazimierz or the pleasant leafy streets just outside the city centre. These lodgings have been featured for their excellent service, wide-ranging facilities or unique character.

Throughout the listings certain hotels have been highlighted as DK Choice. These offer a particularly special experience, such as a beautiful location, spectacular views, a historical setting,

outstanding service, a romantic atmosphere or a combination of these qualities. Whatever the reasons, the DK Choice label is a guarantee of an especially memorable stay. Many of these establishments are popular so it is advisable to book well in advance.

DIRECTORY

Internet Booking Sites

Airbnb
W airbnb.com

Booking.com
W booking.com

Hostelworld
W hostelworld.com

Rooms and Apartments

Krakow Apartments
Tel 12 421 48 65.
W krakow-apartments.com

Old City Apartments
Tel 606 941 483.
W oldcityapartments.eu

Sodispar
Tel 600 191 313.
W sodispar.pl

Campsites

Krakowianka
ul. Żywiecka Boczna 2.
Tel 12 268 11 35.
W krakowianka.com.pl

Smok
ul. Kamedulska 18.
Tel 12 429 83 00.
W smok.krakow.pl

Sleek exterior of the Art Hotel Niebieski, located by the river *(see p185)*

Where to Stay

Historical

Okół and Stradom Quarters

Rezydent   zł zł
ul. Grodzka 9
Tel *12 429 54 10*   **Map** 6 D3
W rezydent.krakow.pl
Behind its medieval façade, the
Rezydent's rooms and suites offer
good value for a three-star hotel.

Royal Kraków   zł zł
ul. Św. Gertrudy
Tel *12 421 35 00*   **Map** 6 D5
W hotelewam.pl
Stay in comfortable rooms at
the foot of the Wawel Royal
Castle in this hotel housed in a
19th-century Art Nouveau building.

Wawel   zł zł
ul. Poselska 22
Tel *12 424 13 00*   **Map** 6 D3
W hotelwawel.pl
In a 16th-century building, the
Wawel mixes the old with the
new. The large, well-appointed
rooms have Art Nouveau-style
decor. There is a wellness centre.

Old Quarter

Francuski   zł zł
ul. Pijarska 13
Tel *666 195 831*   **Map** 6 D1
W hotel-francuski.com
This hotel retains an air of pre-
World War I opulence and
features retro furnishings. It has
a fine restaurant.

Pollera   zł zł
ul. Szpitalna 30
Tel *12 422 10 44*   **Map** 6 E2
W pollera.com.pl
An Art Nouveau classic in the
heart of the Old Quarter founded
in 1834 by Kaspar Poller, this hotel
still preserves its old world charm.

**Polski Hotel Pod
Białym Orłem**   zł zł
ul. Pijarska 17
Tel *12 422 11 44*   **Map** 6 E1
W podorlem.com.pl
Conveniently located next to
St Florian's Gate, this hotel
provides traditional, comfortable
accommodation.

Amadeus   zł zł zł
ul. Mikołajska 20
Tel *12 429 60 70*   **Map** 6 E2
W hotel-amadeus.pl
This four-star hotel in a lovely
mansion has plush, antique
furnishings and a retro feel.

Elektor   zł zł zł
ul. Szpitalna 28
Tel *12 423 23 17*   **Map** 6 E2
W hotelelektor.pl
One of the grand old ladies of
the Krakow hotel scene, the
Elektor preserves an old-world
charm. The staff will fall over
themselves to help guests,
royalty or otherwise: illustrious
patrons have included Prince
and Princess Takamodo of
Japan, King Harald V of Norway
and Princess Maha Chakri
Sirindhorm of Thailand.

Pod Różą   zł zł zł
ul. Floriańska 14
Tel *12 424 33 00*   **Map** 6 E2
W podroza.hotel.com.pl
Balzac and Liszt have stayed in
the elegant, high-ceilinged rooms
at this hotel, which is known to
be Krakow's oldest.

Wit Stwosz   zł zł zł
ul. Mikołajska 28
Tel *12 429 60 26*   **Map** 6 E2
W hotelws.pl
Housed in an old townhouse
just off the main Market Square,
this plush hotel has friendly service.

Kazimierz Quarter

Regent   zł zł
ul. Bozega Ciala 19
Tel *12 430 62 34*   **Map** 4 D2
W hotelregent.pl
A simple, stylish hotel located in
a 19th-century building. A hearty
breakfast is served in the hotel's
converted cellar.

Wrought-iron sign outside the Polski Hotel
Pod Białym Orłem

Wesoła, Kleparz and Biskupie

Europejski   zł zł
ul. Lubicz 5
Tel *12 423 25 12*   **Map** 6 F1
W hoteleuropejskikrakow.pl
Founded in the 19th century, this
friendly family-run hotel is near
the railway station.

Polonia   zł zł
ul. Basztowa 25
Tel *12 422 12 33*   **Map** 6 F1
W hotel-polonia.com.pl
An Art Nouveau gem dating to
World War I, the Polonia is a
grand place to stay.

Red Brick Apartments   zł zł
ul. Kurniki 3
Tel *12 628 66 00*   **Map** 2 D3
W redbrick.pl
These self-catering units in a
restored 19th-century building
sleep two to six people. Perfect
for families or groups.

Piasek and Nowy Świat

Maltanski   zł zł
ul. Straszewskiego 14
Tel *12 431 00 10*   **Map** 5 C4
W donimirski.com
A boutique hotel with luxurious
but understated rooms in a
restored Neo-Classical building.

Further Afield

Dwór w Tomaszowicach   zł zł zł
ul. Krakowska 68, Tomaszowice
Tel *12 419 20 00*
W dwor.pl
In a Neo-Classical manor house,
this hotel blends luxury with a
rural atmosphere.

B&B

Okół and Stradom Quarters

Globus   zł zł
ul. Dietla 91
Tel *12 350 62 65*   **Map** 6 F4
W globuskrk.pl
In a converted town house,
Globus offers rooms and
apartments with elegant decor.

Wielopole   zł zł
ul. Wielopole 3
Tel *12 422 14 75*   **Map** 6 E3
W wielopole.pl
A small, friendly B&B in a 19th-century building, with rooms decked out in warm colours.

Old Quarter

Tango House   zł
ul. Szpitalna 4
Tel *12 429 31 14*   **Map** 6 E2
W tangohouse.pl
Tango House is located in the historical heart of the city. Guests can choose from double rooms or two self-catering studios.

La Fontaine   zł zł
ul. Sławkowska 1
Tel *12 422 65 64*   **Map** 6 D2
W bblafontaine.com
La Fontaine offers cosy rooms and family-sized apartments located on the attic floor of an apartment block.

Kazimierz Quarter

Alef   zł
ul. Św. Agnieszki 5
Tel *12 424 31 31*   **Map** 3 C1
W alefhotel.pl
Wooden antique beds, retro furnishings and a hearty breakfast feature at this popular B&B.

Café Mlynek   zł
Pl. Wolnica 7
Tel *012 430 62 02*   **Map** 3 D2
W cafemlynek.com
Small, tasteful rooms are found above this popular vegetarian café, which also hosts concerts and exhibitions.

Klezmer-Hois   zł
ul. Szeroka 6
Tel *12 411 12 45*   **Map** 4 E1
W klezmer.pl
This characterful guesthouse is full of 19th-century artifacts. The restaurant offers a tempting array of Jewish food.

DK Choice

Kolory   zł
ul. Estery 10
Tel *12 421 04 65*   **Map** 4 D1
W kolory.com.pl
The bright, homely rooms at Kolory are decorated with Polish folk art. It is in the centre of the nightlife zone, so ask for a room at the back of the building to minimize street noise. Breakfast is served in Les Couleurs café on the ground floor, whose croissants and coffee rank among the best in Krakow.

The sauna room at the Galaxy hotel

Eden   zł zł
ul. Ciemna 15
Tel *12 430 65 65*   **Map** 4 D1
W hoteleden.pl
Offering large but simple rooms, Eden also has a kosher restaurant and a healing salt grotto.

Wesoła, Kleparz and Biskupie

Jordan   zł
ul. Długa 9
Tel *12 430 02 92*   **Map** 1 C3
W nocleg.jordan.pl
Above a travel agent, Jordan offers simple, pleasant rooms on a lively shopping street near colourful markets.

Piasek and Nowy Świat

Fortuna   zł zł
ul. Czapskch 5
Tel *12 411 08 06*   **Map** 5 B3
W hotel-fortuna.com.pl
In a charming building, Fortuna has decent-sized rooms and large bathrooms. Friendly service.

Modern
Old Quarter

Floryan   zł zł
ul. Floriańska 38
Tel *12 431 14 18*   **Map** 6 E2
W http://floryan.pl
At the top of a historic town house, this highly individual hotel has contemporary design and an intimate vibe. It is located close to the Market Square.

Unicus Hotel   zł zł
ul. Św. Marka 20
Tel *12 433 71 11*   **Map** 6 E2
W hotelunicus.com
In a historic building, Unicus is contemporary on the inside, with a grey and brown colour scheme.

Kazimierz Quarter

Karmel   zł zł
ul. Kupa 15
Tel *12 430 66 97*   **Map** 4 D1
W karmel.com.pl
A welcoming guesthouse with high-ceilinged rooms, and a mix of antiques and modern decor.

Kazimierz   zł zł
ul. Miodowa 16
Tel *12 421 66 29*   **Map** 4 D1
W hk.com.pl
The comfortable modern rooms in this contemporary building feature stained-glass windows with scenes from local history.

Secesja   zł zł
ul. Paulinska 24
Tel *12 430 74 64*   **Map** 3 C2
W hotelsecesja.pl
On the quieter side of Kazimierz, this cosy hotel has Art Nouveau-inspired decor in warm colours.

Columbus   zł zł zł
ul. Starowiślna 57
Tel *12 252 75 50*   **Map** 4 E1
W hotelcolumbus.pl
The Columbus has rooms decked out in warm colours, attentive staff and a good buffet breakfast.

Galaxy   zł zł zł
ul. Gęsia 22a
Tel *12 342 81 00*   **Map** 4 F1
W http://galaxyhotel.pl
A hotel with designer rooms in bright colours, Galaxy also has a pool and a spa centre.

Wesoła, Kleparz and Biskupie

Ibis Budget Stare Miasto   zł
ul. Pawia 11
Tel *12 355 29 50*   **Map** 2 D3
W accorhotels.com
Next to the main railway station, this no-frills hotel has well-equipped but functional rooms.

For more information on types of hotels *see pages 178–81*

Atrium   zł zł
ul. Krzywa 7
Tel *12 430 02 03*   **Map** 1 C3
W hotelatrium.pl
A good option near the railway station, Atrium offers 50 rooms and two suites with kitchenettes.

Batory   zł zł
ul. Sołtyka 19
Tel *12 294 30 30*   **Map** 2 E5
W hotelbatory.pl
This brightly decorated hotel in a quiet location has friendly staff and a cosy atmosphere.

Wyspiański   zł zł
ul. Westerplatte 15
Tel *12 422 95 66*   **Map** 6 F2
W hotel-wyspianski.pl
This large, functional hotel is a reliable option, offering three-star comforts close to the Old Town.

DK Choice

andel's   zł zł zł
ul. Pawia 3
Tel *12 660 00 10*   **Map** 6 F1
W viennahouse.com
Jutting out into the plaza in front of the main railway station like an ocean liner, andel's offers design-conscious, supremely comfortable rooms in harmonious colours. It is a place for spending quality time in rather than just sleeping, though its location opposite the Planty and the Old Quarter makes it a perfect sightseeing base.

Puro Hotel   zł zł zł
ul. Ogrodowa 10
Tel *12 314 21 00*   **Map** 2 D3
W purohotel.pl
Opposite the railway station and the Galeria shopping centre, Puro has sleek, minimalist but well-equipped rooms with large windows.

Piasek and Nowy Świat

Alexander   zł zł
ul. Garbarska 18
Tel *12 422 96 60*   **Map** 5 C1
W alexhotel.pl
This functional hotel has cosy, neat en suite roomse. It is ideally located, just a short walk from the Old Town and other historical landmarks.

Logos   zł zł
ul. Szujskiego 5
Tel *12 631 62 00*   **Map** 1 B4
W hotel-logos.pl
The stylish Logos offers large rooms with great bathrooms. There are sauna and spa facilities.

Kossak   zł zł zł
Pl. Juliusza Kossaka 1
Tel *12 379 59 00*   **Map** 5 B4
W hotelkossak.com
A smart hotel with contemporary design touches. Rooms on the upper floor offer good views of the castle and the river.

Further Afield

Dom Goscinny Przegorzaly   zł
ul. Jodlowa 13
Tel *12 429 71 15*
W dg.uj.edu.pl/przegorzaly
This student campus on the fringes of Las Wolski forest offers tourist accommodation over the summer. Rooms are bright and plain; the surroundings, peaceful.

Easy Chopin   zł
ul. Przy Rondzie 2
Tel *12 299 00 00*
W viennahouse.com
This smart, comfortable hotel is a 20-minute walk from the city centre. It offers brightly coloured rooms, efficient staff and good facilities.

Ruczaj   zł
ul. Ruczaj 44
Tel *12 269 10 00*
W ruczajhotel.pl
Rooms have large windows and enormous beds at this charming hotel in a leafy suburb. It has a sauna and solarium.

Ibis Krakow Centrum   zł zł
ul. Syrokomli 2
Tel *12 299 33 00*
W accorhotels.com
Just a short tram ride from the city centre, this hotel offers spacious, comfortable rooms.

Novotel Centrum   zł zł zł
ul. T. Kościuszki 5
Tel *12 299 29 00*   **Map** 5 C5
W accorhotels.com
Bright rooms, great service and a generous buffet breakfast are the main draws here. There is a gym, sauna and swimming pool.

Luxury

Okół and Stradom Quarters

Copernicus   zł zł zł
ul. Kanonicza 16
Tel *12 424 3400*   **Map** 6 D4
W hotel.com.pl
In a Renaissance town house, this hotel features beautiful historic interiors and spacious rooms, coupled with excellent facilities.

One of the deluxe rooms on offer at the design-led andel's

Pugetów   zł zł zł
ul. Starowislna 15a
Tel *12 432 4950*   **Map** 6 E4
W donimirski.com/hotel-pugetow
Set in an ornate 19th century house, this hotel has original artworks and sumptuous rooms.

Queen Boutique Hotel   zł zł zł
ul. Dietla 60
Tel *12 433 3333*   **Map** 6 E5
W queenhotel.pl
In a 19th-century town house, this hotel offers plush rooms with contemporary furnishings.

Radisson Blu   zł zł zł
Straszewskiego 17
Tel *12 618 88 88*   **Map** 5 C4
W radissonblu.com/hotel-krakow
This hotel, overlooking the Planty, has contemporary design touches and a basement-level spa centre.

Old Quarter

Gródek   zł zł
ul. na gródku 4
Tel *12 431 9030*   **Map** 6 E3
W donimirski.com/hotel-grodek
Adjoining a Dominican convent, the opulent 5-star Gródek offers high-end comfort.

Grand   zł zł zł
ul. Slawkowska 5–7
Tel *12 424 0800*   **Map** 6 D2
W grand.pl
This historic hotel maintains its antique furnishings while offering modern amenities, such as a fitness centre. A babysitting service is available.

Pałac Bonerowski   zł zł zł
ul. Św. Jana 1
Tel *12 374 13 00*   **Map** 6 D2
W palacbonerowski.pl
This 16th-century mansion retains some historic features. The bathrooms are totally modern.

DK Choice

Stary zł zł zł
ul. Szczepańska 5
Tel *12 384 08 08* **Map** 6 D2
W hotel.com.pl
In a 15th-century merchant's house, Stary retains many original features, such as exposed brick and stone, high ceilings and wall paintings. Furnishings are contemporary and bathrooms have the highest quality marble.

Wentzl zł zł zł
Rynek Główny 19
Tel *12 430 26 64* **Map** 6 D3
W wentzl.pl
Named after the famous restaurant on its first floor, the elegant rooms here have views over the main Market Square.

Kazimierz Quarter

Hotel Rubinstein zł zł
ul. Szeroka 12
Tel *12 384 00 00* **Map** 3 E1
W rubinstein.pl
Located on Kazimierz's prettiest square, this hotel has bright rooms with plush upholstery.

Dada Boutique Hotel zł zł zł
ul. Krakowska 30
Tel *88 737 13 71* **Map** 3 D2
W dadahotel.pl
Chic bathrooms and intelligent use of space characterize this intimate design hotel in an adapted 19th-century town house.

**Metropolitan
Boutique Hotel** zł zł zł
ul. Berka Joselewicza 19
Tel *12 442 75 00* **Map** 4 D1
W hotelmetropolitan.pl
This plush, modern hotel offers large rooms in soothing colours and a generous buffet breakfast.

Wesoła, Kleparz and Biskupie

Komorowski zł zł
ul. Długa 7
Tel *505 989 371* **Map** 1 C3
W hotelkomorowski.com
Ideal for a romantic break, this boutique guesthouse has rich colours and lavish furnishings.

Piasek and Nowy Świat

Amber Design zł zł zł
ul. Garbarska 8–10
Tel *12 421 06 06* **Map** 5 C1
W hotel-amber.pl
Murals inspired by the Art Nouveau artist Stanisław Wyspiański adorn the rooms here.

Sheraton Grand Kraków zł zł zł
ul. Powiśle 7
Tel *12 662 10 00* **Map** 5 B4
W sheratongrandkrakow.com
Located by the river and Wawel Royal Castle, the Sheraton offers high-end comfort and service.

Further Afield

Art Hotel Niebieski zł zł
ul. Flisacka 3
Tel *12 297 40 00*
W niebieski.com.pl
Large rooms have all mod cons at this tranquil hotel by the river. Top-notch restaurant food.

Sympozjum zł zł
ul. Kobierzyńska 47
Tel *12 261 86 00*
W sympozium.com.pl
A popular conference hotel with great dining options, a lively bar and spa facilities.

Qubus zł zł zł
ul. Nadwiślańska 6
Tel *12 374 51 00* **Map** 4 E2
W qubushotel.com
Large and superbly equipped, this hotel south of the Vistula is perfect for exploring Kazimierz.

Hostel

Okoł and Stradom Quarters

DK Choice

Mundo Hostel zł
ul. J. Sarego 10
Tel *12 422 61 13* **Map** 6 E4
W mundohostel.eu
Rooms at this boutique hostel have a geographic theme and contain ethnic-influenced *objets d'art* and textiles. There is a communal kitchen. A quieter option than some of the other backpacker places in town.

Old Quarter

Flamingo Hostel zł
ul. Szewska 4
Tel *12 422 00 00* **Map** 6 D2
W krakow.flamingo-hostel.com
A firm favourite, this hostel is off the main square, on a lively street. Free breakfast and Internet.

Tutti Frutti zł
ul. Floriańska 29
Tel *12 428 00 28* **Map** 6 E2
W tuttifruttihostel.com
A mixture of dorms and four-bed rooms is on offer at this central but relaxing hostel.

Kazimierz Quarter

Goodbye Lenin zł
ul. Berka Joselewicza 23
Tel *12 421 20 30* **Map** 4 E1
W goodbyelenin.pl
In a ramshackle old house adorned with Pop Art murals, this is an enjoyable, sociable hostel.

Secret Garden Hostel zł
ul. Skawińska 7
Tel *12 430 54 45* **Map** 3 C2
W thesecretgarden.pl
Hidden away in a quiet corner of Kazimierz, this hostel offers bright dorms and double rooms.

Wesoła, Kleparz and Biskupie

Greg & Tom Hostel zł
ul. Pawia 12–17
Tel *12 422 41 00* **Map** 6 F1
W gregtomhostel.com
This hostel has dorms and double rooms with neat furnishings and a fully equipped kitchen .

Mosquito Hostel zł
Rynek Kleparski 4–6
Tel *12 430 14 61* **Map** 1 C3
W mosquitohostel.com
Mosquito offers a mixture of dorms and private rooms right beside Kraków's liveliest market.

Trendy furniture and décor at the Qubus hotel

For more information on types of hotels *see pages 178–81*

WHERE TO EAT AND DRINK

Krakow has always been known as a good place for eating out. Even during the Communist era, when Polish restaurants were notorious for having very little on the menu, Krakow's culinary culture survived unscathed. Now one of the busiest tourist destinations in the country, Krakow boasts hundreds of restaurants, many of the highest quality. Traditional Polish food is at its best here – whether in the budget canteen restaurants where customers queue up to order at the counter, or in the finer restaurants serving traditional specialities like roast duck with apples. There is a growing number of haute cuisine restaurants offering Mediterranean, French and contemporary Polish cooking, often blended with Asian influences. Italian, Asian, Mexican and South American eateries can all be found in Krakow. Some of the best places in the city are listed on pages 192–5.

Restaurants

Those who enjoy good food in a pleasant atmosphere will not be disappointed in Krakow. Many of the city's restaurants are housed in historic buildings or medieval cellars, usually painstakingly restored and tastefully furnished. Eateries in the bohemian quarter of Kazimierz frequently opt for a range of retro styles, with candles on the table and antique furniture. Restaurants on the main Market Square and on Szeroka Street in Kazimierz have large areas of outdoor seating, although pavement terraces are a rarity elsewhere. Evenings and weekends tend to be particularly busy, so booking a table in advance is advisable. Wherever you go, restaurants are not too formal, and there is no real dress code.

Canteen Restaurants and Vodka-and-Herring Bars

Much of the best local food can be enjoyed in a *jadłodajnia* (also known as a *bar mleczny* or

Del Papá, considered by many to be one of Krakow's best Italian restaurants *(see p193)*

"milk bar"), a budget canteen restaurant where customers order at the counter, choosing from a menu of inexpensive soups, *pierogi*, potato pancakes, pork chops and other Polish staples. The decor is often plain in these places, but prices are rock bottom – visitors can enjoy a three-course meal for as little as 20zł. *Jadłodajnias* often close early – usually late afternoon or early evening, or when the food has sold out.

The Krakow dining scene is witnessing a rise in the number of vodka-and-herring bars, some of which are open round the clock. These places sell spirits and traditional bar snacks (marinated herring being one favourite) for very little money.

Street Food

Krakow pretzels, or *obwarzanki*, are sold by street vendors throughout the city and make an excellent snack. Very much a local speciality, they are traditionally coated with salt crystals, poppy seeds or sesame seeds. You will also see street sellers offering delicious hunks of *oscypek*, smoked sheep's cheese from the Tatra Mountains.

Arguably Poland's favourite street snack, the *zapiekanka* is Poland's answer to the pizza: a halved baguette covered in meat, cheese and vegetables, then toasted. *Zapiekanki* are sold from fast-food kiosks all over the city, notably on plac Nowy, the centre of nightlife in Kazimierz.

Another ubiquitous feature of the Krakow street-food scene is the grilled sausage. The best sausages are sold at the outdoor grill on plac Nowy in Kazimierz and at the kiosk near the Market Hall in Grzegórzecka Street, where they are available until 3 o'clock in the morning.

Eating at Night

The majority of restaurants in Krakow close around 11pm, but several establishments in

The chic outdoor area at Someplace Else, within the Sheraton Hotel *(see p195)*

Pimiento Argentino, with decor in the style of an Argentinian hacienda *(see p193)*

Kazimierz are open till 1 or 2am. Several vodka-and-herring bars in the Old Quarter stay open round the clock. Plenty of street-food outlets keep going beyond midnight, and it is usually possible to pick up a pizza slice or a *zapiekanka* in the Old Quarter or in Kazimierz well into the early hours.

Prices and Tips

The price of food in Krakow's restaurants is below the European average. A three-course meal without alcohol will cost about 100zł per person in all but the most expensive places. However, drinking alcohol with your meal will add a substantial amount to your bill.

Credit cards are becoming ever more popular and should be readily accepted by all the larger restaurants and those located on the main tourist trail. Signs on windows or doors indicate which cards are accepted by the establishment.

All over Poland a customary tip amounts to about 10 per cent of the bill.

Vegetarian Food

The majority of restaurants in Krakow serve at least a handful of vegetarian dishes. Traditional local specialities, such as *pierogi* (dumplings) filled with wild mushrooms,

cheese, sauerkraut or fruit, are very popular, as are all kinds of savoury pancakes, omelettes and *knedle* (potato dumplings). A choice of many colourful and tasty salads is available in all restaurants. Beetroot, carrots, cabbage, cauliflower, celeriac and leeks are traditional Polish favourites. Broccoli, aubergines, celery, endives and courgettes have also been introduced to Polish cuisine. Vegetarian food is available not only from most ethnic restaurants, but also from salad bars, which are very popular and also serve freshly pressed fruit and vegetable

juices. In some restaurants you can create your own salad from a selection of ingredients.

Recommended Restaurants

The restaurants listed on pages 192–5 have been selected across a wide price range to give a cross-section of the most noteworthy places to eat in Krakow. Whether located in the lively main Market Square, the medieval brick cellars of the Old Quarter and Okół or the former Jewish quarter of Kazimierz, each offers excellent food in great surroundings.

The restaurants and cafés in this guide cover an array of possibilities in terms of cuisine, location and atmosphere. They include traditional Polish canteens, trendy restaurants serving modern Polish delicacies, pizzerias, designer bistros, fish and seafood eateries, characterful cafés and fine dining options. The city also has a number of vegetarian and vegan restaurants.

The DK Choice category draws attention to the very best Krakow restaurants. These have one or more exceptional features, such as superb local specialities, excellent value for money, sensational food, a remarkable or unusual location, or a distinctive atmosphere.

The elegant dining area at Copernicus *(see p192)*

The Flavours of Krakow

Polish cuisine, like that of many central European countries, makes heavy use of meat and poultry, which is often served quite plainly with potatoes or rice and cabbage. However, because of the long Baltic coastline and many inland lakes, fish is also likely to feature on many menus. Carp, trout and herring are particular favourites. Around Krakow, in the south, the local forests yield a bounty of quality game, with venison being very popular. The legacy of former rule by Austria is also evident in the south, especially in some of the sophisticated cakes and pastries.

Pickled herring

Barbecuing meat at a street celebration on Palm Sunday

Meat

Pork *(wieprzowina)* is the most popular meat by far in Poland. It usually comes as a steak *(kotlet schabowy)* or on the bone *(golonka wieprzowa)* and also appears in soups, sausages and as hams. Polish hams are generally cured and have a rich, sweet flavour. Ham is mainly served cold as an appetizer with cheese and pickles, though it may also

be eaten for breakfast. Poland also produces high quality veal *(cielęcina)*, which is often dished up with a rich mushroom sauce *(cielęcina po staropolsku)* or with cabbage and raisins.

Poultry and Game

Chicken *(kurczak)* is a staple food in Poland and drumsticks *(podudzie)* are especially popular. Chicken livers *(wątróbka)*, served with a fruit sauce, are considered a delicacy.

A wide variety of game roams the forests of southern Poland. Pheasant *(bażant)*, duck *(kaczka)*, goose *(gęś)*, venison *(comber)*, rabbit *(królik)* and hare *(zając)* are found on many local menus. Availability varies with the season; autumn is the best time to enjoy game.

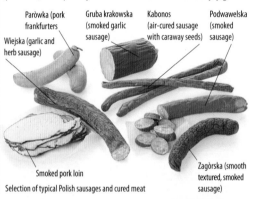
Parówka (pork frankfurters)
Gruba krakowska (smoked garlic sausage)
Kabonos (air-cured sausage with caraway seeds)
Podwawelska (smoked sausage)
Wiejska (garlic and herb sausage)
Smoked pork loin
Zagòrska (smooth textured, smoked sausage)
Selection of typical Polish sausages and cured meat

Local Dishes and Specialities

Many classic Polish dishes are offered at restaurants all over the country, but fish also features prominently on northern menus, while those of the the south offer a range of game. The most varied and cosmopolitan cuisine is found in large cities, such as Warsaw and Krakow, where top chefs run the kitchens of some of the finest restaurants in Poland. The national dish, *bigos*, comes from eastern Poland. It is hearty and warming for the long, bleak winters found there, as is another dish from this chilly region, *pierogi* (pasta dumplings, stuffed with meat, cheese or fruit). Both are influenced by the food of neighbouring Russia. Polish cakes and desserts also tend to be heavy and rich, although most originate in the warmer south, once ruled by Austria.

Green cabbage

Bigos Chunks of meat and sausage are simmered with sauerkraut, cabbage, onion, potatoes, herbs and spices.

A colourful display of locally grown vegetables at a city market stall

Fish

Fish features strongly on menus all over Poland, where herring *(śledź)* is a central part of the diet. It comes pickled, in oil, with onions, with soured cream – in fact, with just about everything. *Rolmops po kaszubsku* (marinated herring wrapped around pickled onion, then spiked with cloves and dipped in soured cream) are widely enjoyed. Other popular fish are freshwater trout *(pstrąg)* – served simply grilled with boiled potatoes; carp *(karp)* – often accompanied by horseradish sauce; and salmon *(łosoś)*. A treat in early summer is smoked salmon served with spears of fresh asparagus *(łosoś wędzony ze szparagami)*, which is then in season.

Vegetables

Poland produces many fine quality vegetables. The hardy cabbage *(kapusta)* remains the country's top vegetable. It is used in so many ways, including raw in salads and simply boiled to partner meat or fish. Cabbage soup

Braided ring-shaped *obwarzanki* (Krakow pretzels) on sale in a bread shop

(kapuśniak) and sauerkraut are on every menu. Potatoes are also a staple. They come boiled, baked and mashed, though rarely roasted. Peppers are popular too, often served stuffed with rice and minced meat or pickled in summer salads. Root vegetables such as carrots, parsnips, swede (rutabaga), turnips and beetroot make their way into a range of dishes. Mushrooms grow wild all over Poland and come both cooked and pickled as a tasty addition to many meals.

SNACKS

Sausages A wide range of smoked and unsmoked varieties are on offer at the profusion of street stalls and snack bars that can be found on most city streets.

Precles (pretzels) Another favourite street snack, these are popular, freshly baked, at train and bus stations first thing in the morning.

Zapiekanki Often referred to as Polish-style pizzas, these are tasty, open-top baguettes, spread with cheese and tomato, then toasted and served piping hot. They are also a common item on street-stall menus.

Smalec This snack consists of fried lard, liberally sprinkled with sea salt, and eaten with chunks of crusty bread. It can be found as a bar snack in most pubs and makes a good accompaniment to beer.

Pierogi These ravioli-style dumplings may be stuffed with meat, sauerkraut, mushrooms, cheese or fruit.

Barszcz This beetroot soup, flavoured with lemon and garlic, may be served clear or with beans or potatoes.

Poppy seed roll A rich yeasted dough is wrapped around a sweet poppy-seed filling and baked until lightly golden.

What to Drink in Krakow

In Krakow, as indeed anywhere in Poland, you'll come across many different brands of exquisite vodkas, both clear and flavoured. Beer is quite popular in Poland, with craft-breweries flourishing, and Krakow's bars offer an ever larger choice of unique, delicious beers on tap or in bottles. Poland isn't known for its quality wines but shops and restaurants offer a good selection of brands imported from all over the world, especially from Europe and the New World.

Cracovia, one of the best Polish clear vodkas

Vodka

Vodka distilled from potatoes or grain is a Polish speciality. Such brands as clear *Wódka Wyborowa* and dry *Żubrówka* (flavoured with bison grass from the Białowieża forest) are both world-famous. The variety of vodka brands produced in Poland may be bewildering. Clear *Cracovia*, which has been produced in Krakow for some years, is very popular. *Starka* is definitely the oldest brand among quality vodkas. For centuries *starka* was made from unrectified grain spirit, which was aged for at least six years in reused oak wine-casks. Today, bottles of aged *starka* are very rare and command high prices.

Other popular spirits include *Wiśniówka*, or cherry vodka; and

Starka krakowska vodka

Dzięgielówka, a dry vodka flavoured with angelica root

Żołądkowa, an amber-coloured vodka flavoured with herbs and used as a digestif. Good kosher plum brandy or *Śliwowica* is traditionally made in the mountain villages southeast of Krakow and has a very high alcohol content. The best is said to be *Śliwowica łącka* from the village of Łącko, 70km (43 miles) south of Krakow.

Vodka plays an important role in Polish social life, and

is frequently offered to guests or drunk when making new friends, and toasts are common. Vodka is usually downed in one gulp rather than sipped gradually, although visitors unaccustomed to its alcohol content should take things at their own speed.

Beer

A vodka glass

Polish breweries have developed rapidly over the years. The production of quality beer has grown and been modernized. Figures show that Poles are drinking more and more beer and less strong alcohol.

Beers from Okocim, Tyskie and Żywiec are traditionally the most popular in Krakow.

Amaretto liqueur

Plum Łąck brandy

Passover Plum vodka

Senator vodka

Krakus vodka

Harnaś vodka

Żywiec logo with the date of establishment

A dancing couple in traditional costumes from the Krakow region

Żywiec Beer Label

Many brands of beer are produced by the Żywiec Brewery, but bottles with the couple dressed in traditional Krakow costumes sell best.

Brackie beer from Żywiec

Lezajsk beer from Żywiec

Beer from the Okocim Brewery

All these breweries produce palatable lager-style beers and dark porters. Smaller breweries (such as Brackie from Cieszyn, Browar Fortuna from Miłosław or Leżajsk from the town of the same name) produce lagers with slightly more

Pre-1939 advertisement of the Okocim Brewery

character. The 2010s have witnessed an upsurge in the production of craft beers, and almost every city in Poland features a handful of boutique breweries producing pale ales, wheat beers and fruit-flavoured brews. Pinta, Trzech Kumpli, Piwo Warownia and Pracownia Piwa are just some of the craft brewers whose beers are well-distributed all over the country. A small but growing number of pubs and restaurants are also brewing their own beer on-site. In addition, there has been an increase in the avail-ability of Czech beers in Krakow. Beer drinkers are presented with a fine choice: the best bars in Krakow stock a wide range of beers in bottles, and there is a growing number of multi-tap pubs that offer a selection on draft.

Wine

Although vineyards were cultivated in the Krakow area quite successfully, they disappeared in the 15th century. Large quantities of quality wine were produced until World War II in the Zaleszczyki region on the then Romanian border. Today only a few vineyards can be found near Zielona Góra in the far west of the country, which means that Poland's wine production is negligible. Any visitor to Krakow wishing to drink wine will find a large selection of imported wines both in shops and restaurants.

Wine comes from many countries, including France, Italy, Spain and Austria, as well as California, Australia, Chile and New Zealand. Hungarian wine, however, is to be recommended in Krakow, and not only because of its budget price. For centuries Krakow was a place where Tokay wines were stored for ageing, in barrels housed in large cellars beneath Market Square, before being exported all over the world.

Non-Alcoholic Drinks

Mineral water, sparkling and still, is the most popular non-alcoholic drink. Many brands of mineral water come from the springs in the mountain foothills or highlands not far from Krakow. Fruit juices are also quite popular. Cold-pressed apple and blackcurrant juices are Polish specialities. The slightly fizzy lemonades and fruit juices made by local Polish firm John Lemon are certified gluten- and preservative-free.

Apple juice

Blackcurrant juice

Where to Eat and Drink

Okół and Stradom Quarters

Balaton   **zł zł**
Hungarian   **Map** 1 C5 & 6 D4
ul. Grodzka 37
Tel *12 422 04 69*
A plain-looking restaurant, Balaton has long been around and still serves the best goulash soups and *pörkölts* (paprika-rich stews) in town. Savour them with wine from the excellent Hungarian list.

Il Calzone   **zł zł**
Italian   **Map** 2 D5 & 6 E3
ul. Starowiślna 15a
Tel *12 429 51 41*
This is the restaurant to visit for a range of high-quality fish and pasta dishes, plus a long menu of inexpensive pizzas. There is a terrace for outdoor dining.

Smak Ukrainski   **zł zł**
Ukrainian   **Map** 1 C5 & 6 D4
ul. Grodzka 21
Tel *12 421 92 94*
Hearty meat-and-potato dishes and dumplings from Poland's eastern neighbour are served by costumed staff in a lively cellar. Wash them down with a selection of Ukrainian beers.

Copernicus   **zł zł zł**
Fine dining   **Map** 1 C5 & 6 D4
ul. Kanonicza 16
Tel *12 424 34 21*
This atmospheric hotel restaurant specializes in superlative modern Polish cuisine and lots of game.

Kurka Wodna   **zł zł zł**
Contemporary Polish   **Map** 6 D4
ul. Kanonicza 15
Tel *730 700 248*
Classic Polish recipes are given a modern touch, with rabbit, lamb

and duck dominating the menu, accompanied by a fine selection of Hungarian wines. The lovely courtyard seating is a major draw.

DK Choice

Miód Malina   **zł zł zł**
Traditional Polish   **Map** 6 D4
ul. Grodzka 40
Tel *12 430 04 11*
Occupying lovely barrel-vaulted rooms decorated in raspberry shades of red, Miód Malina ("Honey Raspberry") is one of the most welcoming places to eat in Krakow. Traditional Polish festive fare is the main focus, with generous portions of meat and poultry followed by delicious desserts.

Pod Aniołami   **zł zł zł**
Traditional Polish   **Map** 6 D3
ul. Grodzka 35
Tel *12 421 39 99*
Classic Polish recipes, superbly prepared, are served in meticulously restored medieval cellars that were once home to goldsmiths' workshops.

Pod Baranem   **zł zł zł**
Polish   **Map** 2 D5 & 6 E4
ul. Św Gertrudy 21
Tel *12 429 40 22*
There are few better places in Krakow for Polish cuisine with a modern European twist, made with locally sourced ingredients.

Pod Nosem   **zł zł zł**
Contemporary Polish   **Map** 6 D4
ul. Kanonicza 22
Tel *12 376 00 14*
The best in modern Polish cuisine, including lots of game and Baltic fish dishes, is served in a tapestry-

Welcoming, traditional decor of the Polish restaurant Miód Malina

Price Guide
Prices are for a three-course meal per person, with a half-bottle of house wine, including tax and service.

zł	under 50zł
zł zł	50zł to 80zł
zł zł zł	over 80zł

rich dining room. The wine list covers all corners of the world.

Trattoria La Campana   **zł zł zł**
Italian   **Map** 1 C5 & 6 D4
ul. Kanonicza 7
Tel *12 430 22 32*
The rustic cellars filled with candlelit tables are perfect for a romantic dinner.

Old Quarter

Ambasada Śledzia   **zł**
Polish   **Map** 6 D3
ul. Stolarska 8/10
Tel *662 569 460*
An outstanding example of the vodka-and-snack bars cropping up all over Poland, the "Herring Embassy" serves marinated herring dishes at rock-bottom prices.

Camelot   **zł**
Café-patisserie   **Map** 6 D2
ul. Św. Tomasza 17
Tel *12 421 01 23*
This mildly bohemian café with a cabaret club downstairs is famous for its good coffee, fine cakes and delicious apple pie.

Chimera   **zł**
Polish   **Map** 5 C2
ul. Św. Anny 3
Tel *12 292 12 12*
At this buffet restaurant in a medieval cellar, guests pay according to the size of their plates. It is ideal for sampling a variety of different dishes. Vegetarian options aplenty.

Przypiecek   **zł**
Traditional Polish   **Map** 6 D1
ul. Sławkowska 32
Tel *12 422 74 95*
This is something of a temple to the humble *pierogi* (stuffed dumplings), which are served with a range of fillings. The savoury, sweet and baked versions are all well represented.

U Babci Maliny   **zł**
Traditional Polish   **Map** 6 D1
ul. Sławkowska 17
Tel *12 422 76 01*
Krakow has no shortage of queue-at-the-counter budget

restaurants, and this is one of the best, serving all manner of classic Polish fare in a folksy bench-filled basement.

Chłopskie Jadło
Traditional Polish zł zł Map 6 D3
ul. Grodzka 9
Tel *12 421 85 20*
Polish classics dominate the menu at this characterful, folk-styled restaurant, with plenty of meat dishes in heavy sauces. There is also a long list of typical Polish alcoholic spirits.

CK Dezerter
Eastern European zł zł Map 1 C5
ul. Bracka 6
Tel *12 422 79 31*
Large portions of meaty Polish and Austro-Hungarian classics are served at this charming restaurant. The soups are terrific, and cabbage has never tasted as good as in the sauerkraut here.

Czerwone Korale
Traditional Polish zł zł Map 6 D1
ul. Sławkówska 13–15
Tel *12 430 61 08* **Closed** *lunch Sat & Sun*
Decorated with dolls in Polish costume and pictures of folk-dancing villagers, this is the perfect place to feast on traditional fare. All dishes are reasonably priced.

La Petite France
Café-patisserie zł Map 6 E2
ul. Szpitalna 20
Tel *602 466 566*
A combined delicatessen and café, this ideal lunchtime spot is dominated by the aroma of fresh cheeses and charcuterie. As well as strong coffee, La Petite France serves some of the finest quiches in Poland.

Urara
Japanese zł zł Map 6 D2
ul. Św. Tomasza 19/4
Tel *531 855 053*
Sushi, sashimi and *shabu-shabu* (Japanese hotpot of thinly sliced meat and vegetables) are dished up in the bright and breezy dining room of Urara. The affordable eatery also prepares a small range of meaty mains.

Aqua e Vino
Italian zł zł zł Map 6 D1
ul. Wiślna 5/10
Tel *12 421 25 67*
The dishes at this outrageously trendy restaurant appear as carefully designed as the interior. Expect imaginative takes on classic recipes made from fresh ingredients, and superb desserts.

Diners enjoying their meal accompanied by live music at CK Dezerter

DK Choice

Cyrano de Bergerac
Fine dining zł zł zł Map 6 D1
ul. Sławkowska 26
Tel *12 411 72 88*
This is a world-class French restaurant set in two elegant rooms, with a quiet patio for the summer. The food is exquisite (leave room for the extravagant desserts) and the service impeccable. Look out for affordable set-menu lunches on weekdays.

Da Pietro
Italian zł zł zł Map 6 D2
Rynek Główny 19
Tel *12 422 32 79*
The quality food here is made with ingredients imported from Italy. Its location is unrivalled and al fresco dining is available during the warmer months..

Del Papá
Italian zł zł zł Map 6 D2
ul. Św. Tomasza 6
Tel *12 421 83 43*
This is one of Krakow's best Italian eateries, with a menu that features classic meat dishes as well as Mediterranean seafood.

Farina
Seafood zł zł zł Map 6 D1
ul. Św. Marka 16
Tel *12 422 18 60*
An informal, Mediterranean-themed restaurant, Farina specializes in fish and seafood. Fine white fish is served grilled, pan-fried or baked.

Gródek
Fine dining zł zł zł Map 6 E3
ul. Na Grodku 4
Tel *12 431 90 30*
Polish and international cuisine prepared with flair is served in the brick-lined basement of the historic Gródek hotel.

Hawelka
Traditional Polish zł zł zł Map 6 D2
Rynek Główny 34
Tel *12 422 06 31*
For fine Polish cuisine in a historic setting, it is difficult to do better than Hawelka, which has been serving roast duck and other classics since 1876 and is considered a local institution.

Leonardo
Italian zł zł zł Map 6 E2
ul. Szpitalna 20-22
Tel *12 429 68 50*
Exquisite cuisine, including superb pasta dishes, is served in this basement dining room decked out to look like a Mediterranean piazza.

Marmolada
Traditional Polish zł zł zł Map 6 D3
ul. Grodzka 5
Tel *12 422 02 33*
Classic Polish cuisine and Italian pizzas are on the menu at this smart restaurant. A profusion of candles and cut flowers provide a soothing ambience. There is live classical music on Saturday and Sunday evenings.

Miód i Wino
Traditional Polish zł zł zł Map 6 D1
ul. Sławkowska 32
Tel *12 422 74 95*
Enjoy classic Polish food in a traditional setting, with waiting staff in folk costumes and wooden-bench seating. This is a good place for meat feasting washed down with local beer.

Noworolski
Café-patisserie zł zł zł Map 6 D2
Rynek Główny 1/3
Tel *515 100 998*
This beautifully preserved Art Nouveau treasure attracts both locals and visitors eager for a cup of coffee and a slice of something sweet. Try the *sernik* (cheesecake).

Pimiento Argentino
Argentinian zł zł zł Map 6 D2
Rynek Główny 30
Tel *12 433 62 85*
Meat-lovers will relish the steaks freshly imported from Argentina to this grill restaurant. The menu includes everything from beef empanadas to ribeye steaks.

Pod Różą
International zł zł zł Map 6 E2
ul. Floriańska 14
Tel *12 424 33 81*
Under a glass-covered atrium at the Pod Różą hotel, this restaurant combines tradition and creativity in its dishes. Game is a speciality.

For more information on types of restaurants *see pages 186–7*

Szara   zł zł zł
International   **Map** 6 D2
Rynek Główny 6
Tel *12 421 66 69*
An imposing place with vaulted ceilings, crisp linens and a grand menu that spans the globe, Szara has a reputation for quality.

Szara Gęś   zł zł zł
Traditional Polish   **Map** 6 D3
Rynek Główny 17
Tel *12 430 63 11*
Feast on goose, suckling pig or venison in the opulent dining room of this traditional restaurant. Be sure to leave room for the signature grey goose dessert.

Trzy Rybki   zł zł zł
Fine dining   **Map** 6 D2
ul. Szczepańska 5
Tel *12 384 08 06*
The cosy flagship restaurant of the Stary hotel serves a seasonally changing menu of European fare.

Wentzl   zł zł zł
International   **Map** 6 D3
Rynek Główny 19
Tel *12 429 52 99*
Savour Polish and European food in a historic setting with oak floors, high ceilings and lavish fabrics.

Wierzynek   zł zł zł
Traditional Polish   **Map** 6 D3
Rynek Główny 15
Tel *12 424 96 00*
Claiming to be the oldest restaurant in Krakow, Wierzynek serves sumptuous Polish fare in elegant, wooden-beamed rooms.

Kazimierz Quarter

Fabryka Pizzy   zł
Italian   **Map** 4 D2
ul. Jozefa 34
Tel *12 433 80 81*
The "Pizza Factory" serves some of the tastiest and best-value thin-crust pizzas in Poland, plus a good selection of pasta dishes.

DK Choice

Pierożki u Wincenta   zł
Polish   **Map** 4 D2
ul. Bożego Ciała 12
Tel *506 806 304*
Pierogi are among Poland's most emblematic dishes, yet they rarely receive the culinary attention they deserve. A tiny restaurant, "Pierogi Mr Vincent" offers only *pierogi*, each stuffed with all kinds of creative fillings, including exotic spicy versions.

Polakowski   zł
Polish   **Map** 4 D1
ul. Miodowa 39
Tel *12 421 07 76*
This popular order-at-the-counter restaurant offers the best in Polish cooking, including *bigos*, *pierogi* and *żurek* (rye soup), plus pancakes and Jewish specialities.

Dawno temu na Kazimierzu zł zł
Traditional Polish   **Map** 4 E1
ul. Szeroka 1
Tel *12 421 21 17*
Enjoy classic Polish and Jewish fare in a room full of retro furnishings and memorabilia.

Genji Sushi Premium   zł zł
Japanese   **Map** 6 E5
ul. Dietla 55
Tel *12 429 59 59*
This restaurant offers a full range of Japanese dishes. The decor is Far Eastern too, with one room carpeted in dried rushes.

Horai   zł zł
Asian   **Map** 4 D2
pl. Wolnica 4
Tel *12 430 03 58*
The menu at Horai spans the entire Asian continent, with solid standards across the board. The Thai curries are especially strong.

DK Choice

Nolio   zł zł
Italian   **Map** 4 D2
ul. Krakowska 27
Tel *12 346 24 49*
Housed in a historic mansion that has been given a modern makeover, Nolio serves excellent thin-crust pizzas made from carefully sourced ingredients – the mozzarella comes from the traditional buffalo-farming areas of Italy. Jazz and blues provide the perfect soundtrack to the dining experience. The place is always busy, so book in advance.

Trezo   zł zł
Traditional Polish   **Map** 4 D1
ul. Miodowa 33
Tel *12 374 50 00*
Classic meat, poultry and fish dishes are presented with style in an interior that mixes modern minimalism with exposed brick. Live music at weekends.

Zazie Bistro   zł zł
French   **Map** 4 D2
ul. Józefa 34
Tel *500 410 829*
Everything from onion soup and bouillabaisse to mussels with fries is served here. With low prices and little space, the place is often busy.

The warmly lit, exposed brick-walled interior of Trezo

Klezmer Hois   zł zł zł
Jewish   **Map** 4 E1
ul. Szeroka 6
Tel *12 411 16 22*
Quality Jewish and Central European fare is served in this restaurant filled with bric-a-brac. There is Klezmer music nightly.

DK Choice

Studio Qulinarne   zł zł zł
Contemporary Polish **Map** 4 D2
ul. Gazowa 4
Tel *12 430 69 14*
Studio Qulinarne uses traditional Polish ingredients, Mediterranean style and the odd touch of Oriental spice to conjure up an original menu. Game and seafood feature strongly. The bright interior is filled with bookshelves and wine bottles; the garden is one of Krakow's loveliest.

Wesoła, Kleparz and Biskupie

Glonojad   zł
Vegetarian   **Map** 6 E1
pl. Jana Matejki 2
Tel *12 346 16 77*
This homely order-at-the-counter café serves hearty vegetarian dishes, including curries, burritos and samosas.

Jarema   zł zł zł
Eastern European   **Map** 2 D3 & 6 E1
pl. Matejki 5
Tel *12 429 36 69*
Cuisine from the eastern margins of what used to be the Polish–Lithuanian commonwealth are on the menu here, including plenty of hearty meat dishes sourced from old recipe books.

Piasek and Nowy Świat

Green Way   zł
Vegetarian   Map 5 B2
ul. Krupnicza 22
Tel *604 957 142*
A good-value buffet restaurant, Green Way serves all kinds of meat-free fare, including filling soups, generous salads and tasty savoury pancakes.

Mamma Mia   zł
Italian   Map 5 C1
ul. Karmelicka 14
Tel *12 430 04 92*
A classy pizzeria that draws local families in droves, Mamma Mia opts for authenticity rather than experimentation in its traditional pizza toppings. There are also many pasta alternatives.

Smakołyki   zł
Traditional Polish   Map 5 C4
ul. Straszewskiego 28
Tel *12 430 30 99*
Located opposite the main university building, this modern, bright canteen restaurant is the ideal place to try filling, inexpensive Polish favourites such as potato pancakes, stuffed cabbage leaves and *barszcz*.

CK Browar   zł zł
Traditional Polish   Map 6 D1
ul. Podwale 6–7
Tel *12 429 25 05*
Krakow's oldest brew-pub, this large brewery-restaurant is an excellent place to enjoy local favourites such as sausages and *bigos*, plus the house-brewed ales.

Dynia Resto-Bar   zł zł
International   Map 5 B2
ul. Krupnicza 20
Tel *12 430 08 38*
The "Pumpkin" excels in pasta dishes, salads and fresh cakes. There is also a kids' menu. The restaurant has a wonderful walled garden.

Międzymiastowa   zł zł
International   Map 5 A1
ul. Dolnych Młynów 10/7a
Tel *577 304 450*
Featuring a post-industrial interior with huge factory windows, this buzzing restaurant has a menu that includes pizzas, burgers, risottos, pastas and fish dishes.

Pod Norenami   zł zł
Asian/Vegetarian   Map 5 B2
ul. Krupnicza 6
Tel *661 219 289*
Sushi, ramen soups and excellent Thai curries are the reasons

why guests make repeat visits to this delightful eatery. It also prepares vegan dishes.

Veganic   zł zł
Vegetarian   Map 5 A1
ul. Dolnych Młynów 10
Tel *668 468 469*
Creative vegetarian and vegan cuisine are dished up in an artfully distressed former factory space. There is a varied breakfast menu and light lunch bites.

Zielona Kuchnia   zł zł
Organic   Map 1 B3
ul. Grabowskiego 8/9
Tel *12 634 55 22*   **Closed** *Mon*
The emphasis at this sleek eco-restaurant is on organic produce and naturally reared meats. There are also vegetarian options.

Biała Róża   zł zł zł
International   Map 1 C5 & 5 C4
ul. Straszewskiego 16
Tel *12 421 51 90*
This convivial restaurant between the Philharmonic Hall and Wawel Hill serves Polish classics with French and Italian influences.

The Olive   zł zł zł
Mediterranean   Map 3 B1 & 5 B4
ul. Powiśle 7
Tel *12 662 10 00*
The Sheraton Hotel's showpiece restaurant offers refined Polish and Mediterranean fare, especially fish and seafood. Try Polish specialities such as roasted duck stuffed with veal and vegetables. Good wine list.

Someplace Else   zł zł zł
Mexican   Map 3 B1 & 5 B4
ul. Powiśle 7
Tel *12 662 16 70*
The bar of the Sheraton offers an affordable menu of Mexican

specialities, plus burgers and chicken wings. Sporting events are shown on the big screen. Al fresco seating is available in the garden during summers.

Further Afield

Manzana   zł
Mexican   Map 4 E3
ul. Krakusa 11
Tel *514 786 813*
This is the place for tacos, burritos, fajitas and other Mexican classics. It also has the biggest selection of tequila in Krakow.

Stylowa   zł zł
Traditional Polish
osiedle Centrum C bl. 3 (Aleja Róża)
Tel *12 644 26 19*
One of the few restaurants in Nowa Huta, Stylowa is like a step back in time, with its 1980s decor and old-fashioned (but delicious) meat-and-potatoes menu.

U Ziyada   zł zł
International
ul. Jodłowa 13
Tel *12 429 71 05*
Perched high on a hill, this café-restaurant on the edge of Las Wolski forest has superb views across the Vistula River and serves quality Polish, European and Kurdish cuisine.

Zakładka   zł zł zł
French   Map 4 E3
ul. Józefińska 2
Tel *12 442 74 42*   **Closed** *Mon lunch*
Just across the river from the Kazimierz Quarter, this bistro offers a creative and seasonally changing menu. You can also pop in simply for a sandwich and a glass of wine.

The airy interior of the Olive, located inside the Sheraton Hotel

For more information on types of restaurants *see pages 186–7*

Cafés and Bars

Krakow's cafés are an important part of everyday life and are often institutions in their own right. It would be unthinkable to deny a Krakovian his or her daily 15 minutes or so spent chatting with a friend or reading a newspaper in a café. The majority of cafés have regular customers, who come year in, year out to their chosen place, every day except at weekends.

Cafés

Due to Krakow's Habsburg heritage, a strong café tradition prevails across the city. Situated in the heart of the Old Quarter, **Kawiarnia Noworolski** is one of the longest established cafés – it dates back to the end of the 19th century. Housed in the Cloth Hall, with its entrance facing the Mickiewicz Monument, its interior is modelled on the cafés of Vienna. A visit to **Jama Michalika** (see p116), renowned for the Zielony Balonik (Green Balloon) Cabaret, is a must.

Elsewhere in the city there is a wealth of modern inter-nationalized coffee chains, with espressos, cappuccinos and lattes on the menu. For a bit more character, visitors should seek out the quirky cafés frequented by locals, which often provide speciality coffees and a home-cooked selection of snacks, main meals and cakes. Running west from the Old Quarter, ul. Krupnicza has plenty of places to choose from for a quick pick me-up or to relax for an hour or two. Hidden behind the Józef Mehoffer House Museum (see p149) is the charming **Meho Café**, with outdoor seating in the building's pretty gardens. The cool **Tektura** and **Karma** serve some of the best coffee in the city – and food, too. In Kazimierz, **Café Młynek** has a laidback vibe and offers vegetarian versions of hearty Polish food. Polish coffeehouse chain **Columbus Coffee** is another reliable choice.

Krakow's very large student population is one of the main reasons the city's cafés continue to thrive. Students of all subjects, ranging from art to philosophy, can be found lounging around in the cafés that surround the old university buildings. These include **Nowa Prowincja**, with its legendary hot chocolate – hot chocolate fans should also head for **Pijalnia Czekolada Wedel** in the Old Quarter.

A particular Krakow speciality is the bookshop café, where tables and chairs are spread among the bookshelves. **Massolit** is a warren of rooms filled with books and nooks, perfect for browsing and relaxing with a book and slice of cake. **Kawiarnia Literacka**, **Bona** and **De Revolutionibus** are also outstandingly relaxing examples of the genre.

The art of cake- and dessert-making remains strong and there are some gorgeous examples at patisseries such as **Słodki Wentzl**. Look out for apple cake (szarlotka), a Krakow favourite. Tasty canapés served on bread from the highlands and tea with home-made raspberry syrup are just two specialities of the **Café Camelot**. The walls here are decorated with pictures by the celebrated Polish naive artist Nikifor. The **Dym** (Smoke) is next door, serving delicious Pischinger cake.

Street Cafés

Most of the eateries in Market Square (Rynek Główny) open street bars and cafés in the spring and summer. The square is thus transformed into a huge open-air café for thousands of customers.

A little away from the square, the corner of ul. Św. Tomasza and ul. Św. Jana is a tiny pavement café paradise. The street café set up by the **Black Gallery** is very busy at night, sometimes till the early hours.

The butchers' stalls in the centre of plac Nowy in Kazimierz serve Polish favourites until after dark: some of the best sausages in the city are grilled here, and the zapiekanki or pierogi make great stomach fillers pre- or post-drinks.

Bars

Again, Krakow's huge student population ensures that there are all manner of bars catering for every possible taste. The main drinking areas are the Old Quarter and the former Jewish district of Kazimierz, where many bars stay open until the early hours and have a pronounced bohemian edge. In Kazimierz, the streets surrounding the lively plac Nowy have a wide variety of drinking spots, including vodka bars, craft beer, multi-tap joints and some that epitomise the alternative, bohemian vibe that prevails around the area. Among the "classically Kazimierz" bars, featuring rickety furniture, lace tablecloths and candle-light, is **Singer** (the original Kazimierz bar that started the trend). Several tables here have old Singer sewing machines affixed to them, lending the place a unique charm. By day, Singer is a great place to relax; by night, the music and dancing carries on until the early hours. Also embracing the retro-bohemian ambience are **Alchemia**, **Eszeweria** and **Mleczarnia**; all three are great options for an evening drink.

The popularity of craft beer has had an enormous impact on Krakow's drinking scene and there is an abundance of brew pubs to pick from. Though the choice – and quality – of the beer is unquestionably excellent, one brew pub can be very difficult to distinguish from the next: post-industrial decor – plenty of sanded wood and exposed brickwork – prevails in most. Some of the establishments making themselves heard, however, include **Browar Lubicz** and **Stara Zajezdnia**. Multitaps serving all manner of guest beers from Poland and beyond include the aptly named **House of Beer**, **Multi Qlti Tap Bar** and **Beer Gallery**. One of the first bars to set up inside Tytano – a former tobacco factory turned trendy cultural centre – is

Weźża Krafta, Krakow's biggest multitap bar and hugely popular with the alternative crowd.

Those in search of cocktails should head to **Mash Room** or **Baroque**, both of which specialize in shaking up a

good drink. **Afera** and **Black Gallery** both offer DJ nights, live music and late opening hours. **Piekny Pies** is perfect for those that want to party til dawn; expect a real mix of music from grunge to motown.

DIRECTORY

Afera
ul. Sławkowska 13.
Map 1 C4 (6 D1).
Tel 12 421 17 71.

Alchemia
ul. Estery 5.
Map 4 D1.
Tel 12 421 22 00.

Antycafe
ul. Sławkowska 12.
Map 1 C4 (6 D2).
Tel 506 48 18 88.

Baroque
ul. Św. Jana 16.
Map 1 C4 (6 D2).
Tel 12 422 01 06.

Beer Gallery
ul. Warszauera 10.
Map 4 D1.
Tel 601 408 870.

Black Gallery
ul. Mikołajska 24.
Map 2 D4 (6 E2).
Tel 724 630 154.

Bomba na Placu
pl. Szczepański 2/1.
Map 1 C4 (5 C1).
Tel 782 60 19 99.

Bona
ul. Kanonicza 11.
Map 1 C5 (6 D4).
Tel 12 430 52 22.

Browar Lubicz
ul. Lubicz 17J.
Map 2 E4.
Tel 12 353 99 44.

Bunkier Café
pl. Szczepański 3A.
Map 1 C4 (5 C1).
Tel 12 431 05 85.

Café Camelot
ul. Św. Tomasza 17.
Map 1 C4 (6 D2).
Tel 12 421 01 23.

Café Młynek
pl. Wolnica 7.
Map 4 D2.
Tel 12 430 62 02.

Carpe Diem II
ul. Sławkowska 6a.
Map 2 D4 (6 E2).
Tel 12 426 10 80.

Charlotte Chleb i Wino
pl. Szczepański 2.
Map 1 C4 (5 C1).
Tel 600 807 880.

Columbus Coffee
ul. Starowiślna 27.
Map 2 D5 (6 F4).
Tel 600 797 415.

De Revolutionibus
ul. Bracka 14.
Map 1 C5 (6 D3).
Tel 530 769 530.

Dym
ul. Św. Tomasza 13.
Map 1 C4 (6 D2).
Tel 12 429 66 61.

Eszeweria
ul. Józefa 9.
Map 4 D2.
Tel 517 491 927.

House of Beer
ul. Św. Tomasza 35.
Map 1 C4 (6 D2).
Tel 530 129 147.

Jama Michalika
ul. Floriańska 45.
Map 2 D4 (6 E2).
Tel 12 422 15 61.

Jazz Rock Café
ul. Sławkowska 12.
Map 1 C4 (6 C1).
Tel 12 430 59 59

Karma
ul. Krupniczka 12.
Map 1 B4 (5 B2).
Tel 662 387 281.

Kawiarnia Literacka
ul. Krakowska 41.
Map 4 D2.
Tel 513 158 167.

Kawiarnia Noworolski
Rynek Główny 1,
Cloth Hall.
Map 1 C4 (6 D2).
Tel 515 100 998.

Mash Room
ul. Dolnych Młynów 10/7.
Map 1 B4 (5 B1).
Tel 530 053 551.

Massolit
ul. Felicjanek 4.
Map 1 B5 (5 B4).
Tel 12 432 41 50.

Meho Café
ul. Krupnicza 26.
Map 1 B4 (5 B2).
Tel 600 480 049.

Mleczarnia
ul. Meiselsa 20.
Map 4 D1.
Tel 12 421 85 32.

Multi Qlti Tap Bar
ul. Szewska 21.
Map 1 C4 (5 C2).
Tel 12 341 58 47.

Nowa Prowincja
ul. Bracka 3–5.
Map 1 C5 (6 D3).
Tel 12 430 59 59.

Pauza
Stolarska 5/3.
Map 6 D3.
Tel 608 601 522.

Piękny Pies
ul. Bożego Ciała 9.
Map 4 D2.

Pierwszy Lokal na Stolarskiej
ul. Stolarska 6.
Map 1 C5 (6 D3).
Tel 12 431 24 41.

Pijalnia Czekolady Wedel
Rynek Główny 46.
Map 1 C4 (6 D2).
Tel 12 429 40 85.

Pod Papugami Irish Pub
ul. Św. Jana 18.
Map 1 C4 (6 D2).
Tel 12 422 61 01.

Singer
ul. Estery 20.
Map 4 D1.
Tel 12 292 06 22.

Słodki Wentzel
Rynek Główny 19.
Map 1 C4 (6 D3).
Tel 12 429 57 12.

Stara Zajezdnia
ul. Św. Wawryńca 12.
Map 4 D2.
Tel 664 323 988.

Tektura
Krupnicza 7.
Map 1 B4 (5 B2).
Tel 797 827 807.

U Louisa
Rynek Główny 13.
Map 1 C4 (6 D3).
Tel 12 617 02 22.

Vis-a-vis
Rynek Główny 29.
Map 1 C4 (6 D2).
Tel 12 422 69 61.

Weżże Krafta
ul. Dolnych Młynów 10/3.
Map 1 B4 (5 B1).
Tel 12 307 40 50.

SHOPS AND MARKETS

Krakow has always been a favourable place for merchants and recent reforms have stimulated trade. Unlike in other Polish cities, most of the prewar buildings in Krakow have remained in private hands. After 1989 the number of new shops surged with house owners either opening shops themselves or letting premises out. A profusion of shop-signs appeared on façades, inner courtyards and basements.

Quality soon took over and big Western names also began to appear. Today one can hardly tell the difference between a Krakow shop and its Viennese or Parisian counterpart. The area around Market Square is especially good for shopping offering a variety of elegant shops, little traffic and many cafés. For something a bit more unique, markets and street stalls offer a good alternative, as well as a lively atmosphere.

Shopping Hours

In Poland, unlike in many other Western European countries, there is no law regulating the hours of trade. Each shop owner decides for themselves when to open and close their shop, and this is regarded as a necessary part of a free-market economy. Grocers open in Krakow at 6 or 7am and close at 7pm at the earliest. Many remain open until 10pm or longer, and a dozen or so shops are open 24 hours. Other types of shops are generally open between 10am and 7pm on weekdays, but on Saturdays close at 2 or 3pm. All shops within the Planty green belt tend to trade on Sundays for similar periods to those on Saturdays. All shops are customarily open on the Sunday preceding Christmas and Easter Day. Supermarkets are at their busiest on Friday afternoon and evening. The great number of tourist shops in the centre attract

Pictures for sale, displayed on the wall near St Florian's Gate

customers all the time regardless of the day of the week but Saturdays are possibly the busiest.

How to Pay

Throughout Poland, cash is the most popular form of payment though most shops and restaurants do accept major credit cards. It is advisable to carry small change for small purchases as some places may not accept large notes. All prices displayed are inclusive of VAT.

Department Stores and Shopping Malls

Jubilat, built in the mid-1970s, is the largest department store in Krakow. The food department is on the ground floor, and on the other floors you will find household goods, furniture and electrical appliances, clothes, shoes and cosmetics, as well as toys and books. The large **Galeria Krakowska** shopping mall is located by the main train station, and there is another large mall, **Galeria Kazimierz**, on the opposite side of town. Both contain dozens of stores, including international names,

A collectors' fair in Market Square

and at least one large supermarket. A little out of town, but served by many bus routes, is a large branch of the **Factory** clothes discount store.

Right on the Market Square (Rynek Główny) is the **Pasaż 13** shopping centre. Converted from a beautiful old townhouse, it has 17 designer and boutique shops, plus a restaurant.

Krakow now has several large shopping malls further out from the centre, with more opening all the time. They include mega supermarkets, DIY stores and all the usual services you would expect elsewhere in Europe.

Dolls in regional costumes sold in the Cloth Hall

The interior of Massolit Books, located in the Old Town

Markets and Fairs

Krakow's markets are never called bazaars as in other Polish towns. Here the term bazaar has a pejorative connotation. In Krakow locals go to the "square" to buy fruit and vegetables, cheese, meat, fish or other produce from the stallholders.

The Old Kleparz market is the nearest to the city centre. The New Kleparz market sells not only food but also flowers and clothes, while every Tuesday and Friday you will find stalls selling brooms, clay pots and wickerware. The market in Grzegórzecka Street by the Hala Targowa (Market Hall) is the biggest and full of stalls selling meat, fruit and vegetables. On Sundays, the whole of the Hala Targowa area is taken over by a large flea and antiques market, where visitors can browse an enormous array of furniture, crockery and bric-a-brac laid out by sellers on the ground. A covered area contains stalls selling old magazines, books and vintage postcards.

The unique atmosphere of the plac Nowy (New Market) in Kazimierz was used to good effect in the filming of *Days and Nights (Noce i dnie)*, a Polish film after a well-known novel by Maria Dąbrowska of the same title. The late 19th-century round butchers stalls, which are located in the centre of the square, are still in use, and are often surrounded by vegetable and fruit stands. There is an antiques and collectors' market on Saturdays and on Sundays the square becomes an extensive craft and clothes market, where among other things you can buy famous Harris tweed jackets from Scotland and woollen coats and Tyrolean tunics from Austria.

Sales

Seasonal sales are now quite common in a number of larger shops but, in terms of the selection of goods on offer and the prices, they are not as attractive as those in other Western European countries. Goods are no longer reduced because they are imperfect or no longer in fashion, as used to be the case, but because of promotions, end of season sales or the arrival of new collections.

A flower stall in Market Square

Shopping in Krakow

If you are a Western visitor you can expect to find everything in Krakow that you can buy at home. It is no longer necessary to bring items for everyday use. On the other hand you should not expect luxury Western merchandise, such as perfumes, alcohol, designer clothes and shoes, and other branded items, to be cheaper in Poland. You may, however, find bargains in shops and galleries selling handicrafts, silver jewellery, contemporary paintings and prints, as well as leather goods, bric-à-brac and coffee-table books.

Book and Record Shops

There are many excellent bookshops in Krakow. **Massolit Books** sells second-hand and new books in English. It also has a café that serves teas and superb cakes. It's common to find people pouring over books in here for hours on end. This is typical of Krakow, a university city, where the way of life is still heavily influenced by professors and students. Massolit also hosts literary readings, art exhibitions and musical events.

Empik, one of Poland's leading book retailers, has nine branches in Krakow, with the two biggest in the Galeria Krakowska and Kazimierz malls. The **American Bookstore**, specializes in English-language books. Cute, characterful book-shops with a well-chosen selection of English language titles and beautifully illustrated children's books include **Bona**, **Kawiarnia Literacka**, **De Revolutionibus** and **Lokator**. All of these shops also serve coffee and cakes, making them excellent places for a leisurely browse.

The prestigious **Znak** bookshop in Kościuszki Street has a large selection of foreign titles. The **Księgarnia Muzyczna Kurant** in Market Square specializes in music books, scores and recordings.

Antiques

Krakow is possibly the best place in Poland for antiques because the city was saved from destruction during World War II and Krakovians did not have to migrate. Foreigners are advised that exporting pre-1945 antiques from Poland is illegal without special permission, which is very difficult to obtain (see p212). As far as valuable works of art are concerned, as well as objects that form part of the cultural heritage, such as paintings, furniture, jewellery, old prints, rare books and maps, this law is rigorously observed, but less so in the case of objects of lesser value and bric-à-brac, which are plentiful in Krakow.

Antique dealers are mainly located in the area around the Planty. Occasional antique markets take place in Market Square and there is one every Saturday in plac Nowy. Every Sunday, sellers of collectors' items and second-hand books put up their stalls by the Hala Targowa in Grzegórzecka Street.

Folk Art

The annual folk Art Fair in Market Square takes place in September. Dozens of stalls are set up, selling sculpture, earthenware, woven rugs and wood carvings made in various parts of Poland.

The stalls in the **Cloth Hall** offer a large selection of crafts and are a must for the tourist. You will find here colourful, embroidered traditional costumes of the Krakow and Podhale regions, as well as walking sticks from the high-lands, crafted with an axe-like handle; ornate chess sets and jewellery boxes, devotional statues and Jewish objects all carved in wood; paper cutouts, painted Easter eggs, traditional dolls and much more.

Crafts and Contemporary Art

The stands in the Cloth Hall also sell silver jewellery, amber objets d'art, leather items and fabrics for the home. Shopping in this Renaissance hall has the added bonus of sustaining a trading tradition that goes back to the 16th century. The **Calik** gallery is famous for Christmas decorations and attracts customers from all over the world.

Krakow is a great place to pick up some Polish contemporary art, and demand for such works is ever growing. The **Starmach Gallery**, **Zderzak**, **Space Gallery**, **Galeria Mariana Gołogórskiego** and many others all display (and sell) works by contemporary artists. The city wall by St Florian's Gate serves as an open-air gallery, with paintings by local artists of sunsets and sunrises, galloping horses, large-scale nudes and many more displayed for visitors to admire – and purchase. Fans of satirical drawings by **Andrzej Mleczko** will find a visit to his gallery in St John's Street (Św. Jana) very rewarding. The small **LueLue** gallery is a great place to buy beautiful vintage photographs, paintings and postcards. It also offers a selection of graphic designs by contemporary artists. **Galeria Plakatu** houses a large collection of fascinating posters advertising Polish theatre, film and music acts.

Children

Krakow's shopping centres have a few places selling books, games and toys for children. In Galeria Krakowska, near the railway station, **Smyk** is a great all-rounder with a big selection of items to educate and entertain children of all ages. **Dragonus**, a small stall found by the escalators, stocks a huge range of boardgames. In the city centre, the unique **Bajo** celebrates traditional toys – everything is made of wood.

Clothes and Shoes

Large shopping malls such as Galeria Krakowska, Galeria Kazimierz and Bonarka City Center have a number of international clothing brands, and most globally known high-street labels have outlets here. Polish brands, such as **Vistula**, offer reasonably priced suits for men, and **Wólczanka** specializes in shirts. **Linen Dream** sells unique shawls, tunics and coats made by Polish artisans with organic materials. **Forum Design** offers the best all-round selection of clothes and household goods. **IDEA FIX** is a hothouse of Polish design, mixing fashion, art, music and photography.

Kazimerz is home to several design boutiques; **Marka**, **Mapaya** and **Anna Gregory** are among the most interesting. In Podgórze, **Pan Tu Nie Stał** offers a good range of t-shirts, bags and quirky accessories.

Promod offers a good selection of clothes and shoes from both leading foreign brands and designers, as well as Polish names.

The **Zebra Buty** chain of shops is best for Italian shoes.

Jewellery and Accessories

Poland is a known producer of amber and Krakow's **World of Amber** is well-stocked with rings, necklaces and bracelets, as well as more unusual items such as wine stoppers and chess sets. The Cloth Hall is also a good place to pick up an amber trinket or two. Those looking for something really unique have several options. **Lilou** and **Galeria Ora**, in the Old Quarter, have a great selection of delicate and pretty pieces, while **Blazko**, in Kazimierz, has bold, colourful accessories.

Food Shops and Off-Licences (Liquor Stores)

One of the few supermarkets in the centre of Krakow is **Carrefour** in the Galeria Krakowska mall. Large supermarkets such as **Tesco** are located away from the centre and cater for shoppers who come by car. There are super-markets on most of the housing estates, catering for local needs.

Most Krakovians purchase their fruit and vegetables from local stalls and markets. The Stary Kleparz market is the closest to the city centre, just a few minutes' walk away.

A large selection of wines from around the world can be found in the off-licence (liquor store) **In Vino Veritas**, as well as in the drinks depart-ment at the Galeria Krakowska. Those who favour strong spirits should head for **Szambelan** or **Regionalne Alkohole** where a broad range of speciality vodkas can be found.

Lovers of chocolate will be welcomed in the **Wawel** shop in Market Square, selling goods from the local sweet factory, Zakłady Przemysłu Cukierniczego. Many patisseries throughout Krakow offer a wonderful selection of cakes and pastries. The best doughnuts can be bought at **Michałek** and nougat at **Cichowscy**. Look out for *kremówka*, a delicious puff-pastry cake filled with custard and available in the city's main patisseries. **Goralskie Praliny** is a good source of locally made chocolates, while **Toruńskie Pierniki** specializes in the traditional gingerbread associated with the Polish city of Toruń.

Typical Polish delicatessen products such as sausage, ham, cheeses and fruit preserves can be found at **Krakowski Kredens**. **Delikatesy 13** on the market square has a particularly good selection.

For organic and health food from Poland and around the globe try specialist shops such as **Naturalny Sklepik**, **Natura** and **Bacówka**.

Cosmetics

All chemists (drug stores) and supermarkets sell basic cosmetic goods, but expensive international brands are best purchased from specialist shops where expert advice is also available. Guerlain and Yves Rocher have their own outlets and beauty clinics. Well-known foreign brands of perfumes, such as Gucci, Biagotti, Trussardi, Bulgari, Carolina Herrera and Burberry are available from **Sephora**. Another place to find a good selection of brands is in Galeria Krakowska.

Pharmacies

The majority of drugs are available from Polish chemists on prescription only. Prescriptions issued by overseas doctors are generally accepted without any problem. Non-prescription drugs and medicines are readily available throughout the city. In the city centre, there are many chemists in the following streets, among others: Szczepańska, Grodzka or Dunajewskiego. If you need some medication after normal opening hours, then go to one of the chemists that are open 24 hours; their addresses are displayed in all the chemists' shop windows. A 24-hour telephone service (12 94 39) will provide you with general medical information, including the location of the nearest hospital with an accident and emergency unit.

Florists

Krakow would not be Krakow without the flower stalls by the Mickiewicz statue in Market Square. On the day of the great poet's birthday, these street vendors have made it a tradition to lay flowers at the base of the statue in tribute. They also regularly make a gift of flowers to visiting foreign VIPs. On warm summer days you can buy flowers till late into the evening. There are many flower stalls to be found in Nowy Kleparz market and several dedicated florist shops around the city. Alternatively, you can buy bunches of flowers in one of the many 24-hour shops and at petrol stations.

DIRECTORY

Department Stores and Shopping Malls

Bonarka City Center
ul. Kamienskiego 11.
Tel 12 298 60 00.

Factory
ul. Rożańskiego 32.
Tel 12 297 35 00.

Galeria Kazimierz
ul. Podgórska 34.
Map 4 F1.
Tel 12 433 01 01.

Galeria Krakowska
ul. Pawia 5.
Map 2 D3 (6 F1).
Tel 12 428 99 00.

Jubilat
al. Krasińskiego 1–3.
Map 1 B5 (5 B4).
Tel 12 619 33 00.

Pasaż 13
Rynek Główny 13.
Map 1 C4 (6 D2).
Tel 12 617 02 27.

Book and Record Shops

American Bookstore
Slawkowska 24a.
Map 6 D1.
Tel 795 207 825.

Bona
ul. Kanonicza 11.
Map 1 C5 (6 D4).
Tel 12 430 52 22.

Bunkier Sztuki
pl. Szczepański 3A.
Map 1 C4 (5 C2).
Tel 12 422 10 52.

De Revolutionibus
ul. Bracka 14.
Map 1 C5 (6 D3).
Tel 530 769 530.

Empik
ul. Pawia 5 (Galeria Krakowska).
Map 2 D3 (6 F1).
Tel 12 451 03 85.

Inter Book
ul. Karmelicka 27.
Map 1 B3.
Tel 12 632 10 08.

Kawiarnia Literacka
ul. Krakowska 41.
Map 4 D2.
Tel 513 158 167.

Księgarnia Muzyczna Kurant
Rynek Główny 36.
Map 1 C4 (6 D2).
Tel 12 422 98 59.

Lokator
ul. Mostowa 1.
Map 4 D2.

Znak
ul. Sławkowska 1.
Map 1 C4 (6 D2).
Tel 12 422 45 48.

Rare and Second-Hand Books

Antykwariat AB
Rynek Główny 43.
Map 1 C4 (6 D2).
Tel 12 421 69 03.

Antykwariat Fundacja Judaica
ul. Meiselsa 17.
Map 4 D1.
Tel 12 430 64 49.

Antykwariat księgarski
ul. Stolarska 8/10.
Map 1 C5 (6 D3).
Tel 12 422 62 88.

Krakowski Antykwariat Naukowy
ul. Slawkowska 19.
Map 1 C4 (6 D2).
Tel 12 421 21 43.

Massolit Books
ul. Felicjanek 4.
Map 1 B5 (5 B4).
Tel 12 432 41 50.

Rara Avis
ul. Szpitalna 11.
Map 2 D4 (6 E2).
Tel 12 422 03 90.

Antiques

Connaisseur
Rynek Główny 11.
Map 1 C4 (6 D2).
Tel 12 421 02 34.

Desa
ul. Floriańska 13.
Map 1 C4 (6 D2).
Tel 12 422 27 06.

Sopocki Dom Aukcyjny
Rynek Główny 45.
Map 1 C4 (6 D2).
Tel 12 429 12 17.

Folk Art

Cloth Hall
Rynek Główny 1/3.
Map 1 C4 (6 D2).

Crafts and Contemporary Art

Autorska Galeria Andrzeja Mleczki (Mleczko Gallery)
ul. Św. Jana 14.
Map 1 C4 (6 D2).
Tel 12 421 71 04.

Calik
Rynek Główny 7.
Map 1 C4 (6 D2).
Tel 12 421 77 60.

Dekor Art
ul. Sławkowska 11.
Map 1 C4 (6 D1).
Tel 515 452 969.

Galeria Jana Siuty
ul. Sławkowska 14.
Map 1 C4 (6 D1).
Tel 12 423 20 07.

Galeria Mariana Gołogórskiego
ul. Grodzka 29.
Map 1 C5 (6 D4).
Tel 12 421 44 19.

Galeria Plakatu
ul. Stolarska 8–10.
Map 1 C5 (6 D3).
Tel 12 421 26 40.

Galeria Związku Polskich Artystów Plastyków (Gallery of the Association of Polish Artists)
ul. Łobzowska 3.
Map 1 C3 (5 C1).
Tel 12 632 46 22.

LueLue
ul. Miodowa 22.
Map 4 D1.
Tel 728 551 024.

Mocak
ul. Lipowa 4.
Map 3 F2.
Tel 12 263 40 17.

Punca
ul. Józefa 3.
Map 4 D2.
Tel 603 195 045.

Space Gallery
ul. Św. Marka 7.
Map 1 C4 (6 D1).
Tel 12 421 89 94.

Starmach Gallery
ul. Węgierska 5.
Map 4 E3.
Tel 12 656 43 17.

Zderzak
ul. Floriańska 3.
Map 1 C4 (6 D2).
Tel 12 429 67 43.

Children

Bajo
Grodzka 60.
Map 1 C5 (6 D5).
Tel 12 429 14 42.

Dragonus
ul. Pawia 5 (Galeria Krakowska).
Map 2 D3.
Tel 535 723 073.

Smyk
ul. Pawia 5 (Galeria Krakowska).
Map 2 D3.
Tel 22 461 02 19.

Clothes and Shoes

Anna Gregory
ul. Józefa 2.
Map 4 D2.
Tel 600 696 621.

Forum Design
ul. Dolnych Młynów 10.
Map 1 B4 (5 A1).
Tel 730 740 025.

IDEA FIX
ul. Bocheńska 7 .
Map 4 D2.
Tel 12 422 12 46.

**Linen Dream
(Lniane Marzenie)**
ul. Grodzka 59.
Map 1 C5 (6 D4).
Tel 790 46 61 03.

Mapaya
ul. Józefa 3.
Map 4 D2.
Tel 501 351 444.

Marka
ul. Józefa 5.
Map 4 D2.
Tel 12 422 2965.

Pan Tu Nie Stał
ul. Nadwiślańska 9.
Map 4 E2.
Tel 667 432 671.

Promod
ul. Floriańska 18.
Map 1 C4 (6 D2).
Tel 694 462 950.

Vistula
ul. Pawia 5 (Galeria
Krakowska).
Map 2 D3 (6 F1).
Tel 783 781 589.

Wólczanka
ul. Pawia 5 (Galeria
Krakowska).
Map 1 C4 (6 D2).
Tel 783 781 688.

Zebra Buty
Rynek Główny 7.
Map 1 C4 (6 D2).
Tel 722 333 010.

Jewellery and Accessories

Blazko
ul. Józefa 11.
Map 4 D2.
Tel 579 056 456.

Galeria Ora
ul. Św Anny 3.
Map 1 C4 (5 C2).
Tel 781 661 212.

Lilou
ul. Św Tomasza 27.
Map 2 D4 (6 E2).
Tel 12 312 13 93.

World of Amber
ul. Grodzka 38.
Map 1 C5 (6 D3).
Tel 12 430 21 14.

Food Shops

Bacówka
pl. Wolnica 1.
Map 4 D2.
Tel 667 681 105.

Carrefour
ul. Pawia 5 (Galeria
Krakowska).
Tel 12 297 71 00.

Cichowscy
ul. Starowišina 21.
Tel 12 421 02 27.

Delikatesy 13
Rynek Główny 13.
Map 1 C4 (6 D3).
Tel 12 617 02 07.

Goralskie Praliny
ul. Grodzka 8.
Map 1 C5 (6 D3).
Tel 502 525 083.

Krakowski Kredens
ul. Grodzka 7.
Map 1 C5 (6 D4).
Tel 12 696 48 00.

Michałek
ul. Krupnicza 6.
Map 1 B4 (5 C2).
Tel 12 422 47 05.

Natura
ul. Krupnicza 21.
Map 1 B4 (5 B2).
Tel 634 54 66.

Naturalny Sklepik
ul. Krupnicza 9.
Map 1 B4 (5 B2).
Tel 12 422 96 83.

Tesco
ul. Dobrego Pasterza 67.
Tel 506 001 875.

ul. Kapelanka 54.
Map 3 A3.
Tel 12 255 25 57.

ul. Wieliczka 259.
Tel 12 299 01 00.

ul. Wybickiego 10.
Tel 12 633 43 99.

Toruńskie Pierniki
ul. Grodzka 14.
Map 1 C5 (6 D3).
Tel 12 431 13 06.

Wawel
Rynek Główny 33.
Map 1 C4 (6 D2).
Tel 12 423 12 47.

Off-Licences (Liquor Stores)

In Vino Veritas
ul. Łobzowska 26.
Map 1 B2 (5 C1).
Tel 12 606 805 151.

Regionalne Alkohole
ul. Miodowa 28a.
Map 4 D1 (6 F5).
Tel 533 59 33 35.

Strefa Piwa
ul. Krowoderska 37.
Map 1 B2.
Tel 791 821 813.

Szambelan
ul. Gołębia 2.
Map 1 C5 (6 D3).
Tel 12 628 70 93.

Winoteka-Alkohole
Karmelicka 64.
Map 1 B3.
Tel 509 622 064.

Cosmetics

Sephora
ul. Floriańska 19.
Map 1 C4 (6 D2).
Tel 12 421 24 24.

Pharmacies

ul. Dunajewskiego 2.
Map 1 B4 (5 C2).
Tel 12 687 57 47.

Apteka Bonifratrów
ul. Krakowska 50.
Map 4 D2.
Tel 12 426 80 10.

**Apteka
Niezapominajka**
ul. Starowiślna 1.
Map 2 D5 (6 E3).
Tel 12 647 14 48.

Bobilewicz
Grodzka 26.
Map 1 C5 (6 D3).
Tel 12 432 07 60.

Dbam o Zdrowie
ul. Podwale 6.
Map 1 B4 (5 C2).
Tel 12 429 49 43.

Pod Opatrznoscia
ul. Karmelicka 23.
Map 1 B3.
Tel 12 631 19 80.

Pod Złotym Lwem
ul. Długa 4.
Map 1 C2
Tel 12 422 62 04.

Pod Złotym Tygrysem
ul. Szczepańska 1.
Map 1 C4 (5 C2).
Tel 12 422 92 93.

Świat. Apteka
ul. Szpitalna 38.
Map 2 D4 (6 E2).
Tel 12 422 65 34.

Ziko
ul. Dunajewskiego 2.
Map 1 C4 (5 C1).
Tel 12 687 57 47.

Florists

BeA
ul. Łobzowska 33/10.
Map 1 B3.
Tel 601 504 436.

Floristica
ul. Szewska 16.
Map 1 C4 (5 C2).
Tel 12 429 16 10.

Margareta
ul. Długa 74.
Map 1 C2.
Tel 12 633 78 63.

Sofi-Flora
ul. Pawia 5.
Map 2 D3 (6 F1).
Tel 12 628 78 77.

ENTERTAINMENT

Krakow is the cultural capital of Poland, and visitors looking for entertainment may find themselves spoiled for choice. Local theatres are among the best in the country and often host leading international companies. The Szymanowski Philharmonic Orchestra and Choir, and the Capella Cracoviensis have excellent reputations. Theatre, film, music and ballet festivals take place throughout the year, many of which are held in the magnificent interiors and grounds of historic houses and churches. Krakow also has a history of cabaret that goes back some 100 years, attracting both locals and visitors alike. The city's busy nightlife is easily comparable to that offered by Italian or Spanish cities; you only have to walk a couple of minutes to find a variety of nightclubs and bars. Housed in Gothic or Renaissance cellars, renovated factories, or spilling out onto the city's streets and squares, they are often open until very late or even till the early hours of the morning.

Useful Information

Full listings of cultural events in Krakow appear in the *Karnet – Krakowskie Aktualności Kulturalne* monthly, published by **InfoKraków** in both Polish and English. For the electronic version of the *Karnet* see their website on: www.karnet. krakow.pl. Current listings and reviews of cinemas, theatres and other events, as well as a guide to restaurants, discos and clubs (live music) are published on Friday in the *Gazeta Wyborcza* supplement entitled *Co jest grane?* (What's on?). Listings also appear in local newpapers on a daily basis.

Booking Tickets

Tickets for many major events can be purchased from the InfoKraków tourist office. This is also the best place to make enquiries about how and

Actors mid-performance during one of Krakow's many stage productions

where to buy other tickets or to make an advanced booking. Staff at the centre speak English, French, German and Italian. The main online booking site for major entertainment events is www.eventim.pl. The Empik bookshop also sells tickets for many concerts and cultural events. Seats for the Philharmonic Hall and the theatres are available from their respective box offices, which also take advance bookings. Cinema tickets can be booked over the phone. Bear in mind that some performances require booking months in advance.

Ticket Prices

Ticket prices have increased considerably in recent years, but they are still cheaper than in the West. Theatre seats are more expensive in Krakow compared to anywhere else in Poland, and in greatest demand. Average prices can vary from 25 to 40 zł per person. Cinema tickets usually cost between 13 and 20 zł. Museum tickets are good value; in some museums entrance is free on one day of the week.

Night Transport

Bus and tram day-routes stop around 11pm. Night buses and trams operate according to timetables displayed at stops or online; visit www.mpk.krakow.pl for more information. Tickets can be purchased from ticket machines at some stops and on most trams and buses.

Taxis are a better option. A radio-taxi booked over the phone is cheaper than one at a taxi-rank but you can rely on the taxis waiting at the ranks in the city centre. Most taxi drivers are honest, but it is best to avoid the

Musicians wearing costumes of the Krakow region

taxi rank by the main Railway Station. If you require a taxi while in the main Railway Station area, go to the radio-taxi rank situated at roof level above the platforms (use the platform stairway).

Festivals

The city plays host to a multitude of cultural festivals; the only problem is how to choose the most interesting. The open-air Krakow Live Festival will appeal to rock fans, the Krakow Film Festival to film lovers, the Sacrum Profanum festival to classical and experimental music aficionados, the Dragon Festival to children and admirers of grandiose theatrical displays, while enthusiasts of brass instruments may enjoy the International Music Festival of Military Bands.

Walks and Open-Air Events

The tradition of open-air fairs in Krakow goes back to at least the early part of the 19th century when folk festivals were organized on the Błonia fields, then located out of town. One of the attractions was to try to climb a pole smeared in soap; a flask of alcohol and sausages attached to the top of the pole awaited the successful climber. The event has since disappeared but the Błonia is still a venue for public events, of either a traditional or light entertainment nature. Two great cavalry parades in the inter-war years, attended by Marshals Józef Piłsudski and Edward Rydz Śmigły respectively, took place here. The masses celebrated on these fields by Pope John Paul II, and attended by millions of the faithful, are commemorated by a granite block brought here from the Tatra Mountains.

All kinds of concerts, festivals and fairs also take place at the Błonia.

The Jordan Park, situated opposite the Błonia fields, is very popular with parents with toddlers. Doctor Henryk Jordan, a Krakow physician, introduced the idea of playing fields which are now found throughout the country and are named after this celebrated physician.

The Jordan Park in Krakow was the first-ever public playground for small children.

The Wolski Wood (Las Wolski) is not far from Krakow and offers many walking routes (see pp174–5). For Krakovians it is one of the favourite destinations for a day out, though the zoo (see p175) is also popular. At weekends and on public holidays there is no access to the zoo by car, so use bus or taxi services. On weekdays a charge is made to enter the zoo by car.

Summer concerts in the open air are organized in the Wawel Castle courtyard, in the gardens of the Archaeological Museum and in Radio Kraków's amphitheatre as well as in the courtyard of the Collegium Iuridicum and on a temporary stage in Market Square.

A pillar advertising cultural events

The cosy interior of the small Pod Baranami cinema

Out of Town Trips

A number of appealing sights are located within close proximity to Krakow. A trip to the Ojców National Park (see p160), one of the smallest but most beautiful of Polish national parks, is an unforgettable experience. White limestone rocks, such as Hercules's Club, have very unusual shapes.

The Salt Mines at Wieliczka (see p160) have been included by UNESCO on their World Heritage List. The mines and the underground sanatorium housed here are unique. Niepołomice (see p159) has a 14th-century castle and the remnants of an ancient forest where bison are bred. The Benedictine Abbey in Tyniec (see p161) is beautifully located on the Vistula and worth visiting, as is Schindler's Factory (see p158), in the former industrial district of Zabłocie.

Krakow Opera House (Opera Krakowska), incorporating the former riding school building

Theatre, Music, Nightlife and Sports

Krakow is famous for its cultural traditions. The renowned Stary Theatre gained its fame through productions directed by Konrad Swinarski and counts as one of Europe's leading theatre companies. The city is filled with music of every kind, from classical concerts and opera to hip-hop, techno, rock and jazz. Cabarets continue the best of traditions that go back to the beginning of the 20th century. As well as myriad cultural events, Krakow also offers good sporting facilites for those who like to keep active.

Major Venues

Krakow has two state-of-the-art concert venues which can host an extraordinary variety of events. **Krakow Congress Centre (ICE)** is a sleek contemporary building with a silver-grey exterior. It contains a large auditorium, a theatre and an impressive complex of spacious halls. The centre can serve as a venue for cultural events such as concerts, opera, and theatrical and ballet performances. The donut-shaped **Tauron Arena**, just east of the centre, is an even more futuristic-looking structure. A multifunctional indoor sporting and perfor-mance venue, the arena has the capacity to accommodate up to 22,000 people. Event schedules for both venues can be found on their respective websites.

Cultural Organizations

Krakow does not have a theatre company that performs in a foreign language on a perma-nent basis but the city occasionally hosts foreign theatre companies, which perform in their own languages.
A number of bodies, such as the **Institut Français**, the **Goethe Institut**, the **Instituto Cervantes de Cracovia**, the **Istituto Italiano di Cultura** and the Manggha **Japanese Centre of Art and Technology**, are all actively involved in artistic patronage. They usually organize events in the language of their country, and infor-mation about these events can be obtained from **InfoKraków**.

Theatre

The first professional theatre company was established in Krakow in 1781, and today there are many theatres. The most renowned is **Stary Teatr** (Old Theatre), where some of the best actors, directors and set designers work. Performances are mostly based on Polish and other Eastern European classics and Romantic literature.

The **Teatr im. Juliusza Słowackiego** shares the same traditions and types of plays. The building, modelled on the Opéra Garnier in Paris, opened in 1893. Its splendid Art Nouveau interior features a curtain designed by the painter Henryk Hektor Siemiradzki. As an added bonus, spectators may watch the performance from the box originally used by the Austro-Hungarian Emperor, Franz Joseph and his wife Sissi.

The **Krakowski Teatr Scena Stu** gained fame through unconventional performances, sometimes staged in the open air, and other grand productions. In their main venue in aleja Krasińskiego, their performances are pre-dominantly of the classics. Benefit performances celebrating theatre stars take place here, and are broadcast by television. These have became classics in their own right.

The **Ludowy Theatre** in Nowa Huta has a young cast who perform not only in Nowa Huta but also in two other venues in Krakow – in the cellars beneath the Town Hall and in Kanonicza Street.

The **Bagatela Theatre** specializes in light satirical productions. The **Teatr Lalki i Maski Groteska** is primarily a puppet theatre and generally hosts performances for children. It has also staged a number of highly original puppet plays for adults.

The experimental productions of the world-famous Cricot 2 theatre ceased following the death of its radical stage and director, Tadeusz Kantor, in 1990. The **Cricoteka** is a museum that documents the history of this major theatre and the art of Tadeusz Kantor, and includes photographs and set designs. Avant-garde traditions are main-tained by **Teatr Łaźnia Nowa**, a leading contemporary theatre company based in Nowa Huta.

Opera and Ballet

After many years without a permanent venue, the **Opera Krakowska** moved into its premises on ul. Lubicz in 2008. It continues to stage occasional performances at various venues across the city, including the courtyard of Wawel Castle and underground at the Wieliczka Salt Mines. The productions here include Galician all-time favourites by Kalman, Lehar and the Strausses. Small-scale productions are held in the charmingly intimate **Krakow Chamber Opera** in Kazimierz.

For many years, ballet was rather unpopular in Krakow, but regular performances now take place at the Opera Krakowska building.

Cabaret

Cabaret artists are much in demand in Krakow and it is wise to book tickets early to avoid missing out. Opened in 1956, the literary **Piwnica Pod Baranami** is the longest-running cabaret in Krakow and is famous throughout Poland. Despite the death of its founder Piotr Skrynecki in 1997, the cabaret continues and is very popular. The **Loch Camelot** is artistically affiliated to the Piwnica and also performs in cellars.

Cinemas

Krakow has many multiplex cinemas, but the largest and best independent cinema is **Kijów.Centrum**. Besides its regular programme, it is also a venue for a number of festivals, including the Krakow Film Festival and one dedicated to commercials. Food and drinks are available on the first floor. A truly Parisian-style multiplex, the **Kino ARS** is situated at the junction of św. Jana and św. Tomasza. It comprises several auditoria named after historic cinemas, such as Salon, Gabinet, Kiniarnia, Aneks and Reduta. Cafés can be found in all of them.

The small **Pod Baranami** cinema, housed in the Palace of the Rams, is very popular with those seeking independent and art-house films from around the world. Its prime location is an added bonus. After a show, walk a few steps to enjoy a drink in the Piwnica Pod Baranami bar. Among other cinemas worth recommending are the **Kika** and **Mikro**.

Classical Music

The most prestigious concert hall in Krakow is the Szymanowski Philharmonic Hall, home of the **Filharmonia**. Classical music is, however, best enjoyed in the more informal setting of one of the city's many historic houses. Among the many venues are the Wawel Castle, the National Museum in the Cloth Hall and numerous churches. There is a regular programme of chamber concerts at the imposing **St Peter and Paul's Church**. In summer, concerts are also organized outside in such open-air venues as the arcades of the Wawel Castle, Collegium Maius's courtyard, in the former prison of St Michael (now the Archaeological Museum) and in the Radio Kraków amphitheatre, housed in the former Tarnowski Palace. For those prepared to venture out of the city, there are the renowned organ recitals in the Romanesque Benedictine Abbey in Tyniec near Krakow (see p161).

Music Clubs

Any jazz fan visiting Krakow should seek out the **Jazz Club u Muniaka**, which was founded by Janusz Muniak (1941–2016) and is still very popular. Jazz concerts take place at the **Harris Piano Jazz Bar** and **PiecArt** as well as Piwnica pod Baranami.

The main venue for medium-sized alternative rock bands is **Kwadrat**, and there are many smaller venues catering to indie, metal, blues and cover bands. You can check the websites or Facebook pages of **Dali Club**, **Klub Kornet**, **Alchemia** or **Piękny Pies** to find a list of upcoming acts.

Nightclubs

Krakow offers a good selection of nightclubs, although venues can go in and out of fashion with alarming speed. Clubs that have been around for a while and have a good party atmosphere include **Afera Club**, **Frantic** and **Prozak 2.0**. **Kawiarnia Naukowa** and **Zetpete** cater for niche genres of dance music and alternative rock. **Drukarnia** caters for fans of avant-garde hip-hop, grunge and acid jazz music.

If you feel exhausted after dancing the night away at a nightclub, **Free Pub** and **Black Gallery** are good places to go to to relax.

Krakow's nightclubs do not have any specific hour at which they close. In summer, especially, a club-goer may simply leave a club and go straight to work. Visitors should note that not all of the clubs have websites, and it is often a good idea to check for Facebook pages for opening hours, as well as information about what kind of music is being played on a particular night. Entry fees and drink prices are reasonable wherever you go.

Sports

As far as sports facilities are concerned, Krakow has much to offer. The artificial lake in Kryspinów has clean water and is a good place for both beach lovers and windsurfers. A supervised swimming area can be found in the Nad Zalewem Recreation Centre. However, here there is a charge for the use of the centre and the lake's beaches. The sports grounds in Jordan Park are a good place for badminton players.

One of the most popular sporting activities in Krakow is ice skating, and open-air rinks are set up in public places between mid-September and early March. Two of the most popular locations are in the square in front of the **Galeria Krakowska** shopping mall and in Jordan Park. You can hire gear at the entrance to the rink.

Those looking to play a game or two of tennis should head to the courts at **Klub Tenisowy na Bloniach**, **Wola Sport Paradise** or **Nadwislan**.

Horse-riding facilities are available at **Krakowski Klub Jazdy Konnej**, as well as at a number of stables located on the outskirts of the city and further afield.

Increasingly, Krakovians have shown an interest in healthy living. Sauna, sun bed and health and beauty clinics have opened in all parts of the city, as have fitness clubs such as **Relax Body Club**. The **Korona Club**, which is attached to the hotel of the same name, offers a covered swimming pool (filled with sea water), fitness centre and sauna facilities.

If you want to go for a run during your visit, take advantage of Błonia Fields (see p149), the expansive meadow in the middle of the city. The Planty also makes a great circular route.

Billiards can be played in a number of venues throughout Krakow. Billiards and snooker clubs include the **Stage** and **Klub Biliardowy Pik**. There is a bowling alley at the Kazimierz bar and club **Plac Nowy 1**.

DIRECTORY

Booking Tickets

Eventim
🌐 evenim.pl

Empik
ul. Pawia 5 (Galeria Krakowska)
Map 2 D3 (6 F1).
Tel 12 451 03 85.

InfoKraków
ul. Św. Jana 2.
Map 1 C4 (6 D2).
Tel 12 354 27 25.

Major Venues

Krakow Congress Centre (ICE)
ul. Marii Konopickiej 17.
Map 3 B2.
Tel 12 354 23 00.
🌐 icekrakow.pl

Tauron Arena
ul. Stanislawa Lema 7.
Tel 12 349 11 02.
🌐 tauronarena
krakow.pl

Cultural Organizations

The British Council
Rynek Główny 6.
Map 1 C4 (6 D3).
Tel 12 428 59 30.
🌐 britishcouncil.pl

Goethe Institut
Rynek Główny 20.
Map 1 C4 (6 D3).
Tel 12 422 58 29.
🌐 goethe.de

Institut Français
Widok 12.
Tel 505 98 00.

Instituto Cervantes de Cracovia
ul. Kanonicza 12.
Map 1 C5 (6 D4).
Tel 12 421 32 55.
🌐 cracovia.cervantes.es

International Cultural Centre
Rynek Główny 25.
Map 1 C4 (6 D3).
Tel 12 424 28 11.
🌐 mck.krakow.pl

Istituto Italiano di Cultura
ul. Grodzka 49.
Map 1 C5 (6 D4).
Tel 12 421 89 23.

Japanese Centre of Art and Technology
ul. Konopnickiej 26.
Map 3 B1.
Tel 12 267 27 03.
🌐 manggha.pl

Theatre

Bagatela Theatre
ul. Karmelicka 6.
Map 1 B4 (5 C2).
Tel 12 424 52 09.
🌐 bagatela.pl

Cricoteka
ul. Nadwiślańska 2.
Map 4 E2.
Tel 12 422 27 70.
🌐 news.cricoteka.pl

Krakowski Teatr Scena Stu
al. Krasińskiego 16–18.
Map 1 A5 (5 A4).
Tel 12 422 27 44.
🌐 scenastu.com.pl

KTO
ul. Krowoderska 74.
Tel 12 633 89 47.
🌐 teatrkto.pl

Ludowy Theatre
Os. Teatralne 34.
Map 1 B4 (5 C2).
Tel 12 680 21 12.
🌐 ludowy.pl

Stary Teatr
ul. Jagiellońska 1.
Map 1 C4 (5 C2).
Tel 12 422 40 40.
🌐 stary.pl

Teatr im. Juliusza Słowackiego
Pl. Świętego Ducha 1.
Map 2 D4 (6 E1).
Tel 12 424 45 26.
🌐 slowacki.krakow.pl

Teatr Lalki i Maski Groteska
ul. Skarbowa 2.
Map 1 B4 (5 A2).
Tel 12 633 37 62.
🌐 groteska.pl

Teatr Łaźnia Nowa
Os. Szkolne 25.
Tel 12 425 03 20.
🌐 laznianowa.pl

Zależny
ul. Kanonicza 1.
Map 1 C5 (6 D4).
Tel 12 421 71 36.
🌐 stenkrakow.pl

Opera and Ballet

Krakow Chamber Opera
ul. Miodowa 15.
Map 4 D1.
Tel 12 430 66 06.
🌐 kok.art.pl

Opera Krakowska
ul. Lubicz 48.
Map 2 F3.
Tel 12 296 62 60.
🌐 opera.krakow.pl

Cabaret

Loch Camelot
ul. Św. Tomasza 17.
Map 1 C4 (6 D2).
Tel 602 763 680.
🌐 lochcamelot.art.pl

Piwnica Pod Baranami
Rynek Główny 27.
Map 1 C4 (6 D2).
Tel 12 421 25 00.
🌐 piwnicapod
baranami.pl

Cinemas

Agrafka
ul. Krowoderska 8.
Map 1 C3.
Tel 12 430 01 79.
🌐 kinografika.pl

Cinema City
ul. Podgórska 34
(Galeria Kazimierz).
Map 4 F1.
Tel 12 254 54 54.
🌐 cinema-city.pl

Kijów.Centrum
al. Krasińskiego 34.
Map 1 A5 (5 A3).
Tel 12 433 00 33.
🌐 kijow.pl

Kika
ul. I. Krasickiego 18.
Map 3 C4.
Tel 12 296 41 52.
🌐 kinokika.pl

Kino ARS
ul. Św. Tomasza 11.
Map 1 C4 (6 D2).
Tel 12 421 41 99.
🌐 ars.pl

Mikro
ul. J. Lea 5. **Map** 1 A3.
Tel 12 634 28 97.
🌐 kinomikro.pl

Multikino
ul. Dobrego Pasterza 128.
Tel 12 298 46 24.
🌐 multikino.pl

Paradox
ul. Krupnicza 38.
Map 1 B4.
Tel 12 430 00 15.
🌐 kinoparadox.pl

Pod Baranami
Rynek Główny 27.
Map 1 C4 (6 D2).
Tel 12 421 25 00.
🌐 kinopodbaranami.pl

Classical Music

Capella Cracoviensis
ul. Zwierzyniecka 1.
Map 1 B5 (5 C3).
Tel 602 620 698.
🌐 capellacraco
viensis.pl

Centrum Kultury „Dworek Białoprądnicki"
ul. Papiernicza 2.
Tel 12 420 49 50.
🌐 dworek.eu

Filharmonia
ul. Zwierzyniecka 1.
Map 1 B5 (5 C3).
Tel 12 619 87 33.
🌐 filharmonia.
krakow.pl

St Peter and Paul's Church
ul. Grodzka 52.
Map 1 C5 (6 D4).
Tel 695 574 526.

Music Clubs

Alchemia
ul. Estery 5.
Map 4 D1.
Tel 12 421 22 00.
w alchemia.com.pl

Awaria
ul. Mikołajska 9.
Map 2 D4 (6 E2).
Tel 12 292 03 50.
w klubawaria.com

Dali Club
ul. Mazowiecka 21/1.
Map 1 A1.
Tel 12 633 77 55.
w daliclub.pl

Harris Piano Jazz Bar
Rynek Główny 28.
Map 1 C4 (6 D2).
Tel 12 421 57 41.
w harris.krakow.pl

Jazz Club u Muniaka
ul. Floriańska 3.
Map 1 C4 (6 D2).
Tel 12 423 12 05.

Jazz Rock Café
ul. Sławkowska 12.
Map 1 C4 (6 D2).
Tel 514 433 506.

Klub Kornet
al. Krasińskiego 19.
Map 1 A5 (5 A4).
Tel 12 265 65 41.
w kornetklub.pl

Kwadrat
ul. Skarzyńskiego 1.
Tel 12 647 50 78.
w klubkwadrat.pl

PiecArt
ul. Szewska 12.
Map 1 C4 (5 C2).
Tel 12 429 16 02.
w piecart.pl

Piękny Pies
ul. Bożego Ciała 9.
Map 4 D2.

Pod Jaszczurami
Rynek Główny 8.
Map 1 C4 (6 D3).
Tel 12 429 45 38.
w podjaszczurami.pl

U Louisa
Rynek Główny 13.
Map 1 C4 (6 D3).
Tel 12 617 02 22.

Żaczek
al. 3 Maja 5.
Map 1 A4.
Tel 12 622 11 67.
w klubzaczek.pl

Nightclubs

Afera Club
ul. Sławkowska 13/15.
Map 1 C4 (6 D2).
Tel 12 421 17 71.

Apoteka
ul. Meiselsa 24.
Map 4 D2.

Black Gallery
ul. Mikołajska 24.
Map 2 D4 (6 E2).
Tel 724 630 154.

Drukarnia
ul. Nadwiślańska 1.
Map 4 E3.
Tel 12 656 65 60.

Frantic
ul. Szewska 5.
Map 5 C2.
Tel 12 423 04 83.
w frantic.pl

Free Pub
ul. Sławkowska 4.
Map 1 C4 (6 D2).
Tel 12 344 46 56.

Kawiarnia Naukowa
ul. Kalwaryjska 10.
Map 4 D4.

Klub 89
ul. Mari Konopickiej 28.
Map 3 C3.
w osiemdziewiec.com

Prozak 2.0
pl. Dominikański 6.
Map C5 (6 D3).
Tel 733 70 46 50.
w prozakdwazero.pl

Społem Deluxe
ul. Floriańska 53.
Map 1 C4 (6 D2).
Tel 12 341 57 51.

Szpitalna
ul. Szpitalna 1.
Map 2 D4 (6 E2).
Tel 430 66 61.

Zetpete
ul. Dolnych Młynów 10.
Map 1 B4 (5 B1).
Tel 728 828 017.

Swimming Pools

Clepardia
ul. Mackiewicza 14.
Tel 12 415 16 74.

Park Wodny
ul. Dobrego Pasterza 126.
Tel 12 616 31 91.

Wisła
ul. Reymonta 22.
Map 1 A4.
Tel 12 615 15 62.

Ice Skating

Błonia Ice Rink
Jordan Park.
Tel 697 008 340.
w lodowisko-krakowskieblonia.pl

Galeria Krakowska
Plac Jana Nowaka Jezioranskiego.
Map 2 D3.

Tennis Courts

Klub Tenisowy Na Błoniach
Na Błoniach 1.
w nabloniach.com

Nadwiślan
ul. Koletek 20. **Map** 3 C1.
Tel 12 422 21 22.
w nadwislan.com

Wola Sport Paradise
ul. Koło Strzelnicy 5.
Tel 12 425 3900.
w wolasportparadise.pl

Horse-Riding

Krakowski Klub Jazdy Konnej
ul. Kobierzyńska 175.
Tel 12 262 14 18.

Krakus
ul. Kąpielowa 51.
Tel 12 654 73 26.
w wlkskrakus.pl

Pegaz
ul. Łowińskiego 1.
Tel 12 425 80 88.
w ojkpegaz.pl

Pod Żubrem
Niepołomice, Targowa 5.
Tel 603 642 725.
w kjkpodzubrem.pl

Stadnina Podskalany
ul. Podskalany 61, Tomaszowice.
Tel 606 91 50 09.

Health, Fitness and Sauna Clubs

Forteca Climbing Centre
ul. Racławicka 60.
Tel 509 228 998.
w cwf.pl

Korona Club
ul. Kalwaryjska 9–15.
Tel 12 656 53 89.
w korona.krakow.pl

Relax Body Club
ul. Mogilska 70.
Map 2 F3.
Tel 12 411 03 60.

Yoga International
ul. Św. Marka 34
Map 6 E2.
Tel 692 41 41, 47.
w yogainternational.com

Billiards and Snooker Clubs

Frame Snooker & Bilard
ul. Smolki 11A.
Map 4 D3.
Tel 12 423 57 06.
w framekrakow.pl

Klub Biliardowy Pik
ul. Estery 18.
Map 4 D1.
Tel 12 349 08 14.
w klubpik.pl

The Stage
ul. Łobzowska 3.
Map 1 B2 (5 C1).
Tel 12 681 63 85.

Bowling

Plac Nowy 1
Plac Nowy 1.
Map 4 D1.
Tel 12 442 77 11.
w placnowy1.pl

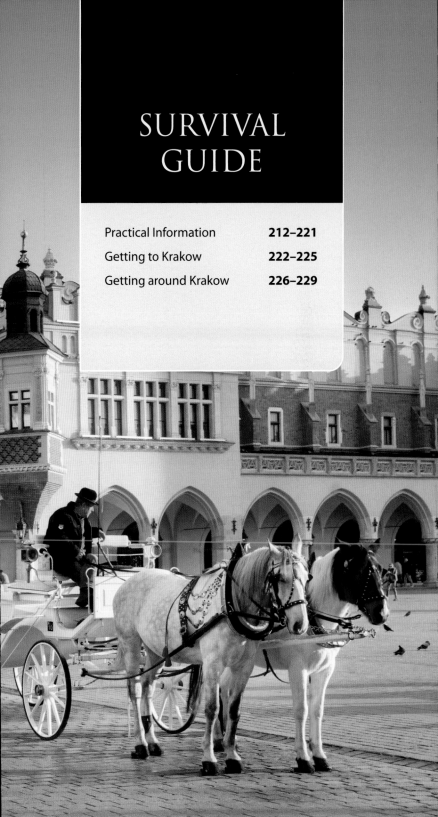

SURVIVAL
GUIDE

PRACTICAL INFORMATION

Krakow attracts more tourists than any other Polish city, and visitor facilities are generally first class. Points of arrival such as the main railway and bus stations have been thoroughly modernized in recent years, and the John Paul II Airport at Balice boasts a speedy rail link to the city centre. Tourist signage makes it easy to find your way around on foot and many of the city's sights are within walking distance from each other. The increased use of bicycles is a sign that Krakow is becoming much more eco-friendly. The communications system is good: postal services are easy to use, and the provision of Wi-Fi access is increasingly widespread. The tourist season lasts all year round in Krakow, but summer is particularly busy thanks to the warm weather.

When to Go

Krakow is a popular destination for visitors throughout the year and tourist facilities are open for business during every season. Spring and summer bring warm weather, when the city is filled with visitors and café tables cover the pavements. Autumn and winter, although cold, can also be a magical time, with Advent markets on city squares and an atmosphere of celebration in restaurants and bars.

Hotel prices are at their highest from Easter to August and around Christmas and New Year. Most theatres and classical-music venues are closed from June to mid-September.

Visas and Passports

Citizens of the European Union, USA, Australia, Canada and New Zealand can enter Poland without a visa, on production of a valid passport, for stays of up to 90 days. Citizens of other countries should check the latest visa regulations with their local Polish embassy. Poland is a member of the Schengen group of European Union countries, which means that there are unlikely to be any border controls at immigration when entering Poland from another Schengen-zone country.

Travel Safety Advice

Visitors can get up-to-date travel safety information from the **UK Foreign and Commonwealth Office**, the **US Department of State** and the **Australian Department of Foreign Affairs and Trade**.

A tourist office in Krakow

Customs Information

If you are travelling to or from another EU country there are few restrictions on items brought in and out of Poland for personal use.

Visitors from outside the EU should check the customs regulations of their home country – there are likely to be limits on the amount of cigarettes, alcoholic beverages, toiletries and gifts that can be taken home. The maximum value of currency that can be brought into or taken out of Poland is €10,000 (or equivalent). Sums in excess of this must be declared to the customs authority. A licence is required to export any item more than 100 years old or any artwork over 50 years old and exceeding more than 16,000zł in value. For more information contact the **Ministry of Culture and National Heritage**. Value Added Tax (VAT) can be claimed back on goods totalling 200zł or more and that are taken out of the country within 30 days of purchase.

Tourist Information

Krakow's municipal tourist office operates information centres at several locations around the city centre. Their locations are shown on the Street Finder maps towards the end of this book (see pp234–9). The main office is in the **Cloth Hall** on Market Square and there are branches on the **Planty**, at ul. Św Jana 2 just off Market Square, in the **Wyspiański Pavillion** on pl. Wszystkich Świętych, and at **John Paul II Airport**. All offices offer brochures with museum and gallery opening times, and lists of accommodation.

Electronic displays with information on the availability of hotels can be found at the main railway station and John Paul II Airport. The tourist office on ul. Św. Jana, provides information on concerts and shows. Hotel and hostel reception desks can be useful sources of information, although they sometimes only advertise tourist companies with whom they have a commercial agreement.

Admission Prices

Admission charges to museums and galleries are modest but may be increased substantially for a temporary exhibition. Reduced rates are available for children, students and senior citizens. Overseas students should carry a valid international student card in order to qualify for a discount (see p214).

Opening Hours

The opening hours of the museums and galleries listed in this guide are given individually for each sight. Most state museums and galleries are closed on Mondays and private galleries of contemporary art are generally closed on Sundays. Opening times vary depending on the day of the week, but late openings are normally on Thursdays.

Churches usually remain open from the first to the last service without closing at midday, but there are some variations. Food stores are open 7am–7pm, but there are no strict rules about opening hours, which are at the owner's discretion. Other shops tend to open between 10am and 7pm. For information on opening times of banks and bureaux de change see p218.

Restaurants are open until 11pm although there are many pubs and bars that serve food and stay open until the early hours. Twenty-four-hour bars serving cheap drinks and snacks are popular with the locals and easy to find.

Tourists in Market Square, with the Church of St Mary in the background

Language

Learning a anguage has undergone something of a boom in recent years, and most young Krakovians speak English and maybe one other world language as well. Older-generation Poles are a bit less forthcoming when it comes to foreign languages, although they will make an attempt to communicate with the few words they may have.

Some taxi companies use drivers who speak foreign languages, so you may, for example, request an English-speaking driver. Staff at museums, hotels and restaurants generally speak English, and possibly also one other major European language. In many cases staff in shops, post offices and banks communicate in Polish only, especially outside the city centre. It is worth making an effort to learn a few words and phrases in Polish; the Phrase Book is a useful place to start (see pp257–8).

Etiquette and Smoking

There are nearly 100 Roman Catholic churches in Krakow and masses take place at all times of day throughout the week. Sightseeing is allowed when there are no services taking places but visitors should refrain from making noise and use cameras discreetly. In some churches, signs banning photography are clearly visible on the door. When visiting places of worship, it is polite to dress modestly: as well as the torso, upper arms and legs should be covered.

Smoking is banned in most public places. Almost all restaurants and cafés are completely smoke-free indoors, although smoking is permitted outside at restaurants and cafés that have a pavement terrace or a garden. Only a handful of bars and clubs have retained a self-contained indoor area where smoking is still allowed.

Accessibility to Public Conveniences

There are free-of-charge public conveniences in big shopping centres such as Galeria Krakowska, next to the main railway station, and Galeria Kazimierz on ul. Podgórska near the Kazimierz Quarter. Pay-to-use toilets are scattered throughout the centre and can be found in the Cloth Hall, on the Planty by Sienna and Reformacka streets, and at the parking area by the Wawel. All restaurants, bars and cafés have facilities. Most of these are free to use if you are a customer, although one or two restaurants do charge.

Taxes and Tipping

It is common to give a tip in cafés and restaurants with waiting staff, although there are no strict rules as to how much this should be. Adding 10 per cent to the bill or rounding it up to a suitable number is considered polite.

Visitors enjoying a drink at one of the street cafés in the Market Square

Travellers with Disabilities

Facilities for people with disabilities are still limited in Krakow. Moving around in a wheelchair is not easy due to the lack of contoured pavements and the large number of cars parked in pedestrian areas. Improvements are being made: some pedestrian crossings have low kerbs, and those equipped with an audio message for the blind is on the increase. Wheelchair access and lifts are available at the city's main railway station.

Good facilities can also be found in a number of museums, including the National Museum in Krakow's Main Building *(see pp150–51)*, most of the National Museum's other branches, and the Japanese Centre for Art and Technology *(see p45)*, as well as in some cinemas and theatres. The main Post Office also offers easy access. All hotels with four stars or above offer at least a couple of rooms for wheelchair users *(see p180)*. An increasing number of trams and buses have low-level entry floors for wheelchair access.

There are several organizations that assist the disabled in Krakow, including the **Polish Association for the Blind** and the **Polish Assocation for the Deaf**. The **Radio Taxi Partner** company operates a fleet of vehicles especially adapted for wheelchair users.

Crowds watching the annual Dragon Parade on Market Square

Travelling with Children

Krakow is an enjoyable and safe environment for children, thanks to the largely pedestrianized city centre and the extensive areas of park in the surrounding areas.

One of the best public playparks is in **Jordan Park**, west of the Old Town. The **Stanisław Lem Garden of Experiments**, east of the centre towards Nowa Huta, is an open-air, hands-on science museum that encourages children to learn about science by playing on large pieces of apparatus.

Groteska Theatre is Krakow's leading children's theatre, whose productions often mix puppets with live action. Groteska also organizes the annual Dragon Parade in June, when puppet monsters descend on Market Square followed by fireworks beside the River Vistula.

Finding child-friendly accommodation in Krakow is usually problem-free *(see p178)*.

Gay and Lesbian Travellers

Although Krakow is more liberal than many other European cities, Poland as a whole is a conservative country and the gay and lesbian scene remains discreet. Krakow has a handful of clubs specifically tailored to the gay and lesbian community, and a broader choice of bars, particularly in the Jewish Kazimierz quarter in the west of the city, that encourage a mixture of all customers. The annual Tolerance March, a gay-pride-style event that takes place in mid-May, attracts many supporters from across the social spectrum – but sometimes draws large numbers of conservative counter-demonstrators.

An ISIC card (International Student Identity Card)

Travelling on a Budget

In comparison to other major European cities, Krakow is not that expensive and with some planning it is possible to get around on a low budget. Many museums and galleries are free at least one day per week so you can save a lot of money on entrance fees if you pick your days carefully.

For young travellers, international youth and student cards such as **ISIC** (International Student Identity Card) and the **European Youth Card** are worth obtaining. Both cards entitle holders to reduced rates in museums, tourist attractions, hotels, hostels and on intercity buses. A wide range of other Krakow businesses offer discounts to bearers of both cards, including car-hire firms, cafés, hairdressers, pizzerias, travel agents and theatres. The logos of the cards are displayed in the windows of those businesses offering discounts.

An ISIC card is available to anyone who is either a full-time student or who is under the age of 26. You can obtain one in

An example of a disabled parking sign in a Krakow street

your home country or through youth-tourism specialists **Almatur** in Krakow, providing you have documentary evidence of your status.

The European Youth Card is available to anyone under the age of 30 and can be bought from numerous outlets throughout Europe, or online via their website.

Time

Poland is in the Central European time zone, which means that Krakow is 1 hour ahead of Greenwich Mean Time, 6 hours ahead of US Eastern Standard Time and 11 hours behind Australian Eastern Standard Time. From late March until late October clocks are set forward 1 hour.

Electricity

The voltage in Poland is 230 volts. Plugs are of the two-pin type, as is the case in most countries in Europe. Buy a European travel adaptor before you leave home.

Responsible Tourism

Travelling responsibly is largely a matter of common sense. Eating in chain restaurants or fast-food outlets increases the likelihood that you will be consuming cheaply supplied products that have not come from ecological sources. If you eat Polish food in Polish restaurants, it is more likely that food has been locally sourced. When shopping for your own food, aim for outdoor markets rather than the large supermarkets. Stall-holders at the Stary Kleparz market at Rynek Kleparski near Planty are far more likely to sell seasonal produce of local provenance, and will frequently advertise the fact by chalking up signs advertising the Polish origin of their vegetables. Organic food shops include Naturalny sklepik at Krupnicza 8 and Natura at Krupnicza 21. Both sell many Polish specialities. Take a multiple-use bag of your own rather than using plastic bags.

If you have rubbish to dispose of, ask locals to direct you to the recycling bins located on many street corners. There is usually a trio of containers set aside for paper, glass and plastics.

Fresh fruit and vegetables at a Krakow food market

DIRECTORY

Personal Security and Health

Krakow is one of the safest cities in Poland. Although the number of reported crimes is generally on the increase, Krakow is a quiet place and visitors can feel safe in most parts of the city. The same safety rules apply here as every-where, so beware of pickpockets, do not leave any property visible in a car and use guarded car parks. The local police take a tough line on rowdy, alcohol-influenced behaviour on the streets. Anyone suffering a minor health problem should seek advice at a pharmacy, while hotels can usually arrange a doctor's visit.

Police officers patrolling Krakow's Market Square

Police

In Krakow the police are assisted by other services, including town wardens and private security guards. Serious crime should be reported to a uniformed officer at a police station. Major police stations are indicated on the Street Finder maps *(see pp234–9)*. Police are often visible, especially on weekend nights when people showing signs of bad behaviour under the influence of alcohol will usually be apprehended. Blue and silver police cars are used for patrolling the streets. Town wardens are unarmed and have no power of arrest. They tend to perform traffic wardens' duties by fining owners of illegally parked vehicles. Private security agencies are generally responsible for security in large shops and public buildings, as well as at public events. They are usually uniformed and should always carry identification badges.

What to Be Aware Of

Krakow is a popular venue for weekend party tourism. Late-night noisy behaviour is a frequent annoyance, but outright public disorder is very rare. Local police are taking an increasingly hard line on drunkenness, and anyone creating a disturbance late at night is likely to be apprehended and fined.

Ambulance

Police car

Fire engine

Ulica Szewska in the Old Quarter is at the centre of the weekend party scene. Most of the bars and clubs here are legitimate, although one or two establish-ments on this strip are notorious for overcharging tourists. Male visitors travelling solo or in small groups should be particularly aware of over-friendly young females suggesting a drink in a nearby bar; a hugely inflated bill will probably be the result.

Anyone found driving under the influence of alcohol will be arrested and must appear in court the following day. Be aware that cyclists riding a bicycle under the influence of alcohol will receive the same treatment as car drivers. The level of alcohol in the blood for both car drivers and cyclists is so low that it is advisable to not drink and drive at all. In the event of a serious road accident you are required by law to call an ambulance, the fire brigade and also the traffic police – *see Directory opposite*.

Petty thieves and pick-pockets are active in crowded bars, on public transport and at busy markets. Keep a close eye on your bag or rucksack, and carry it securely fastened across your body. Passports, wallets and other valuable items should never be carried in a back pocket or in the external pockets of a rucksack. Pickpockets frequently operate in gangs, and a sudden push or other distraction caused by them will hardly ever be accidental.

Valuables should never be left unattended in a car. Car break-ins are a big problem in Krakow. If you can remove the radio and take it with you, you may save your windows from being smashed. A car alarm offers no protection against professional thieves, so guarded parking may be a good option. A number of guarded car parks are available in the centre.

In an Emergency

Call 112 for emergencies requiring medical, police or fire services. An operator will answer (most speak English) and will direct your call. Minor problems can often be treated by trained staff in a pharmacy. Prominent pharmacies are listed in the Shops and Markets directory *(see p203)*; 24-hour pharmacies are listed in the directory below. For more serious injury or illness, head for the casualty unit of one of the big city-centre hospitals.

Police sign

Lost and Stolen Property

If you lose something at a venue in Krakow there is a good chance that staff will keep it for a day or two, in the expectation that you will return. It is a good idea to write your mobile phone number inside bags or wallets – in the event of loss, a good citizen or conscientious policeman may call to inform you that it has been found.

There are several lost property offices in Krakow, one for property lost on public transport and one for items misplaced elsewhere in the city. Items left on aeroplanes, intercity trains or buses will be kept at lost property offices at the airport, railway and bus station respectively. Never leave luggage unattended in public, as this can lead to theft or security alerts.

Hospitals and 24-Hour Pharmacies

Both state and private health care are available in Krakow. First aid is provided free of charge. Other treatment may be subject to a fee, which is usually required in advance, along with showing a passport for identification. It is very important to obtain a receipt for any payment made and it is advisable to take out insurance cover before you travel.

A typical pharmacy (*apteka*, in Polish) window in Krakow

Treatment for minor problems is available at pharmacies located throughout the city. If you require treatment after normal opening hours visit a 24-hour pharmacy. Their addresses are usually displayed in any pharmacy window *(see p201)*. The ambulance service is on call day and night and should be contacted in case of an accident or emergency. There are several hospitals in Krakow including **University Hospital**, east of the city centre. Hospitals with casualty units are shown on the Street Finder maps *(see pp234–9)*.

Travel and Health Insurance

Travel insurance that includes provision for health care is highly recommended. The longer you stay abroad, the more important it is to ensure that you have substantial cover in case of loss, theft or medical emergencies that will require repatriation help.

Many airlines and travel agents offer you insurance when you book your ticket. The Australian-based **World Nomads** is a reputable service that offers travel insurance to citizens of 150 countries.

All EU nationals are entitled to state healthcare in Poland on production of a valid **European Health Insurance Card** (EHIC). In the UK, this can be obtained from a post office or online from the EHIC website. It includes a booklet that details what healthcare you are entitled to, and where and how to claim. You may still have to pay in advance to obtain treatment, and then reclaim the money back later. As not all treatments are covered, it is advisable to take out additional insurance.

Make sure you travel with all relevant insurance documents. Keep a copy in your hotel room or with a reliable family member or friend back home, and itemize any valuables you are taking with you.

DIRECTORY

In an Emergency

Ambulance, Police and Fire
Tel 112.

Lost and Stolen Property

Lost and Found Office
ul. Wielicka 28.
Map 4 F3.
Tel 12 616 5713.

MPK Transport Office
ul. Broźka 3.
Tel 12 254 1150.

Hospitals and 24-Hour Pharmacies

Apteka pod Opatrznością
ul. Karmelicka 33.
Map 5 C1.
Tel 12 631 19 80.

Dbam o Zdrowie
ul. Kalwaryjska 94.
Map 4 D4.
Tel 12 656 18 50.

University Hospital
ul. Kopernika 50.
Map 2 E4.
Tel 12 351 66 01.

Travel and Health Insurance

European Union Health Insurance Card
For UK residents: w ehic.org.uk
For Irish residents: w ehic.ie

World Nomads
w worldnomads.com

Banking and Local Currency

Financial transactions are easy in Krakow. ATMs accepting all major cards are located throughout the city. Foreign visitors will find many bureaux de change in the city centre, offering more favourable exchange rates than the banks. Credit and debit cards are accepted by most of Krakow's shops and restaurants. Signs displayed by the entrance to the establishment indicate which cards are accepted.

Banks and Bureaux de Change

Banks can be found throughout the city, both in and around the centre, as well as on the outskirts. They are usually open 9am–5pm Monday–Friday and many are open until 1pm on Saturday. Banks are often busy so expect to queue. Some branches have a ticketing system – take a numbered ticket at the entrance and wait until the number is displayed before approaching the counter.

Most banks have their own exchange service but better rates are offered by the independent bureaux de change (kantor), which do not charge commission. In Krakow these include **Euro-Kantor**, **JPJ**, **Kantor Exchange** and **Pod Arkadami**. Foreign currency can also be changed at hotels, but rates are more expensive.

Large Polish banks with branches in Krakow include **PKO**, **Bank Zachodni WBK** and **Pekao**. International banks include **Deutsche Bank** and **Raiffeisen**.

Entrance to the PKO Bank, located in Market Square

A typical ATM (bankomat), one of many found around the city

ATMs

ATMs (bankomat) are easy to find in Krakow and instructions are usually available in a choice of languages. The types of card accepted will be displayed on the ATM itself. Check these carefully before inserting your card – the vast majority accept Visa, Maestro and MasterCard. ATM withdrawals will be marginally more expensive than changing cash. The exchange rate for the amount withdrawn in złoty is slightly less advantageous than the one you will receive in a bank or bureau de change. A small fee will be charged by your bank for each ATM transaction carried out when abroad.

Be aware of your surroundings when using an ATM and always shield the keypad when entering your PIN.

Credit and Debit Cards

Credit and debit card payments are accepted in most hotels, museums, restaurants and shops. There may be a minimum expenditure in some restaurants and shops, below which they will not accept credit card payments; ask first. Cards are unlikely to be accepted in markets, suburban railway stations, and in smaller shops and cafés in the suburbs, so it is advisable to carry a small amount of Polish cash.

All major credit cards such as American Express, VISA and MasterCard are widely accepted. Establishments normally indicate which cards they accept by displaying appropriate stickers on their windows.

It is a good idea to notify your bank before you travel so that they expect your card to be used in Poland.

DIRECTORY

BANKS

Bank Pekao
Rynek Główny 31.
Map 1 C4 (6 D2).

Bank Zachodni WBK
Rynek 29.
Map 6 D2.

Deutsche Bank
Rynek 20.
Map 6 D2.

PKO Bank
Starowiślna 22.
Map 4 E1.
Rynek Główny 21.
Map 1 C4 (6 D2).

Raiffeisen
ul. Karmelicka 11.
Map 5 C1.

Bureaux de Change

Euro-Kantor
ul. Szewska 21. **Map** 1 C4 (5 C2).
Tel 12 421 55 65.

JPJ
ul. Wielopole 3. **Map** 2 D5 (6 E3).
Tel 12 429 26 48.

Kantor Exchange
ul. Pawia 12. **Map** 2 D3 (6 F1).
Tel 12 430 33 33.
Karmelicka 1. **Map** 5 C1.
Tel 12 421 35 55.

Pod Arkadami
ul. Grodzka 40. **Map** 1 C5 (6 D5).
Tel 12 421 50 21.

Currency

The Polish unit of currency is the złoty, a term that literally means golden and which dates back to the Middle Ages, when gold pieces were used. Złoty is most commonly abbreviated to zł, although you will see the abbreviation PLN in banks and on your credit or debit card statement. One złoty equals 100 groszy, abbreviated to gr.

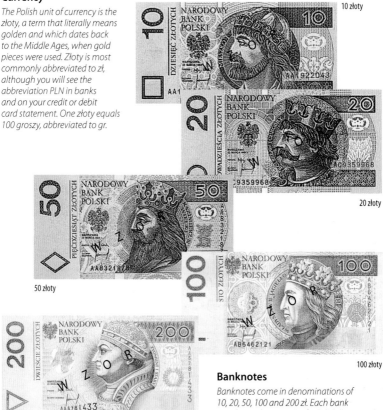

10 złoty

20 złoty

50 złoty

100 złoty

200 złoty

Banknotes

Banknotes come in denominations of 10, 20, 50, 100 and 200 zł. Each bank note bears the portrait of a Polish king.

5 zł

2 zł

1 zł

50 gr

20 gr

10 gr

5 gr

2 gr

1 gr

Coins

Polish coins come in denominations of 1, 2, 5, 10, 20, 50 gr and 1, 2, 5 zł. They all feature on one side a crowned eagle, the emblem of Poland.

Communications and Media

The main Polish telephone service is provided by Telekomunikacja Polska (TP), although there are numerous mobile phone operators such as Plus, Orange and T-Mobile. There are few public telephones in Krakow. Almost all hotels and many cafés, bars and restaurants offer guests free Wi-Fi access, and international newspapers and magazines are widely available. Offices of the efficient Polish postal service (Poczta Polska) are located throughout the city.

International and Local Telephone Calls

With so many Poles using mobile phones, there are hardly any public telephones left in Krakow. Bearing in mind how long it might take you to find the nearest public telephone, it is advisable to not rely on them as an easily accessible means of communication. Telephone calls made from a hotel room are expensive, and in most cases it will be cheaper to use your own mobile phone.

Mobile Phones

Most mobile phones will function perfectly well in Krakow and elsewhere in Poland. However, mobile phones supplied by providers in the US may only have limited global coverage. Contact your service provider for clarification.

To use your mobile phone abroad you will need to check with your provider that the roaming facility has been enabled. Remember that you will be charged for the calls

& tp

Telekomunikacja Polska – the biggest Polish telecoms company

you receive as well as the calls you make, and you will have to pay a substantial premium for the international part of the call. Citizens of countries in the European Union (EU) are no longer expected to pay roaming charges. Citizens of other countries should check with their operator before leaving home about the roaming charges that are likely to be applied. If you have a smartphone, you can cut call costs further by downloading applications such as Skype, WhatsApp and Viber, which allow you to make free calls and send free messages provided you are in a place that has Internet coverage.

If you are staying in the area for a reasonable amount of time, a popular option is to purchase a local SIM card that uses the local mobile phone networks and can be topped up with credit. You can only do this if your handset is "unlocked", as some operators lock their phones to specific networks. Some of the local/

international networks are **Orange, T-Mobile** and **Plus**. Large shopping malls such as Galeria Krakowska and Galeria Kazimierz are good places to look for shops and stalls selling SIM cards and prepaid vouchers for the popular local telephone companies. If you are using a smart phone, beware that charges for data roaming can be high. If you want to make and receive calls while abroad but do not want to be charged for use of the Internet or other data, you can switch this service off and continue using the telephone functions as normal.

Check your insurance policy in case your phone gets stolen and keep your network operator's helpline number handy in case of emergencies.

Internet Access

If you are travelling with a laptop, tablet or a smartphone, there are numerous opportunities to log on to the Internet for little or no cost. Most hotels, cafés and bars provide their guests with Wi-Fi access. In most places it is is free but some establishments, especially upmarket hotels catering for business clients, do charge. Look out for a Wi-Fi sticker in the window and ask about the password. There are also free public Wi-Fi zones across the main Market Square, the main train station, plac Centralny in Nowa Huta, and several other locations around town.

One of the many cafés in Krakow offering Wi-Fi access

Telephone Directories and Dialling Codes

- National (Polish) directory enquiries dial 118 913.
- International directory enquiries dial 118 912.
- Local calls within Krakow first dial 12, the city's area code. For calls within Poland always include the area code.
- To call overseas dial 0 and wait for the tone, dial 0 again followed by the country code, followed by the area code (omit the initial 0), and then the subscriber's number.
- Country codes: UK 44; Eire 353; Canada and USA 1; Australia 61; South Africa 27; New Zealand 64.

For those travelling without a Wi-Fi-enabled device, most hotels and hostels have at least one computer with Internet access in the lobby for guests to use. There are also fewer Internet cafés *(Kafejki Internetowe)* than there used to be now that so many people have access to Wi-Fi options elsewhere, but a handful such as **Garinet** and **Hetmańska** still survive. They offer reasonable rates for Internet use – fares rarely exceed 10zł per hour.

Postal Services

Branches of the post office are scattered liberally throughout central Krakow and the suburbs. The main post office, **Poctzta Głowna**, is situated at the junction of Westerplatte and Wielopole streets. It is open 8am–8pm Monday–Friday, and 8am–2pm Saturday, and offers a wide range of services. You can send letters, faxes, telegrams and parcels, as well as make international money transfers and operator-initiated calls. Stamp collectors can buy from the philatelic counter. A *poste restante* (mail-holding) service is also available. The post office branch near the railway station has a 24-hour counter.

Stamps can be purchased at post office counters and from selected newsagents. Inland letters arrive after 2 to 3 days but international mail can take a week or maybe a little longer. Letters or cards sent via the more expensive express service will arrive sooner. Courier service is the fastest postal method, but is very costly. This service is available from larger post office branches, as well as from **DHL** and other similar courier companies.

A newsstand selling newspapers and magazines in Krakow

Newspapers and Magazines

Foreign newspapers and magazines are available from the larger newsagents and bookshops. The widest choice is available at the **Empik** multimedia store in the Galeria Krakowska mall, which sells English-language and other foreign publications.

The most popular quality newspapers in Krakow are the nationals *Gazeta Wyborcza* and *Rzeczpospolita*, and the local *Dziennik Polski* and *Gazeta Krakowska*. *Dziennik Polski* and *Gazeta Wyborcza* have the best "what's-on" information. English-language monthly the *Krakow Post*, only available online, is a good source of local news.

DIRECTORY

Mobile Phones

Orange
W orange.pl

Plus
W plus.pl

T-Mobile
W t-mobile.pl

Internet Access

Garinet
ul. Floriańska 18. **Map** 2 C4 (6 E2).
Tel 12 423 2233. W garinet.pl

Hetmańska
ul. Bracka 4. **Map** 1 C5 (6 D3).
Tel 12 430 01 08.
W hetmanska24.com

Postal Services

DHL
Tel 6 345 345. W dhl.com.pl

Poctzta Głowna
ul. Westerplatte 20.
Map 2 D5 (6 E3).

Newspapers and Magazines

Empik
Galeria Krakowska, Level -1.
Map 1 D3 (6 F1).
Tel 22 462 72 50.
W empikgroup.com

Krakow Post
W krakowpost.com

TV and Radio

Most hotels have a television in the room offering a handful of Polish-language stations and a choice of German-, English-, Italian- and French-language stations. News channels such as CNN or BBC are more common than entertainment or film channels. Polish TV stations broadcast many English-language films and drama, although the voices are usually dubbed into Polish or read by a single actor.

Popular radio stations include RMF FM (96 FM), Trójka (99.4 FM), Radio Kraków (101.6 FM) and Radio Zet (104.1 FM).

A post office housed in an old palace by the main railway station

GETTING TO KRAKOW

Krakow has good connections with other Polish and European cities. Direct air routes serve John Paul II Airport from Warsaw as well as an ever-increasing number of European and American cities. There are direct trains from Berlin, Prague, Warsaw and other major Polish cities. In addition, Krakow is served by intercity buses from a growing range of European cities and from most cities in Poland itself.

Driving to Krakow is relatively easy and will take you through some wonderful scenery, with plenty of roadside restaurants and petrol stations along the way. Krakow has good, fast road connections if you are approaching from the west. Road routes from the north, south and east however are not in such good condition, and journeys via these routes are generally more time-consuming.

The logo of Polish Airlines

Arriving by Air

Krakow's **John Paul II Airport** at Balice is served by direct flights from a large number of European and Polish cities. Travellers from other continents will find that connections to Krakow – usually involving a change of plane in another European city – are easy to organize.

From the UK there's a choice of **LOT Polish Airlines** and **British Airways** flights from London Heathrow; **Ryanair** from East Midlands, Edinburgh, Leeds-Bradford, Liverpool and London Stansted; **easyJet** from Belfast, Bristol, Edinburgh, Liverpool and London Gatwick; and **Jet2** from Newcastle. From Ireland, Ryanair flies directly from Dublin.

Travellers from North America will need to make at least one stop en route. LOT airlines fly from Chicago, Toronto and New York to Krakow with a transfer in Warsaw. **Lufthansa** offer flights from various North American cities to Krakow with a change of plane in either Frankfurt or Munich. Visitors from Australasia can choose between one-stop flights via a major European hub such as London, or two-stop flights with connections in Singapore or Bangkok. LOT also operate domestic flights to Krakow from Warsaw; while Eurolot

fly to Krakow from Gdańsk, Poznań and Szczecin.

There is another international airport about 110 km (68 miles) northwest of Krakow at **Katowice**, which is served by the budget airlines Wizz and Ryanair as well as Lufthansa. These airlines fly from numerous European destinations, in particular from Eastern Europe.

John Paul II Airport

Situated 15 km (9 miles) west of the city centre, John Paul II Airport is modern, comfortable and easy to get around. Although it has all the facilities that you would expect from an international airport, including cafés, restaurants, shops, money exchange and ATMs, it is small, and doesn't offer the variety found in larger airports. The international terminal is about 1 km (0.5 miles) away from the domestic terminal. There is a regular shuttle bus that transports passengers between the two; the same bus also goes to the airport's small railway station.

There is a tourist information office in the international arrivals hall, and car rental firms operate from their desks in the nearby concourse area.

Katowice Airport

Katowice international airport is located about 110 km (68 miles) northwest of Krakow in Pyrzowice. The airport has two busy passenger terminals. Facilities include souvenir shops, money exchange, duty-free and a post office. Car rental outlets can be found on the ground floor in Terminal A.

Tickets and Fares

Ticket prices vary enormously according to time of year and how far in advance you book. Peak periods such as Easter, June–August and the festive winter season are expensive times to travel whichever airline you book with. In general, tickets booked direct from the airline's website a month in advance or earlier are cheaper than tickets booked through

Krakow's John Paul II Airport

Matusek bus connecting Katowice Airport and Krakow city centre

travel agents or those booked near to your date of travel.

Budget airlines specialize in offering low-cost tickets and should be your first port of call if you are looking for inexpensive deals. Be aware, however, that each item of hold baggage is usually charged extra.

Some airlines offer reductions for children under 12 but this is not standard practice across the whole industry. Children under 2 years old usually travel free, providing they occupy the same seat as the accompanying parent.

Getting into Town

John Paul II Airport is connected to Krakow's main railway station, Kraków Główny (see pp224–5), by fast suburban trains. There is a railway station near the departure terminal of the airport. Trains run every half hour (between approximately 6am and 11pm) and take 20 minutes. Tickets (10zł) can be bought from a machine near the central exit of Terminal 1 or from the conductor on board.

There are two regular bus services from the airport to the railway station: bus numbers 208 and 292, which depart from the airport forecourt. The journey time is about 40 minutes depending on traffic, and although slower than the train, the route runs through parts of west Krakow where several hotels are situated. If you are staying in this area and you have clear directions to your accommodation, these buses are very useful. Between 11pm and 5am, there is also a night bus service, number 902.

Bus tickets (4zł) can be purchased from a newsagent stand inside the airport terminal, from the ticket machine beside the bus stop or from the driver on the bus (coins only) prior to commencing your journey. Large pieces of luggage are subject to an additional charge.

Taxis are located at the terminal's main exit. Here you will find Radio Taxis (see p229). The journey into town takes about 20 minutes but can take longer in rush hour. A Radio Taxi to the centre should cost around 60zł but may cost more at night and weekends. Credit cards are accepted. Expect to pay more if you are travelling to the suburbs, or if you book with an alternative taxi company.

From Katowice Airport, **Matusek** offers a bus service to Krakow central bus station, which takes about two hours. A single ticket costs 44zł if booked in advance or 50zł if bought on board.

DIRECTORY

Arriving by Air

British Airways
w britishairways.com

easyJet
w easyjet.com

Jet2
w jet2.com

LOT Polish Airlines
w lot.com

Lufthansa
w lufthansa.com

Ryanair
w ryanair.com

Airports

John Paul II Airport
Tel 12 295 58 00 or 801 055 000.
w krakowairport.pl

Katowice Airport
Tel 32 39 27 000.
w katowice-airport.com/en

Getting into Town

Matusek
w matusek.com.pl

Pyrzowice Ekspress
w pyrzowiceekspres.pl

Alternatively, you can hire a private car with a driver through **Pyrzowice Ekspress**. For a standard car, with up to four passengers, the journey to Krakow costs 180zł (price is per trip). Cars must be booked at least five days in advance.

Train operating between John Paul II Airport and the city

Escalators to the ticket hall in Kraków Główny, Krakow's main railway station

Travelling by Rail

You can get to Krakow by train from almost any Polish city and town, as well as from many other European cities. Services between Poland's main cities and Krakow are reasonably fast and usually quite comfortable. However, the stretch of track between Krakow and Katowice is relatively slow, and in this particular case travel by road may well be faster.

The Polish rail network is operated by various different companies. Most express intercity trains are run by **PKP InterCity** (Polskie Koleje Państwowe), who operate fast and relatively expensive services, as well as the slightly slower and slightly cheaper TLK (Twoje Linie Kolejowe) services. A number of other express trains are operated by Przewozy Regionalne (and go under the name of Regio). Both Przewozy Regionalne and the regional Koleje Małopolskie operate slower trains that stop at more stations en route.

As a rule, train tickets in Poland are cheaper than in western Europe. Prices vary widely according to class of train, however travelling by express train will be two or three times more expensive than covering the same route on a slower local train.

Tickets for one service will not be valid for travel on another. Buying tickets is relatively straightforward as each of the ticket counters at Krakow's main railway station sell tickets for all of the above companies. Tickets can be bought in advance or on the day of travel from the ticket counters in the main railway station. Queues are common, so allow at least half an hour to buy your ticket. You can also purchase one from the train conductor, but you must inform him that you require a ticket upon boarding the train. Bear in mind that tickets bought from the conductor are 10–20 per cent more expensive than those bought from counters at the station.

InterCity and Express Trains

Trains operated by PKP InterCity offer the fastest and most comfortable way to travel. First and second class seating is available. Seat reservations are obligatory and are made at the time of purchasing the ticket. Express trains operated by Przewozy Regionalnie are not as fast as PKP InterCity and only offer second-class seating although they are much cheaper and also allow bicycles. A PKP InterCity train from Warsaw to Krakow takes just under 3 hours and costs 150zł one-way (200zł in first class). TLK and Przewozy Regionalnie trains from Warsaw to Krakow take 3 hours 15 minutes and only cost 60zł one-way.

PKP InterCity services offer a complimentary hot drink and a pastry, and also have a buffet car and trolley service offering a limited range of drinks and snacks. Other trains do not always carry a buffet car, so buy refreshments before boarding.

Railway Stations

Krakow's main railway station, Kraków Główny, is located in the heart of the city, a 10-minute walk northeast of Market Square. All international and domestic trains pass through this station, and the Krakow airport train terminates and departs from here. The main ticket hall is located under the train platforms and can be accessed from the Krakow bus station immediately to the east, the Dworzec Głowny tram stop, the Galeria Krakowska shopping mall to the west and via a covered walkway from the square in front of the shopping mall. Parking places and taxi ranks are located on the station roof, accessible by lift directly from the platforms.

Station signage is good, with digital displays notifying passengers of train departures and platform numbers. The main ticket hall contains two rows of counters for domestic departures, an information counter, and two counters (clearly marked in Polish and English) for international tickets. Queues at the international ticket counters can be very long in summer.

If catching a train outside central Krakow, beware that smaller railway stations have

An intercity train at Krakow's main railway station

Underground walkway in Krakow's main railway station

poor information displays. Always allow plenty of time to buy your ticket and find the right platform.

Travelling by Coach

Regular coach services to Krakow operate from many Polish and European cities. The main coach station, Dworzec Autobusowy, is located in the city centre, immediately east of the main railway station. Local, domestic and most international coach services operate from this station. The coach station is linked to the Old Town, emerging outside the Galeria Krakowska shopping mall, via the underground pedestrian concourses that connect the bus station with the train station platforms.

The coach station has good facilities and clear timetable information, however there are insufficient ticket windows to deal with demand (especially on summer weekends), and long queues soon build up. International coach tickets can be bought from the coach station or from operating agencies **Jordan** or **Sindbad**.

Coach services are operated by various companies. Those offering prime intercity routes often use more modern, comfortable coaches. Services to nearby towns and villages are also operated by mini-buses. Tickets sell out quickly, especially at weekends. **PolskiBus** runs services to and from Krakow from Warsaw as well as from other Polish and Central European cities. The

Czech operator **Regiojet** has buses running from Prague and Bratislava to Krakow. Tickets are sold online, *see directory*. Pick-up and drop-off points are located in the suburbs of Krakow.

Travelling by Car

Major roads into Krakow are well signposted, but you will need time and patience to find a safe parking space. Prominent car parks in the city are located on the Street Finder maps *(see pp234–9)*.

Driving licences issued in other countries are generally valid in Poland. If you drive in Poland you must carry a valid driving licence and vehicle registration document, as well as a Green Card, which is confirmation of your international insurance cover. If you drive a rental car, a hire certificate is also obligatory. A sticker identifying the country in which the car is registered must be displayed on the vehicle. The wearing of seat belts is compulsory, and children under

12 are not allowed to travel in the front of the car. Headlights must be on, day and night, regardless of the weather.

Road signs at the Polish border indicate strictly observed speed limits (in km). If ignored, foreign drivers are required to pay hefty fines on the spot.

The permitted alcohol content in blood is so low in Poland that drinking and driving should be avoided altogether.

In the event of a break-down, call the **National Road Emergency Service**.

DIRECTORY

Travelling by Rail

PKP InterCity
Tel 19757.
w intercity.pl

Train timetable information
Tel 22 39 19 757.
w rozklad-pkp.pl

Travelling by Coach

Coach timetable information
Tel 703 40 33 40.
w mda.malopolska.pl

Jordan
w jordan.pl

PolskiBus
w polskibus.com

Regiojet
w regiojet.com

Sindbad
w sindbad.krakow.pl

Travelling by Car

National Road Emergency Service
Tel 9637.

A PolskiBus service operating between Warsaw and Krakow

GETTING AROUND KRAKOW

Central Krakow is small and compact so moving around on foot, by bike or by public transport is best. Children in particular will enjoy a sightseeing ride on one of Krakow's blue trams, and tours in a horse-drawn cab are very popular with visitors too. A small electric "meleks" vehicle can also be hired for group sightseeing, with qualified guides who speak foreign languages. Both meleks vehicles and horse-drawn carriages await passengers in Krakow's historic Market Square. If you are visiting attractions outside the city centre, using the public transport system is more environmentally friendly than hiring a car or using taxis. This guide lists the bus and tram routes which you can use to get to the sights described in the Krakow Area by Area section. Maps of Krakow's tram and bus systems can be found on the inside back cover.

Green Travel

There are a great many private cars in circulation in central Krakow, leading to traffic congestion and a shortage of parking spaces. Foreign visitors should try and refrain from adding to this pressure on the local infrastructure and consider alternative ways of getting around the city.

Krakow's centre is easy to navigate on foot and the city is also bike-friendly – the local authorities are trying to extend the number of cycle lanes in busy areas. Otherwise, the electric-powered meleks vehicles available for hire in the Market Square provide an emissions-free alternative to hiring a taxi within the Old Quarter. When exploring further afield, the public transport network is a perfectly adequate way of reaching suburbs such as Nowa Huta or recreation areas such as Las Wolski forest.

Walking

Krakow is ideal for exploring on foot. Much of the city centre is pedestrianized and distances between the main sightseeing areas are small.

Walking from the Old Town to the Kazimierz quarter takes around 20 minutes and there is much to see on the way. The Planty runs round three sides of the Old Town, and the tree-shaded paths offer a pleasant walk from one part of the centre to another.

Pedestrians should take care at zebra crossings as drivers do not always stop.

Cycling

Cycling is a wonderful way to see Krakow, and the number of bike-rental outlets is increasing. Beware that marked cycle lanes are not widespread and cycling on main roads can be unnerving. It is permissible to cycle on the pavement, although pedestrians have right of way. The broad avenues of Planty Park are an ideal way of getting around the Old Town by bike.

A stop and give way road sign

There are several rental outlets around town and your hotel or hostel will know where the nearest one is. Prices depend on the type and age of the bike you are hiring, but you should expect to pay 50–80zł per day. A scheme called **Vavelo** allows you to pick up rental bikes from one of 16 automated bike parks located throughout the city, although registering online is required. If you are hiring a bike for just one day or if you prefer to pay by cash, use **Krakow Bike Tour** or **Bike Trip**.

Driving

Visitors are advised to walk, cycle or use public transport as access to the historic centre is limited to licenced taxis, delivery vans and local residents. Outside the Old Town traffic is busy and parking places are hard to find.

If you do drive, note that congestion is common during rush hours, especially on Friday afternoons. Main roads into the city have numerous traffic lights and junctions causing frequent tailbacks. A ring road runs around the west and south sides of the city, but is yet to be extended all the way round.

Tourists cycling by the Vistula River

Popular excursion routes out of Krakow are well serviced by public transport, although you will need a car in order to explore the countryside in depth. Car hire in Krakow is problem-free, with several car-hire counters in the international arrivals hall of John Paul II Airport, and car-hire deals offered by virtually all of the city's hotels and hostels (see p225). Major car hire companies include **Avis**, **Europcar**, **Hertz** and **Sixt** and the Polish car rental company, **Joka**.

Parking

Parking areas are divided into zones. Most of the Old Town (zones A and B) is a no-parking zone for non-residents, although there is a limited amount of space available for hotel guests – you should enquire about availability when booking your room. Street parking is possible in a belt of territory surrounding the Old Town (zone C), but places are hard to come by. Parking in zone C costs 4zł per hour, payable at roadside parking meters, between 10am and 6pm Monday–Friday, but is free outside that time.

The most convenient car park for the Old Town is at Starowiślna 13 (6–8zł per hour). The largest underground parking garage is near Wawel Castle at Na Groblach

(4.50zł per hour on weekdays, 7.50zł per hour on weekends).

Illegally parked vehicles are prone to clamping. Details of where to pay the fine and get the clamp removed will be posted on the windscreen.

A water tram on the Vistula River

Water Trams

Water trams (*tramwaj wodny*) run during the tourist season from May to October. One service runs between Flisacka (in the suburb of Zwierzyniec) and Kazimierz, passing Wawel Castle on the way. Another less frequent service sails from Flisacka to Tyniec Abbey on the western fringes of Krakow. They function very well as scenic excursions, but are slower than other modes of public transport and should not be used to travel anywhere if you are in a hurry.

Tickets are bought on the boat and cost 10zł one-way on the Flisacka-Kazimierz route and 30zł one-way on the Flisacka-Tyniec route. Buying return tickets works out about 20 per cent cheaper than buying two singles.

Guided Tours

Guided sightseeing tours of Krakow are strongly recommended. The multi-lingual meleks drivers are situated by the Church of St Adalbert in Market Square. Bike-hire and horse-drawn cabs can also be found here.

Top sightseeing spots, such as **Wawel Castle** have their own guides, and many local travel agencies also offer specialist sightseeing tours. **Crazy Guides** focus on the communist past, frequently using old-style Trabant cars as transport. **Cracow City Tours** operate themed tours such as Jewish Krakow and ghost walks, as well as organizing trips to the Auschwitz-Birkenau memorial site. **Discover Cracow** arrange tailor-made city centre and John Paul II tours.

DIRECTORY

Cycling

Bike Trip
ul. Zwierzyniecka 30.
Tel 667 712 054.
w biketrip.pl

Krakow Bike Tour
ul. Grodzka 2. **Map** 1 C5
(6 D3). **Tel** 12 430 20 34.
w krakowbiketour.com

Vavelo
Tel 12 290 33 33.
w vavelo.pl

Driving

Avis
ul. Lubicz 23. **Map** 2 E4.
Tel 12 629 61 08.
w avis.pl

Europcar
ul. Nadwislanska 6.
Map 4 E2.
Tel 12 374 56 96.
w europcar.com.pl

Hertz
Al. Focha 1. **Map** 1 A5.
Tel 12 429 62 62.
w hertz.com.pl

Joka
ul. Zacisze 7.
Map 2 D3 (6 E1).
Tel 12 429 66 30.
w joka.com.pl

Sixt
John Paul II Airport.
Tel 12 639 32 16.
w sixt.pl

Water Trams

**Water Tram
(Tramwaj Wodny)**
Tel 608 496 800.
w tramwaywodny.
net.pl

Guided Tours

**Cracow City
Tours**
pl. Matejki 2.
Map 2 D3 (6 E1).
Tel 12 421 13 33.
w cracowcitytours.com

Crazy Guides
ul. Krakusów 1a.
Tel 500 091 200.
w crazyguides.com

Discover Cracow
Pilsudzkiego 6/9.
Map 1 B5 (5 B3).
Tel 12 357 21 70.
w discovercracow.com

**Wawel Castle
Guide Service**
Wawel 5.
Map 3 C1 (6 D5).
Tel 12 422 16 97.
w wawel.krakow.pl

Buses, Trams and Taxis

Krakow is covered by an extensive public transport network. Trams and buses are frequent on weekdays, with rush hours between 7 and 8am and 2 and 5pm, but less so at weekends and on public holidays. A few trams and buses operate at night. Tickets, valid for both buses and trams, are inexpensive, especially if you opt for a 24- or 48-hour travel pass. A number of private firms operate minibus services, which will stop on request within the inner and outer city. Taxi ranks are located around the Old Town, and their prices are reasonable.

Ticket machine

Tourists planning a route at a Krakow tram stop

Tickets and fares

One type of ticket is used for both trams and buses. Tickets can be purchased from kiosks on the street, from ticket machines at some stops and on most trams and buses. There are two zones: zone 1 covers the city of Krakow and includes all tram and bus routes numbered 100 to 194. Zone 2 covers the outer suburbs, outlying villages and John Paul II Airport.

Several types of ticket are available: in zone 1, a ticket for a single journey by tram or bus is 3.80zł, a ticket for two journeys by bus or tram costs 7.20zł. Tickets valid for unlimited travel within a specific time period include the 20-minute ticket, which costs 2.80zł (useful if you're only travelling a few stops), as well as a 40-minute (3.80zł), 60-minute (5zł), 90-minute (6zł), 24-hour (15zł), 48-hour (24zł) and 72-hour (36zł) ticket. A weekly ticket is also available, which costs 48zł. Family tickets, allowing for unlimited travel for two adults and two children at weekends, cost 16zł. A group

ticket for up to 20 people costs 36zł. If you are travelling to zone 2, a single ticket is priced at 4zł and a ticket for two journeys is 7.60zł. Children under 4 and senior citizens over 70 travel for free.

After boarding, passengers must validate each ticket (even those purchased on board) by inserting it in one of the orange machines. Weekly tickets require the holder to carry identification.

Ticket Inspectors

Tickets are subject to regular checks on Krakow's trams and buses. Ticket inspectors operate in plain clothes but carry ID bearing an MPK symbol and a photograph. A passenger without a valid, punched ticket is liable to pay a fine, which is up to 250zł. Fines may be paid on the spot or at a post office with a penalty ticket. Foreign visitors, however, must pay on the spot.

Machines for checking the validity of your ticket are located throughout the city.

Travelling by Bus

Krakow is well served by buses that take passengers to all parts of the city. Bus routes numbered from 100 to 194 operate in the city centre and those numbered 201 to 297 link the city with outer suburbs and villages. Express buses, which do not go to every stop, begin with a 3 or a 5 and are three digits long. The frequency of buses varies from every few minutes to approximately every 20 minutes Monday–Friday, but they are less regular at weekends and on public holidays.

Bus stops are marked by a blue sign with a picture of a bus on it. When boarding the bus remember to validate your ticket. Approaching stops are read out by a pre-recorded voice and – in the newer vehicles – displayed on an electronic sign. To request a stop, push one of the red buttons near the doors. Some of the more modern buses have low floors, which allow easier wheelchair, pram and pushchair access.

Bus routes beginning with a 6 or a 9 are night buses. These

Interior of main bus station in Krakow

buses run about once an hour and cross the city in all directions. The fare is the same as for any other bus journey.

Private minibus services operate on many routes within the city and in the suburbs. You can purchase a ticket directly from the driver which costs approximately twice the fare of the MPK public transport. Most of these minibuses depart from the main railway station or nearby.

A Krakow tram operating in the city centre

Travelling by Tram

Trams are the main form of public transport in central Krakow, running round either side of the Old Town and fanning out towards outlying suburbs. They are the best means of travelling between the major bus and rail stations, and they are also the quickest way of reaching outlying attractions in the suburbs of Podgórze, 3 km (2 miles) south of the centre and Nowa Huta, 7 km (4 miles) east. Trams run from around 5:15am– 11:15pm daily. Most tram routes operate every 10–15 minutes in the middle of the day, and every 20–25 minutes early in the morning and in the evening. Many vehicles have low floors enabling easy wheelchair access.

The electronic boards at stops use wheelchair symbols to designate which of the arriving trams are wheelchair accessible.

Taxis

Taxis are easy to locate in central Krakow and rates are reasonably low. Various taxi companies are in operation – vehicles vary in colour and make, and have different signs, depending on which company they belong to. All have an identification number clearly marked on the side of the car, as well as an illuminated "taxi" sign on the roof displaying the name of the company.

Taxis wait in taxi ranks rather than driving round the city looking for custom, so it is highly unlikely that you will be able to hail a taxi on the street. Those ordered by phone are usually cheaper than those picked up at a taxi rank.

Taxi ranks can be found all around the Old Town area. The biggest are on ul. Sienna, a short walk east of the main Market Square, and pl. Wszystkich Świętych, close to the Franciscan and Dominican churches. There are also plenty of taxis on or near pl. Nowy

in the Kazimierz quarter. The taxi rank for the main railway station is located on its roof – take the escalator or lift up from the platform.

There is an initial charge of 7zł, followed by 3zł per kilometre. Rates rise by 50 per cent between 11pm and 5am. Bear in mind large items of luggage will increase the fare.

Radio Taxi-Partner runs a fleet of taxis for disabled passengers. These must be booked in advance.

DIRECTORY

Travelling by Bus and Tram

Tram and Bus Information
Tel 191 50.
W mpk.krakow.pl

Taxis

Radio Taxi
Tel 19191.

Radio Taxi Barbakan
Tel 19661.

Radio Taxi-Partner
Tel 19633.

Wawel Taxi
Tel 19666.

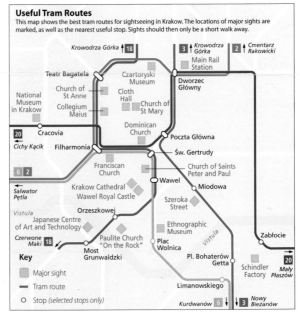

Useful Tram Routes
This map shows the best tram routes for sightseeing in Krakow. The locations of major sights are marked, as well as the nearest useful stop. Sights should then only be a short walk away.

Krowodrza Górka 18 · Krowodrza Górka 3 · Cmentarz Rakowicki 2

Main Rail Station

Teatr Bagatela · Czartoryski Museum · Dworzec Główny

National Museum in Krakow · Church of St Anne · Cloth Hall · Church of St Mary

Collegium Maius · Dominican Church

Cracovia 20 · Poczta Główna

Cichy Kącik · Filharmonia · Św. Gertrudy

6 2 · Franciscan Church · Church of Saints Peter and Paul

Salwator Pętla · Krakow Cathedral · Wawel · Miodowa

Wawel Royal Castle · Szeroka Street

Vistula · Orzeszkowej

Japanese Centre of Art and Technology · Ethnographic Museum · Zabłocie

Czerwone Maki 18 · Paulite Church "On the Rock" · Plac Wolnica · Vistula

Most Grunwaldzki · Pl. Bohaterów Getta 20

Schindler Factory · Mały Płaszów

Key

Limanowskiego

Kurdwanów 6 · Nowy Bieżanów 3

Major sight

Tram route

O Stop (selected stops only)

STREET FINDER

Map references, given for each sight within its individual entry in this guide relate to the map on the following pages only. The same applies to the hotels *(see pp182–5)* and restaurants *(see pp192–5)* listed. The first figure indicates the map number, while the middle letter and the last number refer to the relevant grid. The key map on the right shows Krakow divided into six parts which correspond to the maps that follow. All symbols used are explained in the key. You will find the Street Finder Index on pp232–3. Note that Polish is an inflected language and street names require different name endings (Jan Kowalski but Jana Kowalskiego Street).

Top sights and attractions are indicated on the maps.

Key to Street Finder

- Major sight
- Other sight
- Railway station
- Coach terminal
- Tram stop
- *i* Tourist information
- Hospital
- Police station
- Boat pier
- Church
- Synagogue
- Railway line
- Pedestrian street
- City wall

Scale of Maps 1–4

0 metres	200	
0 yards	200	1:13,000

Scale of Maps 5–6

0 metres	150	
0 yards	150	1:8,500

A hurdy-gurdy man in the Market Square

Stairs leading to the Decius Villa

Church of St Adalbert in Market Square

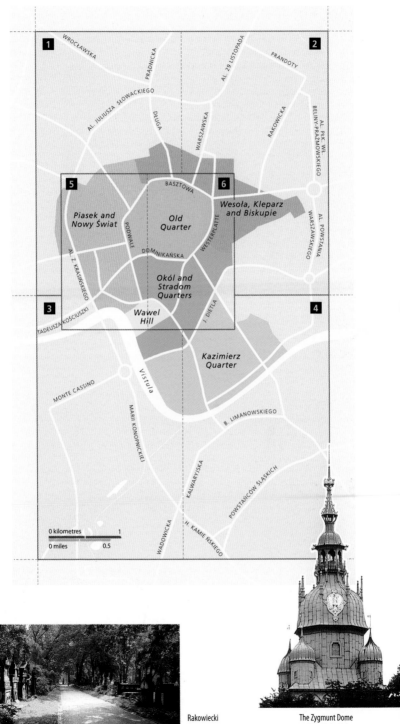

1 WROCŁAWSKA

PRADNICKA

AL. 29 LISTOPADA

PRANDOTY

2

AL. JULIUSZA SŁOWACKIEGO

DŁUGA

WARSZAWSKA

RAKOWICKA

AL. PŁK. WŁ. BELINY-PRAŻMOWSKIEGO

5 BASZTOWA **6**

AL. POWSTANIA WARSZAWSKIEGO

Piasek and Nowy Świat

Old Quarter

Wesoła, Kleparz and Biskupie

PODWALE

DOMINIKAŃSKA

WESTERPLATTE

AL. Z. KRASIŃSKIEGO

Okół and Stradom Quarters

3 TADEUSZA KOŚCIUSZKI **4**

Wawel Hill

J. DIETLA

Kazimierz Quarter

MONTE CASSINO

Vistula

B. LIMANOWSKIEGO

MARII KONOPNICKIEJ

KALWARYJSKA

POWSTAŃCÓW ŚLĄSKICH

0 kilometres 1

0 miles 0.5

WADOWICKA

H. KAMIEŃSKIEGO

Rakowiecki Cemetery

The Zygmunt Dome of the Cathedral

Street Finder Index

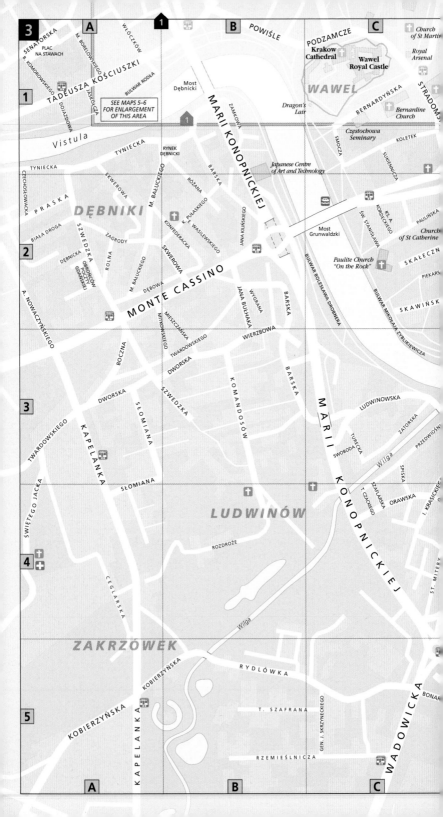

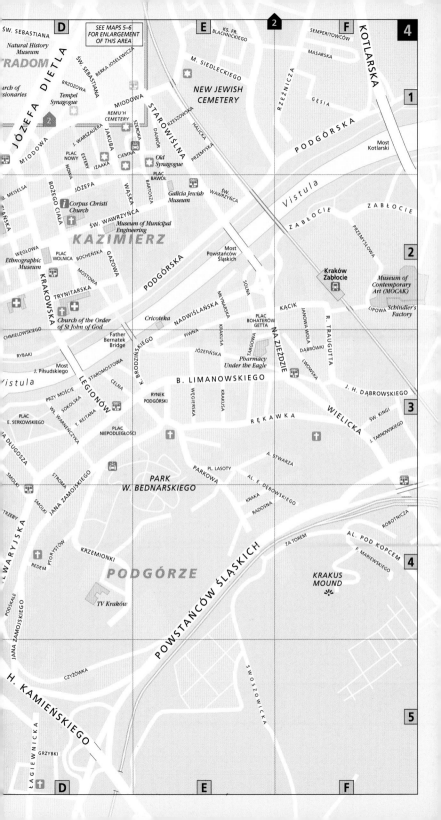

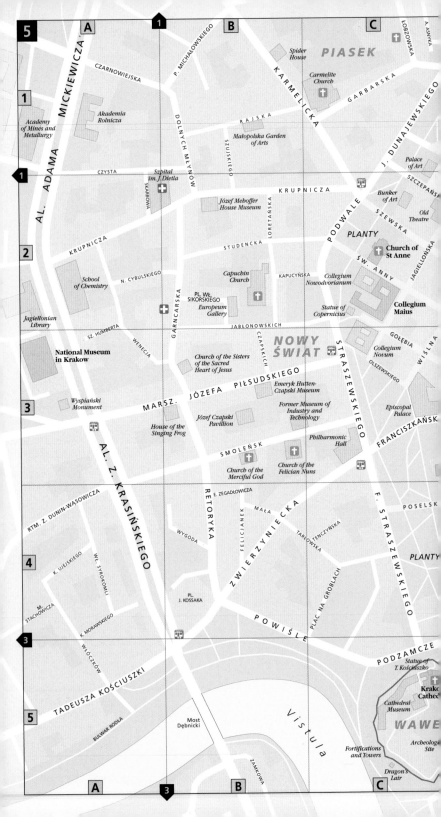

General Index

Acknowledgments

Dorling Kindersley would like to thank the following people whose assistance has made the preparation of this book possible.

Managing Editor Helen Townsend
Managing Art Editor Kate Poole
Senior Managing Editor Louise B. Lang
Art Director Gillian Allan
Additional Photography Jakub Hałun, Jamie Howard, Krzysztof Kotowski, Piotr Kozłowski, Wojciech Kozłowski, Ian O'Leary, Kamil Szymaczek.
Revisions Team Parnika Bagla, Claire Baranowski, Sonal Bhatt, Hilary Bird, Jonathan Bousfield, Arwen Burnett, Caroline Elliker, Eli Estaugh, Rhiannon Furbear, Lydia Halliday, Victoria Heyworth-Dunne, Bharti Karakoti, Elly King, Piotr Kozłowski, Ferdie McDonald, Gordon McLachlan, Casper Morris, Scarlett O'Hara, Catherine Palmi, Susie Peachey, Rada Radojicic, Simon Ryder, Sands Publishing Solutions, Rituraj Singh, Sadie Smith, Jamie Stokes, Hollie Teague, Leah Tether, Conrad Van Dyk, Vinita Venugopal, Deepika Verma, Stewart J. Wild.

Dorling Kindersley wish to thank the following institutions, picture libraries and individuals for their kind permission to reproduce photographs of objects in their care and for the use of other photographic material:
Magdalena Maros the Director, and Krystyna Litewka at the Public Record State Office, Krzysztof Zamorski, Director of the Jagiellonian Library, Stanisław Waltoś the Director, Lucyna Bełtowska and Robert Springwald at the Collegium Maius, Matejko House, St Vladimir Foundation, Katarzyna Balus, Princes Czartoryski Foundation, Jama Michalika, Prelate Janusz Bielański, Krakow Cathedral and Cathedral Museum, Church of the Bernardine Nuns, Bernardine Church, Father Mirosław Pilśniak, OP, Dominican Church, Sister Wanda Batko, Church of the Felician Nuns, Brother Bogumił Stachowicz, OFM, Franciscan Church, Father Edward Stoch, SJ, Church of the Sacred Heart of Jesus in Wesoła, Capuchin Church, Father Dr Bronisław Fidelus, Church of St Mary, Father Jan Mazur, Paulite Church "On the Rock", Church of St Anne, Father Henryk Dziadosz, Church of St Barbara, Church of St Florian, Church of St Catherine, Church of the Holy Cross, Church of St Mark, Church of St Peter and St Paul, Church of St Vincent, Wieliczka Salt Mine, Father Dr Józef A. Nowobilski, the Metropolitan Curia and Archdiocesan Museum, Balice Airport, Archaeological Museum, Andrzej Szczygieł, Director of the Museum of Krakow, Anna Studnicka, National Museum, Natural History Museum, Zbigniew Święcicki the Director, and Mirosław Ciunowicz at the Polish Military Museum in Warsaw, PAP Polish Press Agency, Society of Physicians, Pieskowa Skała Castle.

Dorling Kindersley are grateful to the following individuals for their kind permission to reproduce their photographs:
Jacek Bednarczyk, Olaf Beer, Maja Florczykowska, Michał Grychowski, Stanisława Jabłońska, Dorota i Mariusz Jarymowiczowie, Beata i Mariusz Kowalewscy, Grzegorz Kozakiewicz, Wojciech Mędrzak, Stanisław Michta, Hanna i Maciej Musiałowie, Tomasz Robaczyński, Maciej Sochor, Jan Zych.

All the dishes whose photographs feature in this guide were prepared in the restaurant Pod Aniołami. We wish to thank the owner, Jacek Łodziński for his help. We are also grateful to Marcin Duszyński, Madropol for his kind assistance.

Key: a=above; b=below/bottom; c=centre; f=far; l=left; r=right; t=top.

Works of art have been reproduced with the permission of the following copyright holders: © ADAGP, Paris and DACS, London 2011 *collegium iuridicum* by Igor Mitoraj 78tr. **123RF.com:** kaetana 80tl; qumrran 65tr, 153tl. **AKG-Images:** 20; 165cr; Ullstein Bild-KPA/HIP/ Jewish Chronicle Ltd 127br. **Alamy Images:** AA World Travel Library 158cla, 220br; Kevin Foy 126tl, 189c; David Gee 225tl; Kevin George

113bc; Janusz Gniadek 221ca; Karolek 10cr; kpzfoto 135br; lookGaleria 11bl, 127cb; NurPhoto.com 56bl; G Owston (Poland) 224tl; Pegaz 76, 107tl, 160br, 213bl; Magdalena Rehova 168; David Sanger Photography/ David Sanger 189tl; Paul Springett 72clb; Peter Svarc 10bl; Krystyna Szulecka 188cl; VIEW Pictures Ltd 147br, 159ca; John Warburton-Lee Photography 40; Jan Wlodarczyk 210-211; David Wootton 158bc. **Andel's:** 184tr. **Archaeological Museum:** 22clb, 22bc, 23cr, 23cb, 23bl, 42b. **The Art Archive:** Laurie Platt Winfrey 127cra. **Art Hotel Niebieski:** 181bl. **Auschwitz-Birkenau Memorial & Museum:** 164tr, 164cl, 164bl, 165tc, 166clb, 167cr, 166br; Ryszard Domasik 164tl, 165crb, 166cla, 167tl, 167tr; Jarek Mensfelt 166tr. **Carlsberg polska:** Chris Biggs 191c. **Cathedral Museum:** 24–5c, 26cla, 27cla, 46cl, 62ca, 64c. **Collegium Maius:** 27cb, 33b, 108–9. **Cool Tour Company:** 226bl. **Copernicus Restaurant:** 187br. **Corbis:** Bettmann 127tl; Historical Picture Archive 126tr. **Czartoryski Museum:** 45bc, 114–15. **CK Dezerter:** 193tc. **Del Papa:** 186c. **Dreamstime.com:** Agneskantaruk 45tl; Roksana Bashyrova 93tl; Artur Bogacki 89tr, 227tr; Mike Clegg 74–5; Dimaberkut 12tr, 55bl, 56cra; Anna Duda 99b; Dziewul 58–9, 161tr; Santiago Rodríguez Fontoba 44cr; Jorg Hackemann 19br; Jborzicchi 43cb; Thomas Jurkowski 85b, 120; Katatonia82 63tl; Maryna Kordiumova 117tl; Serhii Kvasha 5clb; Serhii Liakhevych 90t; Mbonaparte 128br; Mychadre77 5c; Krzysztof Nahlik 2–3, 154, 161b; Neirfy 13tr; Nightman1965 162tl; Michal Nowak 4crb; Diana Opryshko 158tr; Puchan 213tr; Tatiana Savvateeva 60; Radovan Smokon 18cla; Jacek Sopotnicki 13bl, 172bl; Studiobarcelona 54cl; Simon Thomas 229cla. **FM Dutton, uk:** 215cra. **Encyclopaedia Judaica:** 126cl. **Flamingo Hostel:** 180tr. **Edyta Gawron:** 126br. **Getty Images:** Maurice Alexandre F. P. 112CLB, Lonely Planet 192bl, Chan Srithaweeporn 57cra; **Groteska Theatre:** Anna Kaczmarz 214tr. **Hotel Fortuna:** 178bl. **Hotel Galaxy:** 179bc, 183tr. **iStockphoto. com:** martin-dm 176–7. **Jagiellonian Library:** 22–3c, 26clb, 28tl, 28cra, 28b, 32b, 32crb, 30br, 34cb, 152bl. **Dariusz Jedrzejewski:** 11tr. **Kraków Airport:** 222br; 223br. **Krakow Festival Office:** 212cr. **Matejko House:** 25cr. **Metropolitan Hotel Krakow:** 179tr. **Museum of Krakow:** 20, 21b, 29ca, 31cb, 36b, 37ca, 37cr, 42cr, 43cr, 94tr, 101br; Emeryk Hutten Czapski Museum 148tr. **Muzeum Historyczne Miasta Krakowa:** Ignacy Krieger 126clb, 126cb, 126crb. **National Museum:** 8–9, 24bc, 25tc, 26b, 27cr, 31br, 32bl, 32–3c, 33cr, 34cl, 34tc, 34–5c, 35t, 35tr, 36cl, 36–7c, 39bl, 42tr, 42cl, 43tr, 43cra, 52tc, 53tl, 52cl, 104tr, 104c, 105, 149cla. **Novotel Krakow Centrum:** 179tr. **Pimiento Argentino:** 187tl. **PKO Bank Polski:** Wojciech Czerniewicz 218cr, 218bl. **Pod Baranami:** 205tr. **Polskibus. com:** 223br. **Polski Hotel Pod Bialym Orlem:** 178cra, 182bc. **Polskie Koleje Panstwowe S.A.:** PKP InterCity 224br. **Public Record State Office:** 26–7c, 26bl. **Qubus:** 185br. **Rex Shutterstock:** Fumie Suzuki 199cl. **Robert Harding Picture Library:** Bennet Dean 12bc, Henryk T. Kaiser 130. **Secret Garden Hostel:** 180bl. **Sheraton Krakow Hotel:** The Olive 195br, SomePlace Else 186bl. **STA Travel Group:** 214cra. **SuperStock:** age fotostock / age fotostock 156tl, Henryk T. Kaiser / age fotostock 142. **Tel Aviv Museum of Art:** *Jews Praying in the Synagogue on Yom Kippur* by Maurycy Gottlieb, oil on canvas, gift of Sydney Lamon, New York 126–7c; **Telekomunikacja Polska:** 220c. **Topfoto. co.uk:** Roger-Viollet 167br. **Trezo:** 194tr. **Urzad Miasta Krakowa:** P. Krawczyk 228tr. **Hotel Wyspianski:** 181tr. **s Żywiec group:** 191cl; 191fcl.

Front endpapers: Alamy Images: Pegaz Rc. **Dreamstime.com:** Thomas Jurkowski Rbr, Serhii Liakhevych Lbl, Tatiana Savvateeva Lcrb. **Robert Harding Picture Library:** Henryk T. Kaiser Rtr. **SuperStock:** Henryk T. Kaiser / age fotostock Lcla.

Sheet map cover: Alamy Stock Photo: Jan Wlodarczyk.
Cover: front main and spine t – Alamy Stock Photo: Jan Wlodarczyk; back – Dreamstime.com: Sergii Figurnyi

All other images © Dorling Kindersley. For further information see: www.dkimages.com

Phrase Book

Summary of Pronunciation in Polish

ą a nasal *"awn"* as in *"sawn"* or *"an"* as in the French *"Anjou"* but barely sounded

c *"ts"* as in *"bats"*

ć, cz *"ch"* as in *"challenge"*

ch *"ch"* as in Scottish *"loch"*

dz *"j"* as in *"jeans"* when followed by **i** or **e** but otherwise *"dz"* as in *"adze"*

dź *"j"* as in *"jeans"*

dż *"d"* as in *"dog"* followed by *"s"* as in *"leisure"*

ę similar to *"en"* in *"end"* only nasal and barely sounded, but if at the end of the word pronounced *"e"* as in *"bed"*

h *"ch"* as in Scottish *"loch"*

i *"ee"* as in *"teeth"*

j *"y"* as in yes

ł *"w"* as in *"window"*

ń similar to the *"ni"* in *"companion"*

ó *"oo"* as in *"soot"*

rz similar to the *"s"* in *"leisure"* or, when it follows **p**, **t** or **k**, *"sh"* as in *"shut"*

ś, sz *"sh"* as in *"shut"*

w *"v"* as in *"vine"*

y similar to the *"i"* in *"bit"*

ź, ż similar to the *"s"* in *"leisure"*

Emergencies

Help!	**pomocy!**	*pomotsi*
Call a doctor!	**zawołać doktora!**	*zawowach doctora*
Call an ambulance!	**zadzwonić po pogotowie!**	*zadzvoneech po pogotovee*
Police!	**policja!**	*poleetsya*
Call the fire brigade!	**zadzwonić po straż pożarną!**	*zadzvoneech po stras posarnAWN*
Where is the nearest phone?	**Gdzie jest najbliższa budka telefoniczna?**	*gjeh yest nlbleezhsha boodka telefoneechna*
Where is the hospital?	**Gdzie jest szpital?**	*gjeh yest shpeetal*
Where is the police station	**Gdzie jest posterunek policji?**	*gjeh yest posterunek politsyee*

Communication Essentials

Yes	**Tak**	*tak*
No	**Nie**	*n-yeh*
Thank you	**Dziękuję**	*jENkoo-yeh*
No thank you	**Nie, dziękuję**	*n-yej jENkoo-yeh*
Please	**Proszę**	*prosheh*
I don't understand.	**Nie rozumiem.**	*n-yeh rozoom-yem*
Do you speak English? (to a man)	**Czy mówi pan po angielsku?**	*chi moovee pan po ang-yelskoo*
Do you speak English? (to a woman)	**Czy mówi pani po angielsku?**	*chi moovee panee po ang-yelskoo*
Please speak more slowly	**Proszę mówić wolniej.**	*proseh mooveech voln-yay*
Please write it down for me.	**Proszę mi to napisać.**	*prosheh mee to napeesach*
My name is…	**Nazywam się…**	*nazivam sheh*

Useful Words and Phrases

Pleased to meet you (to a man)	**Bardzo mi miło pana poznać**	*bardzo mee meewo pana poznach*
Pleased to meet you (to a woman)	**Bardzo mi miło panią poznać**	*bardzo mee meewo pan-yAWN poznach*
Good morning	**Dzień dobry**	*jen-yuh dobri*
Good afternoon	**Dzień dobry**	*jen-yuh dobri*
Good evening	**Dobry wieczór**	*dobri v-yechoor*

Good night	**Dobranoc**	*dobranots*
Goodbye	**Do widzenia**	*do veedzen-ya*
What time is it…?	**Która jest godzina?**	*ktoora yest gojeena*
Cheers!	**Na zdrowie!**	*na zdrov-yeh*
Excellent!	**Wspaniale**	*wspan-yaleh*

Shopping

Do you have…? (to a man)	**Czy ma pan…?**	*che ma pan*
Do you have…? (to a woman)	**Czy ma pani…?**	*che ma panee*
How much is this?	**Ile to kosztuje?**	*eeleh to koshtoo-yeh*
Where is the… department?	**Gdzie jest dział z…?**	*gjeh yest jawuh z*
Do you take credit cards? (to a man)	**Czy przyjmuje pan karty kredytowe?**	*chi pshi-yuhmoo-yeh pan karti kreditoveh*
Do you take credit cards? (to a woman)	**Czy przyjmuje pani karty kredytowe?**	*chi pshi-yuhmoo-yeh panee karti kreditoveh*
bakery	**piekarnia**	*p-yekarn-ya*
bookshop	**księgarnia**	*kshENgarn-ya*
chemist	**apteka**	*apteka*
department store	**dom towarowy**	*dom tovarovi*
exchange office	**kantor walutowy**	*kantor valootovi*
travel agent	**biuro podróży**	*b-yooro podroozhi*
post office	**poczta,**	*pochta*
	urząd pocztowy	*ooZHAWNd pochtovi*
postcard	**pocztówka**	*pochtoovka*
stamp	**znaczek**	*znachek*
How much is a postcard to…?	**Ile kosztuje pocztówka do…?**	*eeleh koshtoo-yeh pochtoovka do*
airmail	**poczta lotnicza**	*pochta lotneecha*

Staying in a Hotel

Have you any vacancies? (to a man)	**Czy ma pan wolne pokoje?**	*chi ma pan volneh poko-yeh*
Have you any vacancies? (to a woman)	**Czy ma pani wolne pokoje?**	*chi ma panee volneh poko-yeh*
What is the charge per night?	**Ile kosztuje za dobę?**	*eeleh koshtoo-yeh za dobeh*
I'd like a single room.	**Poproszę pokój jednoosobowy.**	*poprosheh pokoo-yuh yedno-osobovi*
I'd like a double room.	**Poproszę pokój dwuosobowy.**	*poprosheh pokoo-yuh dvoo-osobovi*
I'd like a twin room.	**Poproszę pokój z dwoma łóżkami.**	*poprosheh pokoo-yuh z dvoma woozhkamee*
I'd like a room with a bathroom.	**Poproszę pokój z łazienką.**	*poprosheh pokoo-yuh z wazhenkAWN*
bathroom	**łazienka**	*wazhenka*
bed	**łóżko**	*woozhko*
bill	**rachunek**	*raHoonek*
breakfast	**śniadanie**	*shn-yadan-yeh*
dinner	**kolacja**	*kolats-ya*
double room	**pokój dwuosobowy**	*pokoo-yuh dvoo-osobovi*
full board	**pełne utrzymanie**	*pewuhneh ootzhiman-yeh*
guest house	**zajazd**	*za-yazd*
half board	**dwa posiłki dziennie**	*dva posheewuhkee jen-yeh*
key	**klucz**	*klooch*
restaurant	**restauracja**	*restawrats-ya*
shower	**prysznic**	*prishneets*
single room	**pokój jednoosobowy**	*pokoo-yuh yedno-osobovi*
toilet	**toaleta**	*to-aleta*

Eating Out

A table for one, please.	**Stolik dla jednej osoby proszę.**	*stoleek dla yednay osobi prosheh*
A table for two, please.	**Stolik dla dwóch osób proszę.**	*stoleek dla dvooh osoob prosheh*
Can I see the menu?	**Mogę prosić jadłospis?**	*mogeh prosheech yadwospees*

Can I see the wine list?	**Mogę prosić kartę win?**	mogeh prosheech karteh veen
I'd like…	**Proszę**	prosheh
Can we have the bill, please?	**Proszę rachunek?**	prosheh raHoonek
Where is the toilet?	**Gdzie jest toaleta?**	gjeh yest to-aleta

Menu Decoder

baranina	mutton, lamb
barszcz czerwony	beetroot soup
bażant	pheasant
befsztyk	beef steak
bigos	hunter's stew (sweet and sour cabbage with a variety of meats and seasonings)
bukiet z jarzyn	a variety of raw and pickled vegetables
ciasto	cake, pastry
cielęcina	veal
cukier	sugar
cukierek	sweet, confectionery
dania mięsne	meat dishes
dania rybne	fish dishes
dania z drobiu	poultry dishes
deser	dessert
flaki	tripe
grzybki marynowane	marinated mushrooms
herbata	tea
jarzyny	vegetables
kabanos	dry, smoked pork sausage
kaczka	duck
kapusta	cabbage
kartofle	potatoes
kasza gryczana	buckwheat
kaszanka	black pudding
kawa	coffee
kiełbasa	sausage
klopsiki	minced meat balls
lody	ice cream
łosoś	salmon
łosoś wędzony	smoked salmon
makowiec	poppy seed cake
naleśniki	pancakes
piernik	spiced honeycake
pierogi	ravioli-like dumplings
piwo	beer
prawdziwki	ceps (type of mushroom)
przystawki	entrées
pstrąg	trout
rolmopsy	rollmop herrings
sałatka	salad
sałatka owocowa	fruit salad
sok	juice
sok jabłkowy	apple juice
sok owocowy	fruit juice
sól	salt
śledź	herring
tort	cake, gâteau
wieprzowina	pork
wino	wine
woda	water
ziemniaki	potatoes
zupa	soup

Health

I do not feel well.	**Źle się czuję.**	zhleh sheh choo-yeh
I need a prescription for…	**Potrzebuję receptę na…**	potzheboo-yeh retsepteh na
cold	**przeziębienie**	pshef-yENb-yen-yeh
cough (noun)	**kaszel**	kashel
cut	**skaleczenie**	skalechen-yeh
flu	**grypa**	gripa
hayfever	**katar sienny**	katar shyienny
headache pills	**proszki od bólu głowy**	proshkee od booloo gwovi
hospital	**szpital**	shpeetal
nausea	**mdłości**	mudwosh-che
sore throat	**ból gardła**	bool gardwa

Travel and Transport

When is the next train to…?	**Kiedy jest następny pociąg do…?**	k-yedi yest nastENpni pochAWNg do…
What is the fare to…?	**Ile kosztuje bilet do…?**	eeleh koshtoo-yeh beelet do
A single ticket to … please	**Proszę bilet w jedną stronę bilet do…**	prosheh beelet v yednAWN stroneh beelet do
A return ticket to … please	**Proszę bilet w obie strony do…**	prosheh beelet v obye strony do
Where is the bus station?	**Gdzie jest dworzec autobusowy?**	gjeh yest dvozhets awtoboosovi
Where is the bus stop?	**Gdzie jest przystanek autobusowy?**	gjeh yest pshistanek awtoboosovi
Where is the tram stop?	**Gdzie jest przystanek tramwajowy?**	gjeh yest pshistanek tramvl-yovi
booking office	**kasa biletowa**	kasa beeletova
station	**stacja**	stats-ya
timetable	**rozkład jazdy**	rozkwad yazdi
left luggage	**przechowalnia bagażu**	psheHovaln-ya bagazhoo
platform	**peron**	peron
first class	**pierwsza klasa**	p-yervsha klasa
second class	**druga klasa**	drooga klasa
single ticket	**bilet w jedną stronę**	beelet v jednAWN stroneh
return ticket	**bilet powrotny**	beelet povrotni
airline	**linia lotnicza**	leen-ya lotna-yeecha
airport	**lotnisko**	lotn-yeesko
arrival	**przylot**	pshilot
flight number	**numer lotu**	noomer lotoo
gate	**przejście**	pshaysh-cheh
coach (bus)	**autokar**	awtokar

Numbers

0	**zero**	zero
1	**jeden**	yeden
2	**dwa**	dva
3	**trzy**	tshi
4	**cztery**	chteri
5	**pięć**	p-yENch
6	**sześć**	shesh-ch
7	**siedem**	sh-yedem
8	**osiem**	oshem
9	**dziewięć**	jev-yENch
10	**dziesięć**	jeshENch
11	**jedenaście**	yedenash-cheh
12	**dwanaście**	dvanash-cheh
13	**trzynaście**	tshinash-cheh
14	**czternaście**	chternash-cheh
15	**piętnaście**	p-yENtnash-cheh
16	**szesnaście**	shesnash-cheh
17	**siedemnaście**	shedemnash-cheh
18	**osiemnaście**	oshemnash-cheh
19	**dziewiętnaście**	jev-yENtnash-cheh
20	**dwadzieścia**	dvajesh-cha
21	**dwadzieścia jeden**	dvajesh-cha yeden
22	**dwadzieścia dwa**	dvajesh-cha dva
30	**trzydzieści**	tshijesh-chee
40	**czterdzieści**	chterjesh-chee
50	**pięćdziesiąt**	p-yENchjeshAWNt
100	**sto**	sto
200	**dwieście**	dv-yesh-cheh
500	**pięćset**	p-yENchset
1,000	**tysiąc**	tishAWNts
1,000,000	**milion**	meel-yon

Time

today	**dzisiaj**	jeeshl
yesterday	**wczoraj**	vchorl
tomorrow	**jutro**	yootro
tonight	**dzisiejszej nocy**	jeeshAYshay notsi
one minute	**jedna minuta**	yedna meenoota
half an hour	**pół godziny**	poowuh gojeeni
hour	**godzina**	gojeena

Days of the Week

Sunday	**niedziela**	n-yejela
Monday	**poniedziałek**	pon-yejawek
Tuesday	**wtorek**	vtorek
Wednesday	**środa**	shroda
Thursday	**czwartek**	chvartek
Friday	**piątek**	p-yAWNtek
Saturday	**sobota**	sobota

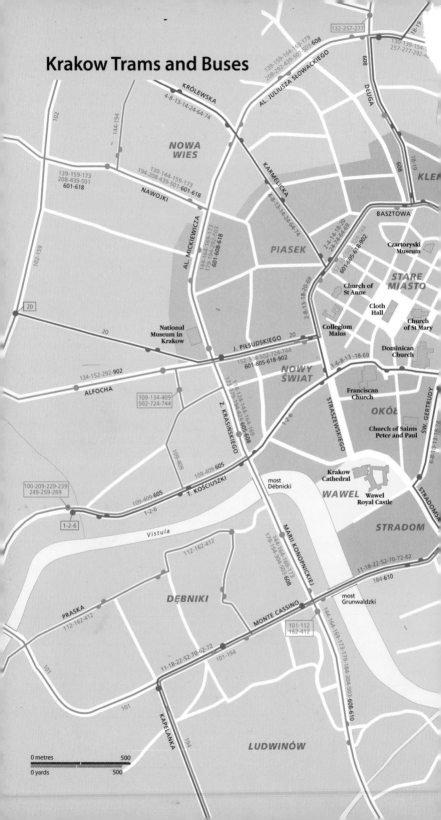